English Poetry and Modern Arabic Verse

English Poetry and Modern Arabic Verse

Translation and Modernity

Ghareeb Iskander

I.B. TAURIS
LONDON • NEW YORK • OXFORD • NEW DELHI • SYDNEY

I.B. TAURIS
Bloomsbury Publishing Plc
50 Bedford Square, London, WC1B 3DP, UK
1385 Broadway, New York, NY 10018, USA
29 Earlsfort Terrace, Dublin 2, Ireland

BLOOMSBURY, I.B. TAURIS and the I.B. Tauris logo are trademarks of Bloomsbury Publishing Plc

First published in Great Britain, 2021
This paperback edition published in 2022

Series design by Adriana Brioso

Cover image Statue of Badr Shaker Sayyab, 1971 by Miran al-Saadi.
(© Ahmed Mahmoud, CC BY-SA 3.0)

A catalogue record for this book is available from the British Library.

A catalog record for this book is available from the Library of Congress.

ISBN: HB: 978-0-7556-0724-2
PB: 978-0-7556-3993-9
ePDF: 978-0-7556-0725-9
eBook: 978-0-7556-0726-6

Typeset by Deanta Global Publishing Services, Chennai, India

To my parents

Contents

Preface viii
Acknowledgements xi

Introduction 1
1 The Arabic waste lands 19
2 Translating Whitman's *Song of Myself* into Arabic 59
3 Al-Sayyāb's translational contribution 101
4 Conclusion 145

Notes 153
Bibliography 156
Index 169

Preface

My journey as a poet-translator started during my master's degree when I studied nine English translations of al-Sayyāb's *Unshūdat al-Maṭar* in 2009.[1] This experience opened my eyes to the interaction between the original poem and its translations, creatively and culturally. I was keen to know how English translations of al-Sayyāb's poem could manipulate their readers on these two levels in a specifically Iraqi system. My second attempt was in 2013. I was invited by Reel Festivals to a workshop called *Found in Translation* between four Scottish (or based in Scotland) and four Iraqi poets to translate each other. The discussion was through interpreters because most of the British poets did not know Arabic, and vice versa. In this way, the poems were produced by a creative rather than a translational process. The discussion about the poems deepened our knowledge not only of the language of the 'other' but also of our own language; it also raised our awareness of the poetic potential each language contributes. The dialogic 'approach' which dominated the workshop resulted in a new third language. The source poem is not simply transferred from one language to another; rather, it is allocated in a new process. This approach helped to involve all poets in the process, especially those who had no translational experience.

The outcome of this project was first presented at the British Council's *Niniti* Literature Festival (Niniti means Lady of Life in Sumerian) and later published as a bilingual book called *This Room Is Waiting* (2014). I translated poems by Krystelle Bamford, William Letford and Jen Hadfield into Arabic. Hadfield translated my poem 'On Whitman' in which I personalized his '*Song of Myself*':

أغني نفسي
في أغنيتكَ الأخيرة
أغني نفسكَ
في أغنيتي الأخيرة
كيف سنكتبهما إذن؟

العشب الذي اقترحته نسياناً يتذكر الآن
الفرح الذي يسبق الكلمة

I sing myself
In your final song
I sing you
In my final song
How can both
Be written then?
The grass you suppose to be oblivion
Remembers now
The delight the forerunner of the word.

(Iskander, tr. Hadfield, 2014: 102–3)

This translation was a collaborative job between writer and translator. In addition, the process of the translation and the discussion, in particular about Walt Whitman as a central theme of the poem, led to a discussion of his influential role, especially in Arabic modernity. It was this experience which first gave me the idea of studying the impact of world modern poets on Arabic modernity as an academic subject. But the most exciting element in this project was when the Scottish poet John Glenday translated part of my poem '*Gilgamesh's Snake*', which is a personal response to the Sumerian *Epic of Gilgamesh*. Subsequently, we developed and enhanced our collaboration to translate the whole book. It won the 2015 University of Arkansas Arabic Translation Award and was published as a bilingual collection by Syracuse University Press in 2016. As Buil stated, 'a bilingual lay-out is always a challenge for the translator, and more so when both versions are presented *en face*' (Buil, 2016: 402). However, as the writer and co-translator, I was fortunate to engage in this collaboration with Glenday, and this joint approach served to ensure that the English translation met the Arabic original. Glenday was rigorous in following poetic aspects of the original, including the form of my poem in the Arabic prosodic system, certain linguistic usages and their cultural significances. Nevertheless, as a poet-translator, Glenday was 'free' to choose what he thought could be poetically presented in the target language. For example, he chose to translate 'الفجر الغريب' as 'the unfamiliar dawn':

غنّى كلَّ شيء:
غنّى الأرصفةَ النائمة

والفجر الغريب.
غنّى روحه وجسده.
حبيبته وأمه
غنّى الملائكة والشياطين.

He sang the sum of things:
The drowsing pavement,
The unfamiliar dawn.
He sang his soul and his body.
His lover and his mother.
He sang angels, he sang devils.

(Iskander, tr. Glenday, 2016: 4–5)

For the same reason, I changed some words and punctuation in the original to match the translation. In other words, translation can also inspire reinterpretation of the original. As this study proposes, I will show the organic relationship between translation and creativity.

I also translated into Arabic a selection of poems by the Noble Laureate Derek Walcott (1930–2017) titled *Hunā Yakmun al-Farāgh* (Here is the emptiness) and published it in Damascus in 2015. My primary motivation in tackling Walcott was the sense of 'affinity' I felt for his writing. The contemplative sense of the world which we find in his later poems describes his 'local' Caribbean life, and yet it appears as a 'universal' concept emotionally. Thus, his poetics have obvious echoes with the works of present-day Arab poets.

As a result of all these experiences, I decided that the next step in this journey would be an investigation of the relationship between translation and modernity in both Western and Arabic cultures, which is now this book.

Acknowledgements

This book is based on my doctoral dissertation presented to the School of Oriental and African Studies (SOAS), the University of London, completed in 2018. I would like to thank my supervisor Professor Stefan Sperl for his time, dedication and wonderful spirit.

I also would like to thank my supervision committee Dr El-Desouky and Dr Feng for their valuable suggestions. My appreciation goes to my examiners Dr Robin Ostle from the University of Oxford and Professor Rebecca Ruth Gould from the University of Birmingham for their suggestions which contributed significantly to the development of this study.

Last but not least, I wish to thank my friends and family for their endless support, and my son, Hussain, who joined us in the middle of this journey to bring infinite love and joy.

Introduction

Translation, as a general concept, functions in most activities: writing, speaking, art, music, design and so on. All of them are regarded as forms of translation. We communicate with each other, whether artistically or ordinarily, by translating ideas, feelings and so on. Literature and translation have always worked hand in hand. History shows us that these two activities were practised in various ways in the classical world as ancient civilizations interacted with each other. Thus, the Sumerian *Epic of Gilgamesh* and other philosophic and scientific texts were translated into Babylonian languages. Greeks translated some Babylonian and Egyptian texts. Babylonians translated texts from Persia and so on. Translating literature was at the heart of their interaction since some sciences and philosophies were embodied or written in literary forms.

Furthermore, the history of literature has shown us that many poetic movements have been based on translation. In the West, Roman poets 'indirectly' translated Greek literature into their works. For example, Homer's *Iliad* resembles Virgil's *the Aeneid* on thematic and stylistic levels. In an introduction to his translation of the *Aeneid*, David West notes that 'the first words of *the Aeneid* are "I sing of arms and of the man . . ." (*arma virumque cano*). Since *the Iliad* is the epic of war, and the first word in *the odyssey* is "man", Virgil has begun by announcing that he is writing an epic in the Homeric style' (West, 2003: xi). Hence, for some Roman poets such as Horace, as Lawrence Venuti notes, 'the function of translating is to construct poetic authorship, and the immediate goal is a good poem in Horatian or Roman terms' (Venuti, 2004: 5). It seems that was the only way for classical Greek literature to be 'translated' and hence to survive. Likewise, Latin literature survived through these translations, enabling it (and any target language) to develop new literary tools and techniques. This is because 'translation is a source of inspiration, rather than an end in itself; it stimulates reflection and acts as a point of departure for further research' (Delisle and Woodsworth, 2012: 95). The importance of translation goes beyond literature. It also applies to Western science as Henry Fischbach states: 'translation was the key to scientific progress as it unlocked for each successive inventor and discover the mind of predecessors who expressed their innovative thoughts in another language' (Fischbach, 1992: 194).

Similarly, in Middle Eastern culture, translation was important for both literature and science. This was clearer after the spread of Islam, when translation was used as a means to learn about the philosophy and science of other cultures, especially Greek, Persian and Indian. However, the rise of translation as an essential movement in Arabic culture began in Baghdad in the ninth century when the Caliph al-Ma'mūn established *Bayt al-Ḥikma* (the House of Wisdom), a time when Greek texts in science and philosophy were being translated into Arabic. The House of Wisdom created an 'international' translational movement involving some five languages: Arabic, Greek, Syriac, Persian and Sanskrit. Abū 'Uthmān al-Jāḥiẓ (*c.* 781–868), who is considered to be the first translation theorist, described the movement as follows:

> The books of India have been transferred (*nuqilat*), and the Greek philosophies have been translated (*turjimat*), and the literatures[1] of the Persians have been converted (*ḥuwwilat*). [As a result,] some of these [works] have increased in excellence and some have not[2] lost a portion [of their original quality].
>
> (Translated by Yücesoy, 2009: 536)[3]

Al-Jāḥiẓ's translational system comprises three types: transference, translation and transformation. Translating al-Jāḥiẓ's terms into English would widen the semiotic chain of each of these terms. Thus, *nuqilat* can be translated into 'move', 'transport', 'transplant', 'shift', 'convey'; *turjimat* into 'interpret', 'treat', 'expound'; and *ḥuwwilat* into 'change', 'turn' and so on (ibid.). Therefore, al-Jāḥiẓ's critical system, as Hayrettin Yücesoy notes, was 'aware that translation is not an uncritical transfer from monolithic language A to monolithic language B, but rather it is a creation of new meaning by transforming the source text through interfering with it' (ibid.). Interestingly, al-Jāḥiẓ did not use 'rigid' categories such as 'right' or 'wrong', 'faithful' or 'unfaithful', 'free' or 'unfree' which, according to Andre Lefevere, have dominated 'the European educational system' since Rome (Lefevere, 1992: 6). Instead, he used descriptive, critical, non-normative terms such as 'developed' 'completed' and so on. Not only is this system still valid, but almost all modern translational schools use similar concepts. For example, for Ezra Pound, as Weissbort notes, translation is 'a form of criticism, the highest in his view since it represents a fusion of the creative and the critical' (Weissbort, 1989: x).

In his statement, al-Jāḥiẓ claims that poetry is untranslatable; it can only be 'converted'. Its themes can be transferred from a language to another, but not its poetic form:

> Poetry cannot be translated and does not render itself to transmission. And whenever it is converted into another language its concinnity (**naẓm**) is broken, its meter is rendered defunct, its beauty evaporates, and that something that inspires wonder and admiration simply absents itself. This is unlike the case with expository prose, though it is likewise true that what was originally written as such is superior to and more genuine in its constitution than prose that has been written by converting metrically balanced poetry.
>
> (Translated by Jackson, 1984: 101–2; see also *Kitāb al-Ḥayawān*, 1965: 75)

Here, al-Jāḥiẓ speaks about the translatability of prose in a practical way, as he had seen the importance of translating Greek philosophy into Arabic and its impact on Islamic culture as a whole. However, his view on the untranslatability of poetry has no basis as there is no mention in the historical record of any such activity at that time. Thus, al-Jāḥiẓ's stance on the translation of poetry is based not on evidence but on his loyalty to Arabic poetry. He states that 'excellence with regard to the art of poetry is limited to the Arabs and those who speak the Arabic language' (ibid.: 101). However, pre-Islamic Arabs did not live in isolation; the Romans and Persians were their neighbours, and translation was the only means to interact with each other. Artistically, poetry was the only literary form for Arabs. Hence non-Arabs could not ignore it because it was part of Arab life. In addition, the pre-Islamic poetry, which was considered to be a 'pure' Arabic form, was not free from hidden 'foreign' features as it had been, to use al-Jāḥiẓ's terms, *nuqilat* or *ḥuwwilat* to Arabic poetry and even *turjimat* into Arabic. Some Arab poets were originally Persian, and they had 'translated' some of their 'wisdoms' into an Arabic poetic form. The original form of a poem is, as al-Jāḥiẓ posits, impossible to translate, but it is not impossible to translate a poem on other levels. Al-Jāḥiẓ himself states that 'If the wisdom of the Arabs were to be translated, the marvellous rhythm would completely disappear. The ideas would all be ideas already expressed by the Persians in their books on wise and sensible living' (Jāḥiẓ, 1969: 133). This statement, if we accept it as is, propounds the notion that Arabic poetry operates at two levels: form (rhythm and rhyme) which is originally Arabic and content which is translated from other cultures. Most importantly, it concedes that poetry can be partially translated from a semantic point of view, and formally completed in the target language. This has been and still is a popular translational approach. However, the phenomenon of the poet-translator in Arabic culture was not considered as an independent and important job as was the case with scientific and philosophic prose until the beginning of the last century when it began to be considered as such by a few poets. In the mid-1950s, translating poetry became more like a modern poetic project with the Lebanese poetry journal *Shi*ʿr, as will be discussed further in the following chapters. In the West, on the other hand, this phenomenon emerged quite early. Steven G. Yao summarizes the translational atmosphere before modernity in the English classical and romantic periods:

> Literary translation functioned primarily as a means for renewing and strategically deploying the authority of the classics, which explains why the most renowned translators in English of earlier eras – Golding and Chapman in the Elizabethan, Dryden and Pope in the Enlightenment, and Browning, Rossetti, and Swinburne in the Victorian – all derive their reputations specifically as translators from their renderings of various Latin and Greek writers and other figures explicitly connected with the classical tradition.
>
> (Yao, 2002: 10)

In the period between the sixteenth and eighteenth centuries, poet-translators mainly translated Roman and Greek literature into 'modern' European languages. Thus, George Chapman and Alexander Pope translated Homer into English; John Dryden translated Ovid and Virgil in the seventeenth century; and in the eighteenth century, Friedrich Hölderlin translated Sophocles into German. Hölderlin's translational work has been considered by many scholars for its importance to his own poetics. Like most poet-translators, as will be investigated in this study, Hölderlin, according to David Constantine, offered 'no theory of translation and had no fixed way of translating either; it varied according to his varying needs' (Constantine, 2011: 81). Nevertheless, his few comments are 'suggestive'. In his letter of March 1794 to his friend Christian Ludwig Neuffer, who was translating Virgil, Hölderlin stated that 'the great

Roman's spirit will surely be a wonderful strengthener of your own. In the struggle with his language yours must become more and more agile and vigorous' (cited in ibid.).

Like al-Jāḥẓ, Hölderlin believes that translation could enrich the target language. He developed this vision in his letter of July 1794: 'Translation does our language good, like gymnastics. It gets beautifully supple when forced to accommodate itself to foreign beauty and greatness and also often to foreign whims' (ibid.). The term 'foreign' is central to Hölderlin's translations. This is reflected, in particular, in his translations of Sophocles's plays. He 'reveals the strangeness of the Greek tragic Word, whereas most "classic" translations tend to attenuate or cancel it' (Berman, 2004: 276).

Friedrich Schleiermacher figuratively describes the necessity of the 'foreign' for his native culture:

> Just as our soil itself has probably become richer and more fertile, and our climate more lovely and mild after much transplanting of foreign plants, so do we feel that our language, which we practice less because of our Nordic lethargy, can only flourish and develop its own perfect power through the most varied contacts with what is foreign.
>
> (Schleiermacher, 1992: 53)

The importance of translation for the target culture was also highlighted by some Arab writers in the first half of the last century. For example, in his essay, 'Let Us Translate' which was published in his book *al-Ghirbāl* (1923), Mīkhā'īl Na'īma encourages Arab writers to translate the world's literary masterworks:[4]

> Let us translate! And glorify the position of the translator because he is a mode of acquaintance between us and the greater human family. It is also because in his revealing the secrets of great minds and large hearts covered by the obscures of a language, the translator raises us from a small limited place, we wallow in its mud to an atmosphere that enables us to see the wider world. Hence, we can live its ideas, hopes, joys and sorrows.
>
> (Na'īma, 1964: 126)

For some poet-translators, enrichment also means that they can use in their translational works what is 'strange' or forbidden, artistically and linguistically. The English poet Edward FitzGerald, who is known more for his translation of *The Rubaiyat* of Omar Khayyam than for his own poems, used some non-English words in his translation. The Argentinian writer Borges explains that translation allows the translator to use what might be forbidden in his native language. He states that when the English poets Dante Gabriel Rossetti and Algernon Charles Swinburne discovered *The Rubaiyat*, they

> felt the beauty of the translation, yet we wonder if they would have felt this beauty had FitzGerald presented the *Rubāiyāt* as an original (partly it *was* original) rather than as a translation. Would they think FitzGerald should have been allowed to say, 'Awake! For morning in the bowl of night . . .'? . . . And I wonder if FitzGerald would have been allowed the 'noose of light' and the 'sultan's turret' in a poem of his own.
>
> (Borges, 2000: 69–70)

For modernists, the concept of 'enrichment' was at the top of their poetic projects in both Western and Arabic cultures. For example, Baudelaire's translation of Edgar Allan Poe, as Marilyn Gaddis Rose notes, allowed the French poet to use

> full expression of desperation, morbidity, excess; full expression, in short, of the extravagance of feelings beyond the strictures of high bourgeois taste exemplified by his mother and stepfather. Poe allowed him to make verbal choice which the reader would not expect. Rhetorically, Poe's prose permitted Baudelaire to express himself rhythmically but with licence.
>
> (Rose, 1997: 31–2)

This is because, as George Steiner explains, the poet-translator through his translation of other poets 'can modernize not only to induce a feeling of immediacy but in order to advance his own cause as a writer. He will import from abroad convention, models of sensibility, expressive genres which his own language and culture have not yet reached' (Steiner, 1975: 351). However, it seems that, to use Ana Mata Buil's words in her essay 'Poet-translators as Double Link in the Global Literary System', 'affinity' is one of the main reasons that a poet translates another poet (Buil, 2016: 406). Thus, Baudelaire translated Poe, Eliot and Perse translated each other, Octavio Paz and William Carlos Williams did the same, Borges translated Whitman, Adūnīs translated Perse and Eliot, al-Sayyāb translated Eliot and Sitwell, Sa'dī Yūsuf translated Whitman, etc. For example, Adūnīs attributes his success in translating Perse to the type of French poet who 'writes poetry as he breaks the world [in order to] reshape it'

(Adūnīs, 2010). In this statement, Adūnīs refers to the poetic kinship between him and Perse. Baudelaire states that he translated Poe because the American writer resembled him: *Savez-vous pourquoi j'ai patiemment traduit Poe? Parce qu'il me ressemblait* (cited in Buil, 2016: 406). Buil adds to 'affinity' two reasons that drive a poet to translate another poet. The first reason is that 'poetry is considered to be translated by poets'. This reason is 'related to the notion that the translation of poetry should be in turn a poetic composition in the target language, and not a meaning-explanation of the original' (ibid.: 402). This also means that poets who themselves approach foreign poetry are more likely able to replace the 'missing' original artistic form than those who are translators but not poets. The second reason involves increasing the symbolic capital of the target text (TT) in translating a certain source text (ST). The latter underlines 'the will [of poet-translators] to win more symbolic capital through translation by association [with influential original poets]' (ibid.: 403; brackets added). This occurs especially when 'the translated poets have a more central position inside [their] literary system' and can therefore 'increase the symbolic capital of their poet-translators, who see their name linked to the consecrated poet' (ibid.: 404; brackets added). In modern Arabic poetics, Eliot and Perse, for example, are always associating with al-Sayyāb and Adūnīs respectively.

These reasons highlight not just the background of this phenomenon but also the importance of the poet-translator in world poetry. Despite this activity for the poet-translator being first and foremost a poetic job, it creates a type of modern creativity across different cultures since 'openness' to other cultures was the favourite modernists' slogan. This movement was established as a reaction to the classicism which glorified tradition and to the romanticism which mainly focused on the poetic 'self' as a source of inspiration for the poet. Thus, the modern poet-translators 'explored alternative sources for such enabling models, employing translation as a strategy by which to underwrite their own cultural ambitions and advance their own aesthetic and ideological ends' (Yao, 2002: 10). Translation aesthetically fulfils poet-translators' own poetics, and ideologically voices their unspoken poetics.

In addition to these artistic and political quests, translation for modernist poets is also a way, to use Walter Benjamin's concept, to relieve the poet's 'existential poverty'. In his book *Baudelaire*, Claude Pichois underlines the importance of translation for Baudelaire as a 'vitalizing' activity and assures himself and his mother that he is working. Explaining Pichois's approach to Baudelaire, Alina Clej clarifies that translation for the French poet is a representation of

> an 'alibi', a means of compensating for his lack of creativity, as well as a form of self-justification: 'a bourgeois guarantee', says Pichois, 'meant to reassure his mother, Ancelle, and himself'. Following Pichois, Baudelaire's 'meager vitality', his 'vertigo' in front of his blank white page, his fear of being confronted with his own 'impotence' forced him into the activity of translation, which provided a prop to his self-confidence. In the case of translation, the score is already given, and the translator's imagination can play along the margins, or weave in and out between the blank spaces of the printed page, like a parasitic plant.
>
> (Clej, 1997: 11; footnote 12)

Unlike previous movements, modernity looks differently at the past and how it can function artistically in the present. This issue has haunted the discourse of modernity since Baudelaire. Paul de Man explains that the French poet viewed modernity as 'an acute sense of the present, as a constitutive element of all aesthetic experience' (De Man, 1989: 156). This can be observed in both his original and translational works. Baudelaire states that 'the pleasure we derive from the *representation of the present* (la représentation du présent) is not merely due to the beauty it may display, but also to the essential "presentness" of the present' (ibid.: 156). Trying to define modernity by its historical and artistic opposites, de Man highlights:

> Among the various antonyms that come to mind as possible opposites for 'modernity' – a variety which is itself symptomatic of the complexity of the term – none is more fruitful than 'history'. 'Modern' can be used in opposition to 'traditional' or even to 'classical'. For some French and American contemporaries, 'modern' could even mean the opposite of 'romantic'.
>
> (ibid.: 144)

But modernity for poets like Rimbaud and Antonin Artaud, as de Man himself explains, is more than the opposite of 'traditional' or 'classical'. It 'exists in the form of a desire to wipe out whatever came earlier, in hope of reaching at last a point that could be called a true present, a point of origin that marks a new departure' (ibid.: 148). However, for other modernists such as Eliot and Pound, to use Roxana Birsanu's words, 'history, more precisely the interdependence of past and present, lies at the core of the modernist concept of culture' (Birsanu, 2011: 181). She adds, 'it is the awareness of the close connection between the two axes that ensures cultural survival and development not only at a European level, but at a universal scale as well' (ibid.). Modernizing the past was at the heart of world modernists, especially the Anglo-American poets such as Pound and Eliot. Like most world modernists, Eliot was a poet-translator as well. He treated the concept of 'tradition' and how it can be observed through 'the creative eye' of the translator to 'digest' and to use it in modern literature:

> If we are to digest the heavy food of historical and scientific knowledge that we have eaten we must be prepared for much greater exertions. We need a digestion which can assimilate both Homer and Flaubert. We need a careful study of renaissance Humanists and Translators, such as Mr. Pound has begun. We need an eye which can see the past in its place with its definite differences from the present, and yet so lively that it shall be as present to us as the present. This is the creative eye.
>
> (Eliot, 1960: 77)

For Eliot and Pound, translation was also a 'fertilizing effect' in two ways 'by importing new elements which may be assimilated, and by restoring the essentials which have been forgotten in traditional literary method. There occurs, in the process, a happy fusion between the spirit of the original and the mind of the translator; the result is not exoticism but rejuvenation' (Eliot, 1917: 102).

For the modernist poets, translation was also a 'vitalising effect' (Eliot, 1960: 73). Steven G. Yao declares that translation for modernist poets was 'much more than either just a minor mode of literary production or an exercise of apprenticeship' (Yao, 2002: 6). Yao adds that although for some poets translation served to satisfy their traditional side, it also is a fundamental part of the modernist movement (ibid.). Indeed, Yao considers Pound the most influential modernist poet because of the uniqueness of his translational work. He describes Pound's work as 'original composition', possessing an 'explicitly and generative, rather than a derivative and supplementary, role in the process of literary cultural formation' (ibid.: 2). Edwin Gentzler states that Pound's translational work centred completely 'on words in action and "luminous" details' (Gentzler, 2001: 15). Daniel Katz explains that 'translation is being viewed as a fundamental element of Pound's work and thought, and not just as an ancillary activity' (Katz, 2007: 71). As Bassnett states, translation for Pound as a modernist poet was, first and foremost, 'a work of art in its own right, for anything less is pointless' (Bassnett, 1998: 64). This demonstrates the crucial role that translation played in shaping English modernism. For modernist poets, translation added a new spirit to their experiences and offered a new way of approaching their own heritage.

These concepts are equally important for Arabic modernists since translating 'other' poetry gave them a sense of freedom on poetic and cultural levels. And the approach to 'tradition' and 'foreign' also formed modern Arabic poetics. In *An Introduction to Arab Poetics*, Adūnīs views modernity as resulting from these two sources:

> Modernity in Arabic poetry had its origins in a climate which brought together two independent elements: awareness of new urban culture which developed in Baghdad in the eighth century, and a new use of the language to embrace this awareness and express it in poetry. It developed in a spirit of opposition to the ancient, at the same time interacting with non-Arab currents. The whole thrust of Arab civilization testifies to this, for it is a synthesis of the pre-Islamic period and Islam, from whence it derives its origins and heritage, and of other cultures – Persian, Greek and Indian – through adoption and interaction, permeated by the most ancient elements deposited in historical memory: Sumerian, Babylonian, Aramaean and Syriac.
>
> (Adonis, 1990: 89)

Adūnīs refers here to what is known in Arabic poetry to be 'the first modernity', namely when poets such as Abū Nuwās and Abū Tammām in the eighth and ninth centuries renewed Arabic poetry formally and stylistically. Formally, Abū Nuwās broke what is called *'amūd al-shi'r*, which can be defined as 'principles and laws stipulated by some critics in the 'Abbāsid period to differentiate good from bad poetry' (Faddul, 1992: 280). Abū Nuwās's revolt, according to Adūnīs, 'violated a firmly-rooted artistic standard which took a socio-cultural form with an authoritative dimension' (ibid.). Stylistically, Abū Tammām introduced new metaphors and images to the poetic language. As we have discussed, the poetic interaction with other cultures, although it existed, was not classified as a translational one as in the case of prose. However, translation played a major role alongside Arabic tradition in 'the second modernity' which developed in Baghdad too in the middle of the last century. Arabic poetry changed not just on a stylistic and a thematic level but also formally. Adūnīs explains:

> The cultural background of Arab poets and critics has derived from two divergent traditions: that of the self (ancient, traditionalist) and that of the other (modern, European-American). These two traditions blur or blot out the values of modernity and creativity in the Arab literary heritage.
>
> (Adonis: 80)

Adūnīs acknowledges that he 'was one of those who were captivated by Western culture' (ibid.). However, the Arabic tradition is present in his works in his application of new techniques. Adūnīs and his pioneering generation view modernity as a dialogic concept between their tradition and Western poetics, and through this concept, Arabic tradition will be, to use Eliot's words, 'so lively that it shall be as present to us as the present'. In addition, Adūnīs was aware of the discursive contexts of modernity although he did not use this term. What I mean by this is that a poetic translational phenomenon should be treated both linguistically and from a sociocultural perspective. Adūnīs states that the only way 'to reach a proper understanding of the poetics of Arab modernity' is by 'viewing it in its social, cultural and political context' (ibid.: 76). This is because 'the problematic of poetic modernity (*ḥadātha*) in Arabic society goes beyond poetry in the narrow sense'. This problematic 'is indicative of a general cultural crisis, which is in some sense a crisis of identity' (ibid.). In *Bayān al-Ḥadātha* (Manifesto of Modernity), Adūnīs states that Arabic modernity cannot function unless it works in harmony with other discourses such as epistemology, psychology and science:

> The problem of poetic modernity in the Arabic language is a central part of the problem of epistemology as a relationship between man and the unknown. It is also a part of the problem of science as a relationship between man and nature, and a part of the problem of technology as a practical experience. Therefore, [poetic modernity] cannot be separated from a general problematic which is linked to both the existence of the Arabs and their destiny as a civilization.
>
> (Adūnīs, 1995: 64)

The Arab modernists were greatly interested in discussing these 'problems'. They were also interested in exchanging, to use Birsanu's words about Eliot, 'ideas . . . as well as the concept of tradition which lies at the core of [their] poetics'. Those modernists 'suggest a constant preoccupation with a form of cultural transfer, namely translation' (Birsanu, 2011: 182). Like Eliot, some Arab modernists, in addition to their main career as poets, worked as literary editors. For example, Yūsuf al-Khāl and Adūnīs established the journal *Shi'r* (Poetry) in 1957. *Shi'r* presented a huge effort to bring together young modernist poets and writers of Arabic culture such as al-Sayyāb, Nāzik al-Malā'ika, Buland al-Ḥaydarī Jabrā Ibrāhīm Jabrā, Sa'dī Yūsuf, Lūwīs 'Awaḍ and Ṣalāḥ 'Abd al-Ṣabūr. Like world modernists, translation for those poets was at the core of their modernity. Thus, the works of Walt Whitman, Pound, Eliot, Baudelaire, Rimbaud, Perse, Auden, Stephen Spender and so on were translated into Arabic by the Arab modernists themselves. This effort created a translational phenomenon in modern Arabic poetics. It is not only the pioneering generation that contributes to and benefits from translating poetry but also the following generations whose poets are almost all translators. Clearly, many poets benefited from world poetry through translations. For example, 'when asked about the poets who have influenced his work, the Palestinian poet Maḥmud Darwish . . . listed, among others, Elouard, Aragon, Nazim Hikmat, Lorca, and Neruda' (Badawi, 1975: 262). M. M. Badawi describes this as an example of 'the international cultural background of the young Arab poet of today' (ibid.).

However, not all translations had the same impact on modern Arabic poetry. For example, Nāzik's translations of the romantic English poets did not influence Arabic poetry. Also, neither al-Khāl's translational selection (1958) nor Tawfīq Ṣāyigh's selection of American poets (1961) had a direct impact on Arabic poetic modernity, although they included poets such as Robert Frost, Wallace Stevens, William Carlos Williams, Archibald MacLeish and E. E. Cummings. Ṣāyigh's translation of Eliot's *The Four Quartets*, as M. J. al-Musawi notices, 'did not have an immediate strong impression on young poets who had already searched for the new and the challenging in every poetry, Arabic, Persian, Turkish, Russian, Spanish, French, or Anglo-American' (al-Musawi, 2006: 234). In my opinion, the reason behind the impact of certain English poems such as Eliot's *The Waste Land*, Whitman's *Song of Myself* and Edith Sitwell's *The Shadow of Cain* on modern Arabic poetry is that these poems were approached discursively in the target culture. They were approached not as 'isolated' linguistic texts but, as a 'world' which has non-linguistic contexts as well. Moreover, these English poems were chosen by Arab poet-translators because of their 'affinities' to Arabic poetic modernity thematically and stylistically although they were created in 'foreign' cultures as will be explained in detail later.

This book is a study of the translations of some major English poems by pioneering Arab poets, including Badr Shākir al-Sayyāb, Jabrā Ibrāhīm Jabrā, Adūnīs Yūsuf al-Khāl, Lūwīs 'Awaḍ and Sa'dī Yūsuf. These translations will form the core of this study. Within this context, I will analyse these translations situationally and textually. Equally important, this study will observe the emergence of a new poetic atmosphere, influenced by these translations, in the pioneers' own output and in the work of other poets. This book will study how these translations have led to changes in modern Arabic poetry from the mid-twentieth century onwards, at both formal and thematic levels. They also led to the creation of new poetic schools:

1. *Al-Shi'r al-Ḥurr* (Free Verse). This school was influenced formally and thematically by modernist English poets, notably Eliot, Pound and Sitwell.
2. *Qaṣīdat al-Nathr* (Prose Poem). Although the impact of French poetry is very significant, especially in terms of this genre's Lebanese proponents, this school was also influenced, in its Iraqi variant, by the American poet Walt Whitman and by others who were inspired by him – for example, Allen Ginsberg.

This book is thus both a translational and a comparative study. It requires a comparative analysis of the STs and the TTs. However, this comparison is of a discursive type, as it analyses both texts according to their backgrounds and their cultural impacts on both systems. As Umberto Eco said, 'translation does not only concern words and language in general but also the world, or at least the possible world described by a given text' (Eco, 2004: 16).

This approach will encompass the three main contexts which operate in any discursive process: situational, verbal and cognitive. Since this study attempts to be comprehensive, I will adopt Michel Foucault's definition of discourse as it serves this purpose. Unlike the linguistic definition which focuses on one level, Foucault's concept is more inclusive and dynamic. In *The Archaeology of Knowledge*, Foucault uses the term 'discourse' to refer to 'the general domain of all statements, sometimes as an individualizable group of statements, and sometimes as a regulated practice that accounts for a number of statements'

(Foucault, 1972: 80). As an authority on Foucault, Sara Mills opines that the French thinker intends that 'discourse' 'can be used to refer to all utterances and statements which have been made which have meaning and which have some effect' (Mills, 2003: 53). According to Mills, Foucault 'used the term discourse to refer to "regulated practices that account for a number of statements"' (ibid.). In addition, there are certain 'rules and structures' which create certain 'utterances' and 'statements' (ibid.). For the analyses undertaken in this book, I have approached these 'rules, utterances and statements' in distinct contexts which can be defined as follows:

1. The situational context focuses on the background and reasons behind choosing these poems. One of the reasons is the crucial role of the STs as modernist poems, not only their native poetic context but in world poetry as a whole. Andrea Kenesei explains that 'the more common features the two cultures share, the easier the adaptation of the poem to the target culture' (Kenesei, 2010: xxi). Arabic culture was ready to receive and adapt such poems. It is also because the subject matter introduced new 'humanistic' themes of importance to world poets. For example, Eliot's *The Waste Land*, which was written in the aftermath of the First World War, found echoes in modern Arabic poetry after the Second World War.
2. The verbal context addresses the linguistic levels of these translations and underlines the stylistic impact of the original texts on the poet-translators' own writings. We will trace this textual inspiration in order to identify the change which occurred in Arabic poetry and to locate it cognitively in the received system. In terms of technicality, a comparative analysis will serve to highlight the translational strategies applied in this context and their poetic nature. However, as Susan Bassnett states, the comparative analysis 'should not be used to place the translations in some kind of league table, rating x higher than y, but rather to understand what went on in the actual translation process' (Bassnett, 1998: 70). Therefore, the question of the 'linguistic' accuracies of these translations, and how close they are to the originals, is of secondary importance. That said, any inaccuracies in these translations will be flagged up if they affect the discursive reception of the ST in the target culture. Here, it is worth mentioning the difference between the text

and discourse. Jacob L. Mey argues that 'discourse is different from text'. In the first instance, this is because discourse 'embodies more than just the text', and secondly 'discourse is what makes the text context-bound, in the widest sense of the term' (Mey, 1993: 187). However, Bronislaw Malinowski adds that text can be studied as a form 'divorced' from its whole discourse (Malinowski, 1935: 8). In fact, the two other discursive contexts can be studied separately, either by highlighting the background of the given texts in a situational context or by underlining their impact on a certain culture in a cognitive sense. However, this type of approach would discursively produce a partial reading. Hence this book aims to study each translation contextually and comprehensively.

3. The cognitive context covers the new cultural roles that these translations played in the target culture. This context is especially important in terms of developing any cultural phenomenon (for many cultures, including in particular Arabic, poetry is the oldest and most important cultural form). Any discourse is incomplete without this context, as it focuses on the resonance of a 'foreign' culture in a 'native' one. Cognitive poetics is so important and popular in literary analysis and is described by many scholars as the 'cognitive turn' of modern studies. A linguistic analysis can no longer approach the complexity of modern texts. Hence the linguistic level of a text is treated initially, albeit it is merely a result of the workings of the cognitive and situational contexts. According to Peter Stockwell, there are six principles of cognitive poetics which can be observed partially or wholly in any discursive process. These principles are experientialism, generalization, stylistics, continuity, embodiment and ecology (Stockwell, 2009: 2–5).

I should mention that the principles of the cognitive context are not used here as 'rigid' abstract ones, but rather as flexible and representative. Stockwell himself explains that 'all of these principles of connection and continuity, a holistic and ecological sense of our place in the world and our literary articulations, entail a key new form of analysis' (ibid.: 5).

In this study, I will adapt and focus on some principles more than others. For example, 'generalization' will be used here as 'common aspects' of Arabic modernity which are influenced by English poetics, that is, how 'common aspects' of the source culture influenced and created 'similar' aspects in the target culture. In addition, 'continuity' is used here as a link between the literary generations of the target culture. This principle can be extended to include the continuity of other cultural forms in modern poetry. For example, using and adapting other semiotic forms is very popular in both English and Arabic poetry. Both principles function cognitively through 'experientialism' which can be regarded as a 'situational' principle, because it explains the reasons for 'discovering' and 'understanding' certain English poems on the part of Arab modernists. These principles obviously function by 'stylistics' as a 'verbal' principle which attracts the readership's initial attention. As we can see, all discursive contexts and cognitive principles often overlap owing to their dynamic natures. Hence, these contexts and principles, alongside other translational strategies, will assist me in developing an analytical discursive approach to the study of Arabic translations of English poetry.

Needless to say, this book will consider the translators' introductions, comments footnotes, interviews and so on. These materials can be used as probes to explain (and sometimes to examine) their translational productions. They can also be used verbally to explain (or develop) a new register and textual variations which have been received by the target language. In addition, these extra-text materials can also be employed to 'situationalize' cognitively the translations by relating them to the environments in which they were constructed. Malinowski terms this 'the context of situation', which includes 'the totality of the culture surrounding the act of text production and reception' (Hatim & Mason, 1990: 36–7). In my opinion, it is more than a 'situational' one, and also shows the organic relationship between the discursive contexts. Finally, this approach should serve to answer the question of this study which consists of three principles:

1. What encouraged pioneer Arab poets to translate these poems in the first place?
2. How did modernist Arab poets approach these poems textually?
3. Why did these poems influence modern Arabic poetry more than others?

These questions will be answered in the Conclusion alongside identifying other translational propositions.

Therefore, the discourse analysis which I advocate here helps to analyse a translated poem as a discursive process, which does not happen in a vacuum 'but rather in the contexts of all the traditions of two literatures' (Lefevere, 1992: 6). Equivalence, as a translational approach whose linguistic aspects had dominated this field in the 1950s and 1960s by Roman Jakobson, Eugene Nida, J. P. Vinay and J. Darbelnet and J. C. Catford (Bassnett, 2002: 34–40), is used here to highlight certain verbal issues that affect the other contexts but not as a primary approach. This is because I am trying to discover why a poem in a certain situation creates a certain culture in its system and functions in a similar 'degree of success in another situation or culture', to use Lefevere's words (Lefevere, 1992: 8). In addition, this book will investigate how poet-translators artistically and thematically manipulate the STs in the target literature. This treatment sometimes goes against the dominant aesthetic themes, such as the political, ideological or religious, and sometimes it is in compliance with them. Hence, this book will be divided into the following chapters and a conclusion.

Chapter 1 is devoted to Arabic translations of Eliot's poem *The Waste Land*. This poem has been translated into Arabic many times. I will study three of these translations which were made by four modernists in the 1950s, and I will argue that translating this poem significantly inspired poetic innovation in Arabic. The importance of this poem in its English system and world poetry is also considered here. In addition, this chapter highlights Eliot's prose writings and the importance of their critical tools for Arab modernists. I selected Eliot because Arab modernists approached him before, more so than any other poet.

Chapter 2 studies three Arabic translations of Whitman's poem *Song of Myself*. The manner in which this poem was received in the target culture will be demonstrated in its three discursive contexts. The question of why Arab modernists approached Eliot before Whitman will be raised in this chapter alongside their different impacts on Arabic poetic modernity.

Chapter 3 deals with al-Sayyāb's translations of major English and Anglo-American poets including Sitwell, Pound and Eliot. By choosing al-Sayyāb I aim to investigate the impact of his translations on his own poetics, as the 'first' modernist, and on modern Arabic poetry in general. Al-Sayyāb's translational work can be regarded as a case study, and therefore it follows Eliot and Whitman.

The Conclusion is intended to contribute to a reformulation of a discursive approach which links Arabic translation and world poetry, and to propose some key features of the analysis of these Arabic translations and underline their crucial roles in establishing Arabic poetic modernity.

1

The Arabic waste lands

Eliot's writings had a major impact on modern poetry across the world. Some scholars define poetic modernity by Eliot's poetry, in large part because of his masterpiece *The Waste Land*. This poem was first published in October 1922 in the opening issue of *The Criterion*, a British literary journal founded and edited by Eliot himself. In November 1922, the poem was also published in *The Dial*, an American modernist magazine. The poem

> was drafted during a rest cure at Margate [in England] . . . and Lausanne [in Switzerland] . . . during the autumn of 1921 by a convalescent preoccupied partly with the ruin of post-war Europe, partly with his own health and the conditions of his servitude to a bank in London, partly with a hardly exorable apprehension that two thousand years of European continuity had for the first time run dry.
>
> (Kenner, 2007: 7–8)

But it seems that most of the poem was written in Lausanne. Eliot himself explains in a letter, dated 25 June 1922, to the American lawyer John Quinn who bought the manuscript of *The Waste Land*:

> I have written mostly when I was at Lausanne for treatment last winter, a long poem of about 450 lines, which, with notes I am adding, will make a book of thirty or forty pages. I think it is the best I have ever done, and Pound thinks so too.
>
> (Eliot, 2011: 681)

The poet also explained that some passages 'date from as far as 1914. Part One probably completed by October 1919. The body of the poem was written and assembled November 1921-January 1922' (cited in Southam, 1996: 126). As a book, the poem was first published in New York by Boni and Liverlight in 1922, and then in London in 1923 by Hogarth Press (which was founded by the English novelist Virginia Woolf and her husband Leonard in 1917 to publish modernist authors).

As its manuscript illustrates, *The Waste Land* is a poem obviously written by Eliot, but its final version was a result of a collaboration with his mentor Ezra Pound. In her introduction to *T. S. Eliot The Waste Land: A Facsimile and Transcript of the Original Drafts including the Annotations of Ezra Pound*, his second wife, Valerie Eliot, highlights Pound's impact on the poem: 'early January [1922] Eliot returned to London, after spending a few days in Paris, where he submitted the manuscript of *The Waste Land* to Pound's maieutic skill' (Eliot, 1971: xxii). Pound described the manuscript of the poem: '*The Waste Land* was placed before me as a series of poems. I advised him what to leave out' (cited in Kenner: 7). Eliot himself described *The Waste Land* as 'a sprawling chaotic poem . . . which left [Pound's] hands, reduced to about half its size, in the form in which it appears in print' (cited in ibid.: 7–8). Both poets did not wait for the poem to be 'completed' and born naturally; instead, they decided to 'deliver' it by a 'caesarean operation'. In a letter to Eliot on 24 December 1921 to discuss his collaboration with Eliot, Pound included his poem 'Sage Homme'[1] which has a double meaning: 'wise man' and 'male midwife'. It seems that Pound preferred the latter:

> These are the poems of Eliot
> By the Uranian Muse begot;
> A Man their Mother was
> A Muse their Sire.
> . . . .
> Ezra performed the Caesarean Operation.
>
> (Pound, 1950: 170)

In *Eliot*, Stephen Spender explains Pound's task in revising *The Waste Land*, or as he puts it, Pound's 'Caesarean Operation': 'What Pound did essentially was to release the energy of the poem and suppress what was distracting, superfluous, slovenly, or rhythmically or imagistically obstructive in it' (Spender, 1975: 93). Pound was, for Eliot, not only a poetic guide but also his cultural mind. In *T. S. Eliot and the Art of Collaboration*, Richard Badenhausen states:

> In March of 1922, T. S. Eliot wrote to Ezra Pound to solicit his assistance in launching *The Criterion*, the influential quarterly Eliot eventually edited for over sixteen years. Eliot envisioned the journal as a vehicle that would allow

> for the collective articulation of the modernist program, yet with a decidedly internationalist slant: the same week he posted the Pound letter, Eliot contacted both Valery Larbaud and Hermann Hesse seeking contributions for the review. In this regard, he was following the lead of Pound, who had earlier understood the importance of trying to unite modernism's work under the umbrella of a single publication.
>
> (Badenhausen, 2005: 61)

The Waste Land was created in such an interactive cultural environment. '[It] is the best-known example of modernist collaboration, an affiliation that was not fully understood until Valerie Eliot's 1971 publication of drafts that detail the evolution of the poem' (ibid.: 62). The manuscript of *The Waste Land* also shows us that the original title of the poem was 'He Do the Police in Different Voices'. This line was borrowed from Charles Dickens's *Our Mutual Friend*. But inspired by Jessie L. Weston's *From Ritual to Romance*, Eliot finally settled on *The Waste Land* which has appeared as the poem's title since its first publication in 1922.

As underlined previously, the phrase 'waste land' was interpreted by some of Eliot's critics as the fall of 'Western civilization' in the aftermath of the First World War (1914–18). As Spender explains, the main theme of *The Waste Land* 'is the breakdown of civilization and the conditioning of those who live within it by that breakdown, so that every situation is a symptom of the collapse of values'. Therefore, it is not a 'private' theme even though 'the personal grief is transcended [and] felt there' (Spender: 106). Stylistically, this theme 'is prevented from being journalistic (expressing the despair of a post-war generation merely) by the vision of the whole past civilization within which the contemporary examples of modern life are enclosed' (ibid.). Thus *The Waste Land* can be regarded as an elegy for post-war Europe intensified by Eliot's mental and physical pains at that time. As Ronald Tamplin explains, this poem 'had mapped and given some structure to the spiritual chaos Eliot perceived outside himself and felt inside himself. It indicated the thirst only and did not slake it' (Tamplin, 1988: 27). This 'chaos' is depicted by 'fragmented' images to reflect the collapsed civilization. Furthermore, the 'fragmentariness' formally 'suited' such a long poem, as Spender suggested. This technique poetically functions in *The Waste Land* when it is 'projected into many scenes, with shifts of centre of attention and mood, lends force to the obsession, gives the poem its apocalyptic visionary force' (Spender: 106). However, these 'fragments are organized in order to stress the contrast between prophetic and contemporary voices' (ibid.). Indeed, the voices of *The Waste Land* are not of one type. On the one hand, this poem was considered a manifesto of modernity, and on the other hand, it, as Seamus Heaney notes, 'reproduced . . . a sense of bewilderment and somnambulism, a flow of inventive expressionist scenes reminiscent of those which Virgil and Dante encounter in the divine comedy' (Heaney, 1989: 98). It also ranged through other cultures such as 'the Eastern texts that Eliot had first come across in his Harvard classes' (Tamplin, 1988: 27). It seems that these Eastern texts helped to present *The Waste Land*, to use Ted Hughes's terms, in its 'most fully, most nakedly' vision which was written by a 'seer of a very rare kind'. Hughes further explains that this poem 'is precisely the clairvoyant quality of [Eliot's] vision of contemporary urban reality, the hallucinated depth and complexity and actuality of it, which sets him apart from, and perhaps a little above, all other poets of the last three hundred years' (Hughes, 1992: 12). Indeed, *The Waste Land*, as the American poet William Carlos Williams described its first publication in America in 1922 by *The Dial*, 'wiped out our world as if an atom bomb had been dropped upon it and our brave sallies into the unknown were turned to dust' (Williams, 1967: 146). C. D. Lewis describes *The Waste Land* as Eliot's greatest work 'and probably a greater one than any other poetry of the century' (Lewis, 1969: 22). But he attributes the influence of this poem 'on present-day verse . . . to its subject matter – more so, perhaps, than to the novelties of technique' (ibid.). Some writers regard *The Waste Land* not as an original poem, in a sense this technique 'will be found in novels and poems by other writers', but, as F. B. Pinion clarifies, 'never in all probability at the same sustained intensity. What is peculiar to *The Waste Land* is the collocation of images and scenes in a manner calculated to evoke feelings and accordant ideas, without overt statements of meaning' (Pinion, 1989: 119).

Indeed, the 'novelty' of Eliot's technique is reflected in his ability to form these 'fragmented' images, ideas and feelings and to orchestrate them in such a unique 'symphony'. I. A. Richards called Eliot's poetic technique 'music of ideas' (Richards, 1960: 233). Alongside his choice of themes, Eliot's technique inspired modernist poets to develop similar styles and subject matters. Modern Arabic poetry was greatly influenced by Eliot's writings. In his essay 'Modern Arabic Literature and the West', Jabrā explains that the impact of Eliot on the generation of pioneering Arab poets

> was eruptive and insistent. This influence came, at first, through his early poetry and was partly responsible for the great change that has since overtaken Arabic forms. This was so because it happened that the people who read him most and translated him and commented on his work were themselves the leading young writers and poets of the new generation.
>
> (Jabra, 1971: 81)

The poets of this generation were fascinated by Eliot 'mainly because he seemed to be an articulate and concise advocate of their incipient thoughts' (ibid.: 82). Therefore, they 'responded so passionately' to Eliot's works, and especially to *The Waste Land*, 'because they, too, went through an experience of universal tragedy, not only in World War II, but also, and more essentially, in the Palestine debacle and its aftermath' (ibid.: 83). Thus, *The Waste Land* was translated in its entirety three times by Arab poet-translators.[2] First, Eliot's poem was translated by Adūnīs and Yūsuf al-Khāl and published in the Lebanese journal *Shi'r* (Poetry) in 1958. Second, it was translated by Lūwīs 'Awaḍ and likewise published in *Shi'r* in 1968.[3] Third, the poem was translated by Tawfīq Ṣāyigh in the 1950s, but he did not publish it during his lifetime. The manuscript of this translation was discovered by his family after his death in 1970. Unfortunately, Ṣāyigh's *Al-'Arḍ al-Kharāb* had to wait a long time to be edited by the Iraqi poet Mūḥammad Maẓlūm and published by al-Jamal Publishing House in Beirut in 2017. According to his own notes, Ṣāyigh approached *The Waste Land* in Beirut in 1951 and finished it in Cambridge in 1953. This translation was only published recently and raises the question of its impact on Arabic poetry from the middle of the last century. Nevertheless, I include it here because it shows Ṣāyigh's early involvement with Eliot's poetry. Therefore, it is worth exploring its textual level as well as Ṣāyigh's contribution to Arabic poetic modernity.

1.1 The situational context

Arab modernist poets began to approach Eliot's writings, especially *The Waste Land*, in the middle of 1940s. It seems that 'Awaḍ pioneered the encounter with Eliot's works when he was asked by Ṭāhā Ḥusayn to write some essays on influential modern English authors 'who had made a mark in their respective fields', with a view to publishing them in *Al-Kātib al-Miṣrī* (DeYoung, 1998: 68).

Thus, ʿAwaḍ published a number of articles in this journal, and his essay about Eliot came to have a huge influence on young Arab poets. In the same essay, he translated the whole text of *The Hollow Men*, and some sections from the middle and the end of 'The Love Song of J. Alfred Prufrock'. The essay also includes his translation of the first fifteen lines of 'Burnt Norton' from Eliot's poem *The Four Quartets*, in addition to a short section from the third part and some other lines from *The Dry Salvages*. As for *The Waste Land*, he translated the first eighteen lines of the poem (De Young: 281). It was later that ʿAwaḍ produced a complete translation of *The Waste Land*. In *Fī al-Adab al-Ingilīzī al-Ḥadīth*, he also published a complete translation of *Ash Wednesday*.

These translations, with their critical introduction, show ʿAwaḍ's strong relation to Eliot. He had contradictory views of Eliot's writing and life, however. On the one hand, the Egyptian communist translator criticizes the sociopolitical beliefs of the Anglo-American poet. As mentioned previously, ʿAwaḍ published an article in 1946 setting out his views of Eliot as a *rajʿī* (reactionary) poet and critic. ʿAwaḍ repeated his views of Eliot in his book. In *For Lancelot Andrewes*,[4] Eliot describes his 'general point of view' as 'classicist in literature, royalist in politics, and anglo-catholic in religion' (Eliot, 1928: ix). ʿAwaḍ singled out for criticism Eliot's statement in *After Strange Gods*:

> The population should be homogeneous; where two or more cultures exist in the same place they are likely either to be fiercely self-conscious or both to become adulterate. What is still more important is unity of religious background; and reasons of race and religion combine to make any large number of free-thinking Jews undesirable. There must be a proper balance between urban and rural, industrial and agricultural development. And a spirit of excessive tolerance is to be deprecated.
>
> (Eliot, 1934: 19–20)

ʿAwaḍ translated this statement and compared 'Eliot's fascist views' to Hitler's ones in *Mein Kampf* (ʿAwaḍ, 1987: 206–7).

On the other hand, ʿAwaḍ expressed his admiration for Eliot's writings. In the same book *Fī al-Adab al-Ingilīzī al-Ḥadīth*, he describes Eliot as the pioneer of English modernism, because his poetry 'was a historical turning point in English poetry' (ʿAwaḍ, 1987: 293–4). ʿAwaḍ theoretically benefited from Eliot's modernity, but he failed to employ it poetically, as we will see in the cognitive context. In *Tradition and English and American Influence in*

Arabic Romantic Poetry, Muhammad 'Abdul-Hai notes that 'Awaḍ's view of Eliot drew on certain English writers, including C. D. Lewis, in his book *A Hope for Poetry* (1939) and his essay 'Revolutionaries and Poetry' (1936). In the essay, Lewis described Eliot bluntly as a 'reactionary bourgeois' who wrote a 'revolutionary' poem (Lewis, 2017: 52).

Like 'Awaḍ (or perhaps inspired by him), al-Sayyāb had a conflicting attitude towards Eliot. In his earlier career as a member of the Iraqi Communist Party (ICP), al-Sayyāb used the same term *raj'ī* to describe Eliot. Al-Sayyāb changed this view later, apparently after he left the ICP, and showed his admiration for Eliot's writings on both stylistic and thematic levels. In *Kunt Shiyū'iyyan* (I used to be a communist), al-Sayyāb criticized himself for having been a communist, claiming that he had to 'defend' communist poets and degrade Western poets such as 'the genius English poet Eliot' (al-Sayyāb, 2007: 105). In addition, many critics considered al-Sayyāb as the most important modernist Arab poet who used and developed Eliot's poetic techniques. Indeed, al-Sayyāb inspired many other poets to do likewise.[5] Interestingly, Sa'dī Yūsuf, whose modernity was inspired by al-Sayyāb's approach to Pound and Eliot, continues to apply the term *raj'ī* to Eliot. In a recent interview, Yūsuf not only rejected the notion of Eliot's importance to modern Arab poets, or even to his own poetics, but also criticized certain poets, notably Jabrā, for introducing Eliot's writings to Arabic culture (Yūsuf, 2014b: 79).

In contrast to 'Awaḍ and al-Sayyāb, Adūnīs and al-Khāl admired Eliot's writings from the start. Their translation of *The Waste Land* appeared in 1958 in *Tī. As. Ilyūt: Tarjamāt min al-Shi'r al-Ḥadīth* (T. S. Eliot: Translations from modern poetry). This book was edited by al-Khāl and printed by the publishing house *Dār Majallat Shi'r*. This book includes, alongside their translation of *The Waste Land*, the Arabic translations of some of Eliot's poems such as 'The Love Song of J. Alfred Prufrock' by Buland al-Ḥaīdarī and D. Stewart, *Ash Wednesday* by Munīr Bashshūr, *The Hollow Men* by Yūsuf al-Khāl and Eliot's verse play *Murder in the Cathedral* by Ibrāhīm Shukr Allah.

The book's postscript notes that the new style created by Eliot was important not only for the English poetic scene but also for the Arabic one. This description forms part of Bashshūr's postscript of his translation of *Ash Wednesday* which was published earlier in *Sh'ir* in spring 1957. Bashshūr observes that 'in his new style, Eliot destroyed what the romantic poets were considering as facts in life' (Bashshūr, 1957: 66). He adds, 'Eliot had started a trend in modern poetry and thought whose effect was not confined to the Anglo-Saxon world, but spread to the French and Latin worlds, to the extent that we could notice its effect on many contemporary Arab poets' (cited in Faddul, 1992: 82–3). *Sh'ir*'s poets were, enthusiastically, among those poets. For example, for al-Khāl, 'it was clear from the concentration on Eliot that his poetry was . . . the poetry that actualized the concept of poetry that he wanted to implement and that he wanted the *Shi'r* poets and Arab poets in general to adopt' (Faddul, 1992: 81). Therefore, al-Khāl encouraged Adūnīs to become involved in translating *The Waste Land* 'in order to introduce him more intimately to the world of Eliot' (ibid.). In his introduction to *Tī. As. Alyūt: Tarjamāt min al-Shi'r al-Hadīth*, al-Khāl records that they started by translating those of Eliot's poems which were the most well known and which had had the greatest impact on contemporary poetry (al-Khāl, 1958a: 3). However, in the same introduction, al-Khāl said that starting with Eliot was unintentional (ibid.: 4). In my opinion, al-Khāl subconsciously selected Eliot first because his writings taught Arab poets how to approach other world modernists. The question of whether to approach Eliot before other poets such as Whitman will be studied in Chapter 2. Al-Khāl opines that 'every forward-thinking poetic movement, such as that adopted by *Shi'r*, should be naturally open to the world . . . this is the proper interaction between cultures which we are inciting to be one of our key purposes' (ibid.: 3). Thus, Eliot was for al-Khāl a 'forward-thinking' poet, unlike for 'Awaḍ. Inspired by the collaboration of Eliot and Pound, al-Khāl's partnership with Adūnīs was fundamental to the establishment of modern Arabic poetry. But it seems that it is al-Khāl rather than Adūnīs who should be 'termed the first conscious promoter of modern poetry; he himself gave it the name of "Modern Poetry" (Al-Shi 'r al-Ḥadīth) in 1957 and described its major attributes' (Jayyusi, 1987: 17). In his Beirut lecture in the spring of 1957, al-Khāl defined in critical terms 'the whole attitude of the moderns and their concepts of poetry, and laid the foundation for the modern [Arabic] movement in clear and sophisticated terms' (ibid.: 17–8). But when he spoke about modern Arabic poetry, it was with the English modernists, namely Eliot and Pound, in mind. Eliot died in 1965, during that year Shi'r was on hold, but when it reappeared two years later, the Lebanese journal published an unsigned obituary of the Anglo-American poet. This obituary was probably written by al-Khāl and Adūnīs together:

> In our absence, in those two years, a face, known to our readers, was missing. Our readers knew him by 'Murder in the Cathedral', 'The Waste Land', 'the Love Song of J. Alfred Prufrock', 'the Hollow Men' and 'Ash-Wednesday'. These works are among his most important poetic works; some of which were published in our journal before being collected in a book [published by Shi'r] which is now out of print. *From the first moment, T. S. Eliot (1888-1965) was present with us, together with his comrades Ezra Pound, Andre Breton, and other main figures of modern poetry. He was a hero who fought alongside us fully armed. He walked in the front defeating the ghosts standing in his way. He knew of us in his last days, and was happy to be one of those poets whose names are related to the renaissance of modern Arabic poetry.* He allowed us to translate and publish some of his poems without asking us for the rights. In this, he was a role model like Andre Breton, Saint John Perse and other poets to whom we opened our windows. Even for Ezra Pound a silent agreement [to publish his poems] was not enough. Moreover, he wrote to us saying: 'Welcome to the Cantos'! *We were badly in need of Eliot, because the renaissance of Arabic poetry needed the things that we learned from him: unique personal human experience connected with the experience* throughout *history of the human being as a human being.*
>
> (*Shi'r*, 1967: 189; in italic translated by Faddul: 81)

The obituary highlights the importance of Eliot for the Arabic poetic 'renaissance' in the middle of the last century. In particular, he was a 'role model' for young Arab modernists. However, al-Khāl was closer to Pound than to Eliot as he considered him a key figure in changing English poetry. Thus, Pound inspired al-Khāl 'to transform Arabic poetry' (Faddul: 76). More than other poets of *Shi*'r, Eliot's modernity is clearly reflected in Adūnīs's writings, although his influence was rarely acknowledged in Adūnīs's interviews and articles. It seemed al-Khāl himself planned this, as he saw in Adūnīs 'the 'Eliot' of his movement in which he planned to play the role of Pound' (ibid.: 102). Thus, some of Adūnīs's poems, which were written after translating Eliot's, such as *Aghānī Mihyār al-Dimashqī* (*The Songs of Mihyar, the Damascene*), were described as an Arabic 'Waste Land'. Adūnīs's novel style is similar to that of al-Sayyāb whose poem *Unshūdat al-Maṭar* is often compared to Eliot's *The Waste Land.*

Like other Arab modernists, Tawfiq Ṣāyigh was aware of the significance of Eliot's writings. The manuscript of his translation of *The Waste Land* shows us that he approached Eliot as early as 1951, but unfortunately, it has no introduction or comments which might have shed light on the process of his work. Ṣāyigh also did not mention his translation of *The Waste Land* in the introduction to his translation of Eliot's *Four Quartets*. However, as Maḥmūd Shuraiḥ notes, in his 14 May 1954 correspondence with his former professor in Oxford, Edwin Honig, Ṣāyigh mentioned that he had just finished his first book *Thalāthūn Qaṣīda* (Thirty poems) and his translation into Arabic of Eliot's *Al-Arḍ al-Yabāb* (*The Waste Land*), and was ready to go to Beirut in the summer for a holiday (Shuraiḥ, 1989: 50). In Beirut, Ṣāyigh did publish his own book, but it seemed he forgot or ignored his translation of *The Waste Land*. We do not know if Ṣāyigh initially used *Al-Arḍ al-Yabāb* as a translation for the title of Eliot's poem before he settled on *Al-Arḍ al-Kharāb*, or if it is an interpretation by Shuraiḥ. But we do know, as the editor of Ṣāyigh's translation of *The Waste Land* notices, that *Al-Arḍ al-Kharāb* as an Arabic title of Eliot's poem was mentioned by Ṣāyigh three times: in his introduction to his translation of *Four Quartets* (1970), in his introduction to Ezra Pound in his translational selection *50 Poems from American Contemporary Poetry* (1963) and in his introduction to Jabrā's book *'Araq wa-Qiṣaṣ Ukhrā* (Wine and other stories) (1956) (Maẓlūm, 2017: 7). Interestingly, the title of this introduction is *'Abr al-Arḍ al-Bawār* (Through the waste land). It is worth mentioning that Ṣāyigh in his article "Al- Shi'r al-Ingilīzī Mu'āṣir" translated the title of Eliot's poem into "الأرض الخربة" using biblical terms as we will shortly underline (Ṣāyigh, 1955: 93). Ṣāyigh's translations of Eliot, alongside those of his modernist colleagues, show the active contribution they made in introducing Eliot's work to the Arab world. Eliot's modernist concepts, in particular those which were associated with *The Waste Land*, dominated Arabic poetry in the latter half of the last century and helped to develop it stylistically and thematically.

1.2 The verbal context

The Waste Land consists of five sections: 'The Burial of the Dead'; 'A Game of Chess'; 'The Fire Sermon'; 'Death by Water'; 'What the Thunder Said', as well as a title, an epigraph and a dedication. In this context, I will first investigate the Arabic translational treatment of the title, the epigraph and the dedication. Second, I have chosen from this 433-line poem the first section 'The Burial of the Dead' and the fourth 'Death by Water' as examples to study them along with their translations. Some lines from the second and third sections will also be analysed in this context to highlight other translational issues.

1.2.1 The title, the epigraph and the dedication

The title of *The Waste Land* was replaced with *Al-Arḍ al-Kharāb* in 'Awaḍ, Adūnīs-Khāl and Ṣāyigh (albeit in the last case, the title does not appear in the manuscript). *Al-Arḍ al-Kharāb* is used as the title, except in few cases, principally, the translations of al-Yūsuf and Lu'lu'a which use *Al-Arḍ al-Yabāb*. Interestingly, Nabīl Rāghib interpreted it as *Arḍ al-Ḍayā'* (The land of loss). Rāghib and al-Yūsuf did not attempt to justify their choices, while Lu'lu'a asserts that Al-*Arḍ al- Yabāb* is better than *Al-Arḍ al-Kharāb* because it is stronger in tone (Lu'lu'a, 1995: 104). However, he did not explain why the former is more poetic than the latter. He himself states that 'waste' as an adjective to go with 'land' was taken from the Old Testament and translated into 'خربة' as exemplified in Ezek. 6.14 (ibid.). In 'classical' Arabic, as Lu'lu'a notices, there is no difference between *Yabāb* and *Kharāb*. For example, in *Lisān al-'Arab* (The tongue of the Arabs) أرض يباب أي خراب (a land which is *Yabāb*, is *Kharāb*). However, in my opinion, in 'modern' Arabic language, *al-yabāb* is denotatively used as a specific adjective which refers to the absence of water (i.e. an arid land), while *al-Kharāb* is connotatively used for several meanings although it is commonly interpreted as 'ruin'. Therefore, *Al-Arḍ al-Yabāb* is a 'literal' translation which decodes *The Waste Land* as a title, while *Al-Arḍ al-Kharāb* is an 'interpretive' one which decodes the central theme of the poem and which goes beyond 'land' to encompass the devastation of men, buildings and civilization as a whole.

As for the epigraph, it was ignored by these poet-translators. Eliot adopted it from *Satyricon* which was believed to be originally written in prose by the Roman writer Gaius Petronius (AD *c.* 27–66), and he wrote it in a mixture of two languages: Latin and Greek:

> Nam Sybillam quidem Cumis ego ipse oculis meis vidi
> in ampulla pendere, et cum pueri illi dicerent:
> Σίβυλλα τί θέλεις; respondebat illa: ἀποθανεῖν θέλω .
>
> (Eliot, 1972: 25)

These lines were, as Grover Smith pointed out, versified in English by Rossetti as follows:

> I saw the Sibyl at Cumae
> (One said) with mine own eye.
> She hung in a cage, and read her rune

To all the passers-by.
Said the boys, 'what wouldst thou, Sibyl?'
She answered, 'I would die'.

(Smith, 1956: 69)

Here, the Sibyl 'symbolizes death in life because the land is dead (ibid.: 69–70). In Greek mythology, the Sibyl of Cumae was a woman of prophetic powers and was 'granted long life by Apollo . . . ; but carelessly she forgot to ask for eternal youth. Hence, she aged and her prophetic authority declined' (Southam, 1996: 133). The translations also ignored the dedication of Eliot to Ezra Pound which is enshrined in English and Italian:

For Ezra Pound
il miglior fabbro.

(Eliot, 1972: 25)

This phrase was translated by Eliot's critics into English as follows:

For Ezra Pound
The better craftsman.

In the dedication, Eliot used 'Dante's tribute to the twelfth-century troubadour poet Arnaut Daniel, emphasizing his superiority over all his Provencal rivals' (Southam: 136). For this part, Pound was the 'closest mentor and critic' to Eliot, and he shaped Eliot's style from the beginning (ibid.: 135). For me, the title, dedication and epigraph are used by the poet not only as illustrative tools to make *The Waste Land* easier to appreciate but also as stylistic features to intensify and multiply the voices of his poem. They have their own poetic values. Therefore, decoding only the main text and ignoring those features will affect the poetics of the ST by producing an incomplete TT. Furthermore, in applying this 'strategy', we lose the historical connection between Eliot's poem and the Greek myth, and the personal connection between Eliot and Pound, who played such a crucial role in moulding *The Waste Land*. The dedication and the epigraph were translated into Arabic by others who can be termed critic-translators. For example, al-Yūsuf translated the epigraph as follows:

أبصرت سيبل بأم عينيّ معلقة في قفص صغير، وحين سألها بعض الأطفال العابرين: ما سيبل.،
"أجابتهم: "أريد أن أموت"

(Al-Yūsuf, 1986: 95)

While Lu'lu'a translated the same epigraph into:

بعينيّ أنا رأيت "سيبيلّا" في "كومي" معلّقة في قارورة، وعندما كان يصيح بها الأولاد: "سيبيلّا. "ماذا تريدين"؛ كانت تجيبهم دوماً: "أتمنى أن أموت

(Lu'lu'a, 1995: 35)

Lexically, Lu'lu'a uses a number of different words, for example, 'قارورة' (flask) instead of 'قفص' (cage) which was used by Rossetti's poetic translation of the same epigraph. The name of the city 'Cumae' was ignored by al-Yūsuf, but Lu'lu'a included it in his translation. It appears in the original and in Rossetti's translation. These different lexical choices obviously led to the differences in the translations of al-Yūsuf and Lu'lu'a on a semantic level. Al-Yūsuf's translation is static, and this is reflected in his choice of the perfect tense, that is, 'سأل، أجاب', whereas Lu'lu'a's is more active. He opts for the use of *kāna* with the imperfect كانت تجيبهم دوماً' and this expresses the past continuous. In other words, it indicates motion in Arabic. The dedication was similarly translated by both critic-translators as:

الى عزرا باوند
الصانع الأمهر

(Al-Yūsuf: 95 and Lu'lu'a: 35)

Lu'lu'a criticized 'Awaḍ and Adūnīs–Khāl for not translating the epigraph and dedication. He felt that their approach 'affects the meaning of the poem and its stylistic value', and this in turn affects its comprehension by the Arabic readership (Lu'lu'a: 74). He explains that although Eliot himself put the epigraph and dedication in different languages and the 'average' English readership questioned this style when the poem was published in 1922, they became part of the poem's style (ibid.: 68). Thus, in Lu'lu'a's view, they should be translated into Arabic so that they can be understood by the 'average' Arabic readership. However, rather than omit the epigraph and the dedication, the modernist poet-translators ignored them. Neglect is not a common translational strategy, while omission is. Omitting a word or phrase means we leave a trace or a pointer to it. Mona Baker explains this strategy by saying there is no harm in applying it, 'if the meaning conveyed by a particular item or expression is not vital enough to the development of the text to justify distracting the reader with lengthy explanations' (Baker, 1992: 40). In addition, the Arab poet-translators, notably Adūnīs–Khāl and Ṣāyigh, did not translate the non-English lines which were used in *The Waste Land*, as we will see in the following section.

1.2.2 'The Burial of the Dead'

'The Burial of the Dead' derives from the Anglican service. The resurrection theme, which was 'proclaimed through Saint Paul's subtly moving assurance that 'the dead shall be raised incorruptible, and we shall be changed', finds here its counterpoint in the rhythmic annual return of spring' (Smith, 1956: 72). Taken as a whole, the first section of *The Waste Land* can be considered an 'exposition in which Eliot establishes both the theme of the "stony rubbish" of modern life set against the prophetic biblical questioning, and also the pattern of his method and procedure, followed in other sections' (Spender, 1975: 106).

All three translations use 'دفن الموتى' for 'The Burial of the Dead'. In fact, almost all the Arabic translations of this poem used this phrase, because of its closeness to the original and its familiarity in the target culture. The Christian and Islamic rituals have many similarities. In ST 1, 2 and 3 the verbs 'breeding, mixing, stirring' were changed from the English present participle form to the imperfect in Arabic by each of the above-mentioned translations. Thus, these verbs were, respectively, replaced by 'Awaḍ with 'ينبت، يخلط، يوقظ', by Adūnīs-Khāl with 'يُنبت، يمزج، يُحرّك' and by Ṣāyigh with 'يبعث، ويمزج، ويُحرك'. The Arabic form is usually used as an equivalent to the English present continuous. In the TT1, 'Awaḍ interpreted the 'hidden' adverb (therefore) into 'ف' and added it to the Arabic distinctive pronoun 'هو' which is also an interpretation of the latent pronoun of the English participle form. Thus, 'Awaḍ's line can be back-translated as follows:

> April is the cruellest month therefore it breeds.

However, this strategy does not help to reflect the dynamism of the original as it was replaced by a stative Arabic form alongside 'ف' as an explanatory tool. Sometimes, the 'invisible' tools of the original are only needed to be understood; they do not need to be interpreted 'visibly'. Such interpretation affects, to use Ezra Pound's words, the 'energy of poetry' which is produced by a certain 'movement of the words'. In this case, such tools are either being poetically interpreted or not. In addition, the English present participle form is usually equivalently replaced by the Arabic اسم الفاعل (active participle).

In ST 1, 'Awaḍ maintains the Latin name of the month 'April' which is used in the Egyptian dialect, while Adūnīs- al-Khāl and Ṣāyigh use the Arabic standard 'نَيسان' which is commonly used in Levantine Arabic. In ST 2, Ṣāyigh interprets 'breeding' as 'يبعث' (resurrects) which semantically suits 'the dead land', while Adūnīs-Khāl and 'Awaḍ replaced it with 'يُنبت' (grow) which is semantically appropriate for the 'lilacs' in the same line. The plant was replaced by Adūnīs-Khāl and Ṣāyigh with 'ليلك' (lilac), as the English and the Arabic use the same name. Interestingly, 'Awaḍ tried to 'localize' his target poem, but he used a different plant – 'الزنبق' (lilies) – to replace it. This is an untenable strategy because 'ليلك' or 'ليلج' are widely used in Arabic.

In ST 3, 'Awaḍ also interpreted 'desire' as 'الشهوة' (lust) which has a sexual connotation in Arabic. It seems that 'Awaḍ offered this reading because it reflects the theme of the opening lines as the birth of the 'lilacs' can be interpreted as a result of a sexual activity. However, Eliot did not use 'lust'; instead, he used 'desire' which was translated by Adūnīs-Khāl into 'رغبة' (desire), and by Ṣāyigh into the plural 'رغائب' (desires). Ṣāyigh applied the same strategy in the same line with 'memory' which he translated into the plural 'ذكريات' (memories). This is also not justified, because the Arabic infinitive 'ذكرى', as translated by 'Awaḍ and Adūnīs-Khāl, semantically and stylistically suits the original. In ST 5, 'Awaḍ uses the incorrect verb form 'أدفأنا' for 'kept us warm', while the Arabic verb is 'دفّأنا' as used by Adūnīs–Khāl. Ṣāyigh translated the same phrase into 'خلّى لنا الدِّفء' ([winter] left for us the warmth'. In the same line, Ṣāyigh replaced 'covering' with two words 'وراح يغمر' (it has begun to flood/ overflow). This choice might be more appropriate for the significance of 'winter' and 'snow' in the original than the literal terms 'دثر' and 'غطى' which were respectively used by 'Awaḍ and Adūnīs–Khāl in TT 5.

In ST 6, 'Awaḍ and Ṣāyigh changed the form of the noun-adjective 'forgetful snow' into an *iḍāfa* construction 'ثلوج النسيان' (the snows of oblivion) in 'Awaḍ's translation and into 'ثلج النسيان' (the snow of oblivion) in Ṣāyigh's. This strategy clearly altered the significance of this line and stylistically changed the 'personification' of Eliot's metaphor to a general one, unjustifiably. Adūnīs-Khāl translated 'forgetful snow' into 'ثلج كثير النسيان'. Here, the translators kept the original form (noun-adjective). However, they replaced the adjective 'forgetful' by two words 'كثير النسيان'. They could have replaced it by one word 'نسّاء', as al-Yūsuf and Lu'lu'a did. In ST 7, 'Awaḍ translated the plural 'tubers' (درنات) by the singular 'درن' (tuber). This strategy is commonly used in

English-Arabic translations, as the English plural noun is changed into an Arabic generic noun. Adūnīs-Khāl changed the plural form of 'tubers' into a singular noun 'كمأة' (truffle). Ṣāyigh formally replaced it by an equal plural form, but he semantically interpreted it as 'جذور' (roots). In the same line, Adūnīs-Khāl and Ṣāyigh semantically and grammatically replaced the noun-adjective 'little life' by 'حياة بسيطة' and 'حياة زهيدة' respectively. 'Awaḍ changed it into an *idāfa* construction 'ذبالة الحياة' (the wick of life). This change occurs not only on the grammatical level but also on a stylistic one as he replaced the everyday word 'little' by the classical (or even archaic) 'ذبالة'. This strategy affected the modernity of the poem. In *The Waste Land*, Eliot constructed varied linguistic levels as he used neutral and colloquial words and phrases to multiply and, to use Ted Hughes's words, to 'dramatize' the voices of the poem. However, 'Awaḍ has not always been loyal to his 'classicizing' strategy, as will be demonstrated in this context.

These first seven lines are thematically constructed on the theme of 'birth and death'. Stylistically, metaphor is the dominant technique that was used to reflect this. From the eighteenth line onwards, the theme has changed to 'memory'. The new theme is stylistically produced by a narrative technique which normally suits it. Translationally, this technique should be easier than the metaphorical one. This is because the relationship between words and their significances is direct and logical. However, in ST 8, 'Awaḍ rendered the German name of 'Starnbergersee' (Starnberg Lake) into 'بحيرة شتارنبرجرزى' (lit. 'lake of Starnberg Lake'). This is because, as Lu'lu'a notes, the German *see* is a lake in English (Lu'lu'a, 1995: 77). Adūnīs-Khāl and Ṣāyigh Arabized it as 'ستارنبرجرسي' and 'ستارن برجيرسي' respectively. In the same line, 'Awaḍ kept the same grammatical order of the nominal sentence 'Summer surprised us' (فاجأنا الصيف), while Adūnīs-Khāl and Ṣāyigh changed that order to a verbal one 'فاجأنا الصيف'. In Arabic, this order is more common than the nominal one. However, both structures are stylistically different, and therefore they imply a different significance. In ST 9, 'Awaḍ replaced the singular everyday word 'shower' with an Arabic classical (if not archaic) plural form 'شآبيب' (showers). This strategy marks the style of the TT as he used an 'outdated' word in a modern poem. Thus, it affects the significance of the ST, although it was lexically replaced by an 'equivalent' item in the TT. The same word was translated by Adūnīs-Khāl and Ṣāyigh as 'وابل' which lexically and semantically mirrors the original image of a sudden shower. In ST 10, 'Awaḍ repeated the same 'strategy' that he used in ST 8 when he simultaneously translated and transliterated 'Hofgarten' into two words 'حديقة الهوفجارتن' (lit. 'the garden of Hof Garden). In English, the German word means Hof Garden. In ST 12, 'Awaḍ altered the feminine first pronoun in Eliot's German line into a masculine:

Bin gar keine Russin, stamm' aus Litauen, echt deutsch,

ما أنا بالروسي، وإنما أنا ألماني من لتوانيا

The German line can be translated, as B.C. Southam suggests, as: 'I am not Russian at all; I come from Lithuania; I am a real German' (Southam, 1996: 142). This is not only problematic lexically but also significant inasmuch as it changes the gender of the narrator of the stanza and therefore its poetic voice, and this affected the whole poem. Adūnīs-Khāl and Ṣāyigh kept this line in its original German. This strategy can be regarded as an 'extended type', to use J. S. Holmes's concept, of 'mimetic' form. Holmes describes 'mimetic form a fiction'. According to him, the poetic 'form cannot exist outside language' (Holmes, 1994: 25). This is correct because it is impossible to retain the whole form of the ST in the TT without it becoming a copy, rather than a translation. However, as just demonstrated, this strategy is not only possible but also effective as it retains both the form and the language of this line in the translated texts to highlight that these linguistic variations are intentionally used here to multiply the poem's voices. In addition, in a complex poem like *The Waste Land*, which uses different languages such as Greek, Latin, Italian and German, these foreign languages can be treated semiotically as para-textual items such as pictures and other visual materials. Pound uses this 'mimic strategy' in his translations of poetry, as he kept the original shape and language of some titles. Eliot's strategy of using foreign languages in his own works inspired some Arab modernists such as Adūnīs, al-Bayātī, Ṣāyigh and Saʿdī Yūsuf to do the same. For example, Yūsuf wrote the title of his poem, 'America America', alongside other words and phrases, in English. This poem in which he addresses the American poet Walt Whitman will be studied in Chapter 2.

In ST 13, Adūnīs-Khāl translates 'when we were children' into 'حين كنا صغاراً'. This phrase, which links the past to the present, influenced Arab modernists to imitate this style in their own poems. For example, al-Sayyāb widely applied this technique, and in *Unshūdat al-Maṭar* he even used almost the same phrase. 'Awaḍ translated it as 'عندما كنا اطفالا', while Ṣāyigh added 'بعد' (then) to the sentence 'وعندما كنا بعد أطفالا'. In ST 14–18, the narrative tone of the poem continues, and these Arabic translations stylistically conveyed that 'tone' and formally used a similar layout of the poem, except for some changes in the length of the lines in 'Awaḍ's translation.

In the following lines, Eliot returns to his metaphorical tone. In ST 20, 'stony rubbish' was interpreted by 'Awaḍ as 'الخُثالة الصخرية' (stony dregs), while Ṣāyigh rendered it as 'المزبلة الصلبة' (stony dump). Adūnīs-Khāl replaced it by 'الركام الحجري' (stony heap). This last translation suits the context of this stanza more than the others because it intensifies 'death' as the main theme; this is embodied in particular in ST 23–4 'dead tree' and 'the dry stone no sound of water' respectively. In addition to 'stony rubbish' in ST 20, the line shifted to address 'son of man'. This loaded Christian expression was translated by Adūnīs-Khāl and Ṣāyigh into 'يا ابن الإنسان' (O son of man). In TT 21, 'Awaḍ interpreted it into an 'Islamic' form 'يا ابن آدم!' (O son of Adam!). This emphasizes the importance of understanding the situational context of the original in regulating the verbal context of the translated poem. In ST 22, 'Awaḍ used the same strategy to replace 'broken images' by an Islamic term 'مهشم الأوثان' (broken idols). Localizing the translation should not mean adding unfamiliar concepts to the poem. Adūnīs-Khāl translated it literally as 'الصور المحطمة' (broken images). Indeed, they applied this approach in most of their translations to convey the beauty of the original without 'injecting' it with alien words. Ṣāyigh interpreted it into 'الأخيلة المُكسَّرة' (broken shadows) which suits the meaning of the rest of this line because 'where the sun beats', it makes shadows.

In ST 30, 'Awaḍ translates 'I will show you fear in a handful of dust' as 'أريك الخوف في قبضة من تراب' (I show you fear in a handful of soil). The translator not only chooses a different word 'تراب' to render 'dust' but also changes the form of the verb from the future 'I will show' to the present 'أريك' (which mistakenly appears in *Shi'r*'s version 'أرك'). This theme was used by many writers, including John Donne, Alfred Tennyson and Joseph Conrad, and it refers, in this poem, as Ethel M. Stephenson explains, not to the fear of death but to 'the fear of what the embryonic life, contained in a handful of dust, is likely to produce' (Southam: 145). In accordance with this notion, Adūnīs-Khāl translated it as 'سأريك الخوف في حفنة من الغبار', while Ṣāyigh added ن of emphasis to the verb 'سأرينَّك الخوفَ في حفنة من الغبار' (I will surely show you fear in a handful of dust). In line with this strategy, Ṣāyigh has doubled the emphasis since 'س' has the same significance in Arabic.

In ST 31–4, Adūnīs-Khāl and Ṣāyigh maintained their strategy of not translating the German quotations from *Tristan und Isolde* (*Tristan and Isolde*), the opera by Richard Wagner (1813–83). Southam explains that these lines are a part of a song sung by a sailor 'about the sweetheart he has left behind' (ibid.), and he translates them as follows:

> The wind blows fresh
> To the homeland.
> My Irish girl,
> Where are you lingering?
>
> (ibid.)

'Awaḍ translates 'Mein Irisch Kind' (my Irish girl) as 'طفلتي الايرلندية', and this indicates that he was not aware of 'the properties' of the original poem 'and its literary dynamic as well as its status in the source system' (Bassnett, 1998: 64). The phrase 'Mein Irisch Kind' was included in German by Eliot for a specific purpose, namely to multiply the poem's voices. By rendering this phrase in Arabic and omitting the original German, 'Awaḍ kills a technique which was much used in *The Waste Land*.

In ST 35, 'Hyacinth' was rendered as different flowers 'الزنابق' (lilies) and 'السوسن' (iris) by Adūnīs–Khāl and Ṣāyigh respectively. It could more correctly be translated as 'الياقوتية'. 'Awaḍ Arabized 'hyacinth' as 'الياسنت'. This strategy was applied wholesale by 'Awaḍ in his translation of *The Waste Land*. In *Thaqāfatunā fi Muftaraq al-Ṭuruq* (Our culture at the crossroads), 'Awaḍ stated that there was no harm in using some foreign words in Arabic. In the last chapter of *Thawrat al-Lugha* (Revolution of the language), he explained that Arabic was not structurally affected when it 'imported' 'pharaoh' from ancient Egyptian or 'Caesar' from Latin in the same way as it is when it 'imports' modern words such as 'television' and 'radio' ('Awaḍ, 1974: 169). According to 'Awaḍ, these borrowed words, although digested and ingested by Arabic, merely serve to expand its vocabulary. The radical change which developed in Arabic can be seen in the new styles of literary writings. These new styles were principally influenced by English and French languages through translation and by Arab writers who were able to approach these languages directly (ibid.: 168–70). Consequently, when he came to translate the third section, 'The Fire Sermon',

'Awaḍ did not hesitate to replace 'weekend, combinations, camisoles, and gramophone' by '،الويك اند الكومبينزون، الكاميزول، فونوغراف' (Eliot, tr. 'Awaḍ: 116). This 'visible' strategy, to use Venuti's term, differentiates from the 'invisible' one he used previously in 'The Burial of the Dead' in order to 'classicize' the style of the TT. He also used a 'classicizing' strategy to translate 'A Game of Chess'. At the end of this section, Eliot even used Cockney to make a pastiche of the voice and shape of this dialect. Instead of conveying this colloquial style by an Arabic 'equivalent', 'Awaḍ replaced 'goonight' and 'good night' by classical expressions 'طابت ليلتك / طابت ليلتكن' respectively (ibid.: 114). By contrast, Adūnīs–Khāl tried to differentiate between these two styles by translating them as 'تصبح على خير' (good night) and 'عمن مساء' respectively (Eliot, tr. Adūnīs-Khāl: 137). In Arabic, the former is regarded as a neutral style, while the latter is a decidedly classical expression. Ṣāyigh's translation did not consider this stylistic transition in Eliot's poem, and therefore he translated these expressions into 'طِبت مساء' and 'طِبتنَّ مساء' (Eliot, tr. Ṣāyigh: 101–2). Interestingly, Lu'lu'a seemed to be the only translator who thoughtfully dealt with 'goonight'. First, he wanted to render it in an Arabic dialect 'because that is what the poet wanted' (Lu'lu'a: 83), but then he 'preferred' to imitate the original 'goonight' by using two attached words in one form 'ليلسعيدة' (ibid.: 44). In so doing, he seeks to 'point out, for the Arabic reader, that this talk is not in the standard language *al-fuṣḥā*' (ibid.: 83).

It is worth mentioning here that Venuti's concepts of visibility and invisibility, which deal with cultural issues, can be developed and applied to evaluate the stylistic differences between the ST and the TT. Applying these contradictory strategies in the same text, sometimes in the same line, affects the TT, however, as we have seen with 'Awaḍ's translation. They either conceal the aesthetic features of the original or interpret them differently to suit the target culture. More importantly, applying or adopting these (or any other) strategies should enrich the target culture poetically. Alas, 'Awaḍ's translational strategies failed to develop poetic techniques that could be positively reflected in his own poems or in modern Arabic poetics in general. Interestingly, 'Awaḍ's critical essays, in particular those on Eliot, had a greater influence on Arab poets than did his own poems. This issue will be discussed in detail in the following context.

In ST 42, Adūnīs–Khāl and Ṣāyigh kept the original of the line which Eliot, again, borrowed from *Tristan and Isolde*, and they left 'Oed' und leer das Meer' in German. This is translated into English by Grover Smith as 'The sea is waste and void' (Smith, 1956: 76), and by Southam as 'Desolate and empty the sea'

(Southam, 1996: 146). The original and its English translations portray a sad and gloomy image, but 'Awaḍ's translation gives different attributes to the sea 'عميق وفارغ هو البحر' (deep and empty the sea). He changed the poetic image by 'injecting', to use Derrida's words, the TT with unnecessary or irrelevant 'supplements'. His approach alienates, or even sometimes kills, the 'spirit' of the original. Kāẓim Jihād concludes that we now know the danger of using the supplement as a translational technique:

> The supplement comes to inject the work with something which does not suit it, claiming that it comes to fill something missing. Therefore, the translator rushes to enrich the content [of a text] which he thinks is poor and full of gaps. Had he used these 'dangerous supplements' (this expression from Derrida taken from Rousseau), representing in the attributive and adjectives, he would only work to impoverish the translated poetic discourse. The gap which should be filled does not necessarily occur in the text, but in the translational procedures that are applied to that text.
>
> (Jihād, 2011: 252)

In ST 43–59, Eliot changes his heroine from the hyacinth girl to Madame Sosostris. Smith clarifies that this woman 'partly symbolizes rebirth, for she is a "wise woman" or midwife' (Smith: 76). It is hard to connect the roles of Madame Sosostris together as they are fragmented in 'surreal' images. Smith himself explains that Madame Sosostris is 'a caricature of her predecessor the hyacinth girl' (ibid.). The Arabic translations of this stanza mostly use an 'equivalent' narrative shape to convey these scattered images. However, In ST 46, 'Awaḍ returns to his colloquial 'strategy' as he replaced 'pack of cards' with an Egyptian spoken word 'كوتشينة'. The same words were translated by Adūnīs-Khāl as 'ورق اللعب' and by Ṣāyigh as 'رزمة أوراق اللعب', while the adjective 'wicked' was translated by 'Awaḍ and Adūnīs-Khāl as 'فظيعة' and 'الخبيث' respectively, while it was ignored by Ṣāyigh. In ST 49, 'Awaḍ renders the Italian female name 'Belladonna' as 'السيدة الجميلة' (the pretty woman). He also uses it as an adjective for the same name 'وهذه بيلادونا، السيدة الجميلة'. In this line, Eliot uses 'Lady' with an uppercase letter, but he uses lowercase for the same word 'lady' in ST 50. Translating English uppercase letters into Arabic is still one of the translational challenges since Arabic has no upper and lower cases. Hence this word was translated in both lines by all translators as 'سيدة'. Interestingly, in the second section 'A Game of Chess', Adūnīs-Khāl underlined the words with capital letters 'HURRY UP PLEASE IT'S TIME' which were repeated in this section five times and was translated as 'اسرعوا ارجوكم حان الوقت'

(Eliot, tr. Adūnīs–Khāl: 135–6). They did not use the same method in the first section, however. Once again, 'Awaḍ classicized this 'neutral' phrase as 'هيا، عجلي فالوقت أزف' (Eliot, tr. 'Awaḍ, 113–14). In ST 50, Adūnīs-Khāl interpreted 'situations' as 'مآزق' (dilemmas). Meanwhile, 'Awaḍ translated it as 'مواقف', and Ṣāyigh kept the original English. In fact, he kept the original for the entire line. This notwithstanding, we should bear in mind that this was, for Ṣāyigh, not necessarily a translational strategy as much as an unfinished translation. In ST 55, 'the Hanged Man' was translated by Adūnīs-Khāl and 'Awaḍ as 'الرجل المشنوق' (the man executed by hanging) and 'المشنوق' (the executed) respectively. This literal approach was applied by many translators of *The Waste Land*, save for Ṣāyigh, who translated it as 'الرجل المُعلَّق' (the hung man). This rendering, as the editor of Ṣāyigh's translation noted, suits the context of the stanza. This is because the image in the Tarot card in ST 47 depicts a man who was hung upside down, but not executed (Maẓlūm: 91).

In ST 60–76, Eliot introduces a different theme. These lines could be entitled 'Unreal City'. This title goes beyond its linguistic usage to shape the whole theme of the stanza. The poet describes 'crowds of people' walking purposelessly over 'London Bridge'. Eliot borrows this image from Baudelaire's poem *Les Sept Vieillards* in which he describes Paris as:

> Fourmillante cité, cité pleine de rêves,
> Où le spectre en plein jour raccroche le passant!
>
> (Cited in Eliot's notes, 1972: 45)

But this city 'is also a hell, for it is inhabited on the one hand by the secular and on the other hand by the spiritually ignorant, like those characterized in the third and fourth cantos of the *Inferno*' (Smith: 78). In ST 60, 'Unreal City' was interpreted by 'Awaḍ as 'يا مدينة الوهم' (O city of illusion) changing the original noun-adjective form to an *iḍāfa* construction in addition to the vocative particle. Adūnīs-Khāl translated it as 'مدينة وهمية' (an unreal city). Interestingly, Ṣāyigh used 'بلدة أوهام' (a town of illusions), by which he is referring to the financial district of London which includes 'London Bridge' and is called the City of London. In ST 68, 'a dead sound' was interpreted by 'Awaḍ as 'صوت خامد' (a silent sound) and translated by Adūnīs-Khāl as 'صوت ميت' (a dead sound). On the other hand, Ṣāyigh translated it as 'صوتا مائتاً' (a dying sound). Maẓlūm suggests that Ṣāyigh was aware of Eliot's style of using the present participle form in preference to using nouns, verbs and even adjectives (Maẓlūm: 92). To some extent, this is true as we can see in the opening stanza of *The Waste*

Land with 'breeding, mixing, stirring, covering and feeding'. However, Ṣāyigh did not translate them as active participles but as the imperfect tense. Moreover, Eliot uses the adjective 'dead' in this line, rather than the imperfect participle 'dying'. The last line of this section is a direct quotation from Baudelaire's introductory poem 'To the Reader' of *Fleurs du Mal* (The flowers of evil). 'Awaḍ renders Baudelaire's line as if it was an 'organic' part of the original. Once more, this 'invisible' strategy affects the stylistic and cultural nature of the ST since the target readership assumes it to be Eliot's line. Moreover, 'Awaḍ did not translate Eliot's notes in which he refers to the original of this line. Unlike 'Awaḍ, Adūnīs–Khāl and Ṣāyigh are loyal to the strategy of retaining the foreign quotations which Eliot used in *The Waste Land*. Thus, they kept Baudelaire's line in its French original, but they omitted mention of the poet. This is because Adūnīs–Khāl and Ṣāyigh did not translate Eliot's notes which appear at the end of *The Waste Land*. Eliot's relationship with French is much deeper than simple loan words or translation.

1.2.3 Death by water

This ten-line section is the shortest one in the 'official' version of *The Waste Land*, but originally it was much longer. The manuscript shows us that Pound encouraged Eliot to delete about eighty lines from this section. It seems that they agreed to keep only one stanza from the first draft. Spender explains that

> When Eliot was persuaded by Pound that he should cancel from the original draft the lines about a voyage and shipwreck, he supposed that he should also cancel 'Death by Water', about Phlebas the Phoenician. However, Pound insisted on his retaining these. On the analogy of musical form they are entirely justified, breaking the mood of the first three sections, opening on to a world which, despite their sadness, is pure and filled with light.
>
> (Spender, 1975: 111–12)

The different mood of 'Death by Water' is attributed to the fact that the section is an English version of the last lines of Eliot's French poem *Dans le Restaurant* (1918):

> Phlébas, le Phénicien, pendant quinze jours noyé,
> Oubliait les cris des mouettes et la houle de Cornouaille,
> Et les profits et les pertes, et la cargaison d'étain:

. . . .
Figurez-vous donc, c'était un sort pénible;
Cependant, ce fut jadis un bel homme, de haute taille.

(Eliot, 2015: 45–6)

Eliot translated these lines into English to form 'Death by Water':

IV. Death by Water

Phlebas the Phoenician, a fortnight dead.
Forgot the cry of gulls, and the deep sea swell
And the profit and the loss.
A current under the sea
Picked his bones in whispers. As he rose and fell
He passed the stages of his age and youth
Entering the whirlpool.
Gentile or Jew
O you who turn the wheel and look to windward,
Consider Phlebas, who was once as handsome and tall as you.

(Eliot, 1972: 39)

In an interview with *The Paris Review*, which was conducted by Donald Hall in 1959, Eliot explains the importance of writing in a 'foreign' language on his own 'native' poetry:

> That was a very curious thing which I can't altogether explain. At that period I thought I'd dried up completely. I hadn't written anything for some time and was rather desperate. I started writing a few things in French and found I *could*, at that period. . . . I did these things as a sort of *tour de force* to see what I could do. That went on for some months. . . . Then I suddenly began writing in English again. . . . I think it was just something that helped me get started again.

(Eliot, 2015: 460)

In *Dans le Restaurant*, however, the poet used French, not only to cure writer's block but so that he could 'translate' it to become an 'original' part of *The Waste Land*. It questions the 'originality' of writing in a non-native language, and it becomes difficult to know what is a translation of what.[6] For his part, Eliot did not mention this 'translation' in his notices of *The Waste Land*, and it seems as if he treated 'Death by Water' or let's say his translation of *Dans le Restaurant* as an 'original'. Perhaps this is because 'Death by Water' 'crystallizes the hidden elegy' of the first section 'The Burial of the Dead', as we have seen, in line 48: 'Those are pearls that were his eyes' (Spender: 112). Similarly, Arab poet-translators treated this section as an organic part of *The Waste Land*.

Here is ʿAwaḍ's translation:

الموت غرقاً

'فلبياس' الفينيقي، وقد مات منذ أسبوعين،
'نسي صوت النورس، طير الشطئان،
ونسي صوت اللج
ونسي الكسب والخسارة.

والتقط عظامه من همس تيار تحت البحر
وفيما هو يعلو ويهبط
مر بمراحل شيخوخته وشبابه
ودخل الدوامة.
يهودياً كنت أم أغلف
يا من تدير العجلة وتنظر صوب الريح
تذكر 'فلبياس' الذي كان مثلك
وسيماً وفارعاً.

(Eliot, tr. ʿAwaḍ, 119–20)

Adūnīs-Khāl translates the same lines as follows:

الموت غرقاً
فلبياس الفينيقي، ميت منذ أسبوعين،
نسي صراخ النورس، وموج البحر العميق
والغُنْمَ والخسارة
تيار تحت البحر
التقط عظامه همساً، فيما هو ينهض ويقوم
قضى مراحل شيخوخته وشبابه
وهو يدخل الدّوامة.
يهوديّاً كنتَ أم غير يهوديّ
أنت يا من تدير الدولاب وتنظر الى مصدر الريح
اعتبرْ بفلبياس الذي كان مرّة جميلًا وطويل القامة مثلك.

(Eliot, tr. Adūnīs-Khāl, 143–4)

While Ṣāyigh translated them thus:

الموت عن طريق الماء
فِلِيباسُ الفِينيقيُّ، الذي مَاتَ لأسبُوعينَ مَضَيا،
نَسِيَ صُراخَ النَّوارسِ وتلاطُمَ البَحْرِ العَمِيقِ
وَالرِّبْحَ وَالخِسَارَة.

تيَّارٌ تحتَ البحْرِ
التَقَطَ عِظامَهُ بِهَمْسٍ. وَبينما ارتفعَ وَسقَطَ
عَبرَ مِرَاحلِ شَيْخوخَتِهِ وَشَبَابِهِ
إذْ دَخَلَ الدوَّامَةَ.
أيُّها الأُمميُّ أو اليَهُودِيُّ
يَا مَنْ تُديرُ العَجَلةَ وتنظرُ إلى اتْجاهِ الرَّيحِ
اعْتَبِرْ بِفِليباسَ، فَقَدْ كانَ يَوماً طَويلًا وَوسِنيْمَاً مِثْلَك.

(Eliot, tr. Ṣāyigh: 116–17)

As we can see, the title was interpreted by ʿAwaḍ and Adūnīs-Khāl as 'الموت غرقاً' (Death by drowning) in line with the central theme of this section. Meanwhile, Ṣāyigh translated it literally as 'الموت عن طريق الماء'. In ST 312, 'a fortnight dead' was translated by ʿAwaḍ as 'وقد مات منذ أسبوعين' (lit. and he already died two weeks ago), changing the adjective 'dead' into an Arabic past tense and adding 'قد' (already). Ṣāyigh also changed the structure of the line to 'الذي مَاتَ لأُسبُوعينَ مَضَيا' (lit. he who died for two weeks past). Moreover, he interpreted the hidden relative pronoun (who) as 'الذي'. Adūnīs-Khāl conveyed the English structure of the original in their translation 'ميت منذ أسبوعين', and al-Khāl defended their approach in his introduction to *T. S. Eliot Tarjamāt min al-Shiʿr al-Hadīth*:

> Translation, particularly translating poetry, is a rigorous and hard work. Some people tend to believe that transferring poetry to another language is an error. Some tolerate it with reservation, and we are among the tolerant. Our only reservation is the commitment to honesty and accuracy in the transformation, especially when the purpose, like our purpose, is a purely scientific one which envisages introducing [world poetry] and benefiting [from it], not pleasure and profit.
>
> (Al-Khāl, 1958a: 5)

However, Adūnīs-Khāl's translational project went beyond the rigid terms of 'honesty and accuracy', which are usually synonymous with a literalness in a negative sense. For Adūnīs-Khāl, translating poetry was a poetic adventure rather than a technical job. Therefore, their translation was intended to create a poetic 'equivalent' of *The Waste Land* in Arabic, and it influenced Arab modernists more than other translations, albeit it has a few linguistic errors. For example, they translated the name of the bird 'O swallow swallow' in line 428 as a verb 'آه إبلعْ إبلعْ' (O gulp gulp) (Eliot, tr. Adūnīs-Khāl: 148), and this became a laughing matter for some translators.

'Awaḍ broke ST 313 into two lines. Furthermore, he 'injected', to use Derrida's term once more, this line with the phrase 'طير الشطئان'[7] (birds of the shores). This strategy not only is a misreading of the original but also affects the translated poem since poetry tends to make images more intense rather than clearer. Although 'Awaḍ used one word 'اللج' to cover the expression 'the deep sea swell' semantically, he once again selected a classical word for this most modern of poems. In his manuscript, Ṣāyigh put three words – 'ارتفاع/ موج/ تلاطم ' before 'swell'. It seems that the editor (who was a poet as well) chose 'تلاطُم' to intensify the poetic image of the TT. In ST 314, 'profit' was translated literally by 'Awaḍ as 'الكسب' and by Ṣāyigh as 'الرِّبْح'. Adūnīs-Khāl interpreted it into 'الغُنْم' which means in this context (booty). In ST 318, 'entering the whirlpool' was rendered literally in the translations under study as 'دخل الدوامة', with the exception of Adūnīs-Khāl, who used a present tense form 'يدخل الدوامة'. Interestingly, some critic-translators approached this line differently. For instance, al-Yūsuf interpreted 'entering the whirlpool' as 'دخل الحوّام'. In Arabic, 'الحوّام' is derived from 'حومة' which means the greatest (or deepest) part of the sea. Lu'lu'a, inspired by the Qur'ānic style, also interpreted it differently as 'يلج الدوّامة' (Lu'lu'a: 51). It seems Lu'lu'a was thinking of the Qur'ān (7:40), which depicts the difficult situation of 'those who reject [God's] signs and treat them with arrogance':

> وَلَا يَدْخُلُونَ الْجَنَّةَ حَتَّىٰ يَلِجَ الْجَمَلُ فِي سَمِّ الْخِيَاطِ
>
> [N]or will they [the sinners] enter the Garden, until the camel can pass through the eye of the needle (brackets added)[8]

In ST 319, 'Awaḍ translated 'gentile' as 'أغلف' (uncircumcised), to give his target poem a more local feel. In Arabic, 'أغلف' is used to describe those who are uncircumcised, in particular Christians. Meanwhile, in the biblical context, the term means a non-Jew. Thus, Adūnīs-Khāl translated it as 'غير يهوديّ', while Ṣāyigh replaced it with 'الأُمميُّ' which is the standard term in the Arabic Bible for 'gentile' (i.e. not Jewish). In ST 321, 'tall' was translated as 'طويلاً' and 'طويل القامة' by Adūnīs-Khāl and Ṣāyigh respectively. 'Awaḍ interpreted it as 'فارعا' which signifies someone who is 'tall' and 'handsome' at the same time. It seems that 'Awaḍ wanted thereby to beautify the target poem.

All these three translations applied a 'verse to prose' strategy for *The Waste Land*. In fact all the Arabic translations of Eliot's poem did likewise, except 'Adnān K. Abdullah and Ṭalāl 'A. Ismā'īl who chose to convey the poem in verse. The 'verse to verse' strategy was defined by Lefevere: when a translator chooses to translate a verse of ST into a verse in the TT 'either in a metre that is not identical with that of the source text, or in some form of "organic verse"' (Lefevere, 1975: 5). In some languages, 'identical' or semi-identical metres exist, for example, in Arabic and Persian, but between English and Arabic there are no identical metres, because their prosodic structures are very different. Abdullah and Ismā'īl chose the Arabic metre *al-rajaz*:

الموت غرقاً
فليباس الفينيقيُ ماتَ منذُ أسبُوعين
نسِيَ تَصخَاب طُيُور النَّورس البحري واللُّجة في الأعماق
والرّبح والخسارة
فكّكَ تيارٌ يغور البحر في همسٍ عظامَه
وحيثُ باتَ صاعداً وهابطاً
مرَّ بشيخوختهِ ومرّ بالشباب وهو يَلجُ الدوامهْ
من اليهُودِ كنتَ أم من غيرهم
يا مَن تُديُر دفّة السفينه
مُحدّقاً حيثُ تَهُبُ الرّيح
تذكّر فليباس
كان وَسيماً فارعاً
مِثلكَ في يوم من الأيام.

(Eliot, tr. Abdullah and Ismā'īl, 2006: 102)

Their work showed that using a metrical translation is not impossible and can be a success, if the translator applies the 'right' metre.[9] The flexibility of al-*rajaz* (its foot *mustaf'ilun* varies) allowed the translators to cover the main stylistic and thematic levels of the original. In 'On Translating Poetry into Arabic, with Special Reference to T.S. Eliot's *The Waste Land*', Abdulla justified their metrical strategy by saying that this section

> reads like a genuine Arabic poem for many reasons: First, the section is simple, straightforward, and direct poetry. There are no technical innovations, nor are there any foreign quotations, foreign names or places, except for the proper name 'Phlebas'. Second, 'Death by Water' with its sad and meditative mood is reminiscent of some great classical Arab poets.
> (Abdulla, 2011: 17)

The classical Arab poets did not use *al-rajaz*, because they considered it unpoetic. However, in modern Arabic poetry the metre is viewed differently, for instance when al-Sayyāb used it in his masterpiece *Unshūdat al-Maṭar*. The metre is also in evidence in other poems by the likes of Adūnīs, al-Bayātī, 'Abd al-Ṣabūr and Darwīsh for instance.

As we have seen, each poet-translator translated *The Waste Land* differently. ʿAwaḍ mainly applied an 'interpretive' strategy in which, as Juliane House explains, 'the translator is licensed to manipulate the original for purpose of experimenting with norms of usage and commenting on the original, rather than translating it in the usual sense of the word' (House, 2009: 21). House argues in favour of this strategy because translation is basically an interpretive process (ibid.). However, ʿAwaḍ's manipulation of the original won few followers. He failed because his translation did not consider the differences between the voices in Eliot's poem stylistically. ʿAwaḍ's *Al-ʿArḍ al-Kharāb* is almost in one voice, although he did use Egyptian colloquial a few times. The latter did not help to convey Eliot's style because he used it randomly. Ṣāyigh's translation, although an unfinished work, conveyed the multiplicity of the original voices and structural layers in a poetic manner to the TT, apart from its 'invisible' treatment of the colloquial techniques. Like Ṣāyigh, Adūnīs-Khāl did not 'visibly' treat the spoken language of the original, but their translation eventually produced an Arabic poetic 'equivalent' of *The Waste Land* by, to use Asʿad Razzūq's words, preserving 'a kind of interior music that comes from the choice of words and syntaxes' (Razzūq, 1959: 90–1) which skilfully reflect the poetics of the original. Therefore, their translations managed to create a seminal work which successfully reflects the status of the poem in the source culture.

1.3 The cognitive context

As we have seen, *The Waste Land* was translated in its entirety some ten times, in addition to a number of partial translations. This reflects the popularity and the impact of the poem in Arabic. As far as I am aware, no other poem has been translated into Arabic so many times. On a global scale, as Jabrā says, 'someone has said that no poem in history has been so widely discussed, interpreted and translated during the author's lifetime as "The Waste Land". Certainly no poem has been so influential' (Jabrā, 1971: 83). Jabrā summarized the impact of Eliot's writings on young Arab poets in the 1950s:

> Until 1950, nothing could be more unlike Arabic poetry than 'The Wasteland': the endless juxtapositions, the sudden jumps, the parodies, the quotations and deliberate misquotations, the mixture of the sublime and the ridiculous, the use of different languages, free verse, rhymed verse, the

> fusion of St. Augustine and Buddha, of Dante and Webster, the high-flown eloquence and the music-hall language, the Fisher King and the Hanged God, Tiresias and Jesus at Emmaus and Phlebas the Phoenician, the 'Unreal City' and the 'falling towers' a veritable orchestration of verbal and symbolic means, all previously quite unknown in Arabic poetry.
>
> (ibid.: 84)

These new techniques 'were some of the many things that opened the poets' eyes to the untried possibilities of style. Skill was no longer a mere matter of rhetoric, but a cunning use of a resourceful technique, which employed variety and surprise' (ibid.).

We may infer that this poem has been able, on a cognitive level, to create the most important principles, namely, to use Peter Stockwell's concepts, 'generalization' and 'continuity' (Stockwell, 2009: 17). However, these principles were not achieved by all the Arabic translations. For example, 'Awaḍ's translation failed to inspire following generations, let alone his colleagues, to adopt a poetic modernity. As early as the 1940s, 'Awaḍ wrote poems in the style of English free verse, which is in turn based on the French *Vers Libre*. According to Eliot's 'Reflections on Vers Libre' (1917), this type of poetry is devoid of pattern, rhyme and metre (Eliot, 1978: 184). 'Awaḍ calls it prose poetry to differentiate it from Arabic free verse, which, as we have seen, is patterned, metrical and even occasionally rhymed, in a flexible and not a rigid way. Thus, it is also called the poetry of *taf'īla* (metrical foot). 'Awaḍ's collection *Plūtūlānd* (Plutoland) (1947/ 1989) contains poems in Arabic and English free verse, Egyptian colloquial and even classical Arabic, and he entitled his critical introduction to this collection *Ḥaṭṭimū 'Amūd al-Shi'r* (Break the pattern of poetry). In it, 'Awaḍ said that two of his prose poems – *Al-Ḥubb fi Sān Lāzār* (Love in St. Lazare) and *Amūt Shahīd al-Jirāḥ* (I die a martyr of my afflictions) – are influenced by Eliot, and not by Walt Whitman 'the creator of the prose poetry' ('Awaḍ, 1989: 25). Here is an example from *Al-Ḥubb fi Sān Lāzār*, which is considered one of his finest:

في محطة فكتوريا جلست وبيدي مغزل.
وكان المغزل مغزل أوديسيوس.
....
جلست وبيدي مغزلي في انتظار بنيلوب التي لا أعرفها
وهل أتت بنيلوب الى رصيف نمرة 8

كلا، لم تأت بنيلوب الى رصيف نمرة 8
هذه الجزيرة العابسة. لقد رأيت الجاريات يدخلن خلجانها مثقلات.

('Awaḍ, 1989: 57–8)

In Victoria Station I sat, a spindle in my hand –
Odysseus' spindle.
. . . .
I sat, spindle in hand, waiting for Penelope, whom I didn't know.
Had she come to gate number eight?
Penelope had not come to gate number eight.
From this forbidding island I saw the ships come laden into harbour.

(Translated by Asfour, 1992: 93–4)

This example shows us that 'Awaḍ's poetry, to use Eliot's words once more, 'is anything but 'free'; it can better be defended under some other label' (Eliot, 1978: 184). This is because 'a great deal of bad prose has been written under the name of free verse . . . only a bad poet could welcome free verse as a liberation from form (Eliot, 1957: 37). Indeed, freeing up the poet from metre and rhyme is not enough to create a new poetic atmosphere in Arabic culture. As a result, his formal 'experiment' failed to inspire other poets to imitate him and to develop new techniques. Neither the colloquial technique which he used in translating *The Waste Land* nor his poetry managed to 'generate any creative response' (Khouri, 1970: 140). Thus, we have rarely seen his poems in the anthologies of modern Arabic poetry, whether in English or Arabic. However, 'Awaḍ's critical writings are valuable inasmuch as they introduced Eliot's poetry to the Arabic poetic scene of the 1940–50s. Moreover, his writings seemed to stimulate poetic development and debate among Arab modernists.

Eliot's experimental language was echoed and appreciated by Arab poets. For example, in a statement published in *Ḥayātī fi al-Shi'r* (My life in poetry) (1969), Abd al-Ṣabūr explains that he admired Eliot's 'linguistic boldness' (الجسارة اللغوية) more than his themes. He explained that when he and his colleagues were young, they believed that their poetic language should be 'selective' and devoid of any colloquial ('Abd al-Ṣabūr, 1969: 90). Reading *The Waste Land*, 'Abd al-Ṣabūr added, 'alerted him to the richness of the spoken language and taught him to be daring in the use of language' (cited in Faddul: 228; see also Abd al- Ṣabūr, 1969: 90–2). His early poems such as *Shanq Zahrān* (Hanging *Zahrān*) and *Al-Mulk Lak* were influenced by Eliot's new language. His 1954 poem *Al-Ḥuzn* ('The Sadness') was also influenced by Eliot's 'colloquial' technique:

يا صاحبي، إني حزين
طلع الصباح، فما ابتسمت، ولم ينر وجهي الصباح
وخرجت من جوف المدينة أطلب الرزق المتاح
وغمست في ماء القناعة خبز ايامي الكفاف
ورجعت بعد الظهر في جيبي قروشْ
فشربت شاياً في الطريق
ورتقت نعلي
ولعبت بالنرد الموزع بين كفي والصديق
قل ساعة او ساعتين
قل عشرة او عشرتين
وضحكت من اسطورة حمقاء رددها الصديق
ودموع شحاذ صفيق

(ʿAbd al-Ṣabūr, 1969: 93)

O my friend, I am sad
The morning came, but neither did I smile, nor did the morning light my face.
I came out of the city and asked for the predestined livelihood
And I immersed in the waters of contentment the subsistence of my day's bread
I returned in the afternoon with some piasters in my pocket
I drank tea on my way
I mended my shoes
I played with dice divided between the palm of hand and the friend
Say an hour or two
Say ten or twenty
I laughed at a silly legend told by the friend
And the tears of a brazen beggar

Lines 220–7, which appear in the third section 'The Fire Sermon', exhibit a marked influence. Unfortunately, 'Abd al-Ṣabūr did not translate *The Waste Land*[10] in full, but he did translate these lines in order to show the contrast between Eliot's 'daring' language and the 'classical' style favoured in Arabic poetry. It is worth quoting in their entirety both the original and the translated stanzas:

At the violet hour, the evening hour that strives
Homeward, and brings the sailor home from sea,
The typist home at teatime clears her breakfast, lights

Her stove, and lays out food in tins.
Out of the window perilously spread
Her drying combinations touched by the sun's last rays,
On the divan are piled (at night her bed)
Stockings, slippers, camisoles, and stays.

(Eliot, 1972: 35–6)

في الساعة البنفسجية، ساعة المساء التي تقود
إلى البيوت، وتعيد البحار إلى بيته من البحر
والتايبيست الى بيتها في موعد الشاي لتنظف المائدة من بقايا
الإفطار، ولتشعل الموقد، وتخرج الطعام من علب الصفيح.
لقد تدلّت من النافذة منشورة خوف السقوط
أطقمها الداخلية، وهي تجف، إذ لمستها أشعة الشمس الغاربة
(وتكومت على الأريكة) التي تتخذها سريراً في الليل
جواربها، وشبشبها، وقمصانها، ومشداتها.

('Abd al-Ṣabūr, 1969: 90–1)

'Abd al-Ṣabūr can be considered one of the Arab poets 'who benefited most from Eliot's views on the need to keep the poetic language close to the spoken language and who utilized folklore in his poetry' (Faddul: 193). Both 'Awaḍ and 'Abd al-Ṣabūr used Egyptian dialect in their translations and own works, but it was 'Abd al-Ṣabūr who applied this technique to the actualities of the Arabic poetic register. It was used not for the sake of experiment, and it therefore functioned more comprehensively than 'Awaḍ's in the received culture, especially in Egypt.

Like 'Abd al-Ṣabūr, al-Sayyāb's relation to Eliot is also 'visible' in Arabic modernity, but it is much deeper than in the case of the other poets. Al-Sayyāb did not stop at imitating or developing Eliot's experimental techniques, although he believed, to use William Carlos Williams's words about Whitman, that the only way to be like Eliot is to write unlike Eliot. Hence, in *Unshūdat al-Maṭar*, which is considered poetically the Arabic 'equivalent' of *The Waste Land*, one feels Eliot's style, but it is difficult to point it out. In the poem, al-Sayyāb considerably developed the technique of *The Waste Land* in order to make it his own. For instance, the Iraqi poet developed the central theme of *The Waste Land* as water, symbolizing life and fertility, and this is clearly illustrated in the fifth section 'What the Thunder Said':

Here is no water but only rock 331
Rock and no water and the sandy road

The road winding above among the mountains
Which are mountains of rock without water
If there were water we should stop and drink

(Eliot, 1972: 40)

This dark image mirrors the drought in Western civilization and life after the First World War. Not only does it describe the lack of water; it also doubts the existence of that water. Metaphorically, this image highlights the 'hollowness' that people felt during that difficult time. In *Unshūdat al-Maṭar*, al-Sayyāb used the symbol of water to depict the aftermath of the Second World War in the Arab world. He 'sees Eliot producing a 'critique' of Western civilization which he could parallel with a critique of his own society' (DeYoung, 1998: 72). However, his 'critique' is not as gloomy as Eliot's, which may reflect his beliefs as a communist at that time. Indeed, he ended his poem in an optimistic voice. He also skilfully localized Eliot's 'water' to manifest the revolutionary change that Iraqi (and Arab) people dreamt about in the 1950s:[11]

في كل قطرة من المطر
حمراءُ أو صفراءُ من أجنة الزهر
وكلّ دمعة من الجياع والعراة
وكلّ قطرة تراق من دم العبيدْ
فهي ابتسامٌ في انتظار مبسم جديد
أو حلمةٌ تورَّدت على فم الوليدْ
في عالم الغد الفتي، واهب الحياة
ويهطل المطر

(Al-Sayyāb: 124)

Every drop of rain
Whether red or yellow flowers bloomed
And every tear from the hungry and the naked
And every drop spilled from the blood of the slaves
Is a smile awaiting fresh lips
Or a rosy nipple on the mouth of the newborn
In tomorrow's young world, life-giver
And the rain pours down.

(Al-Sayyāb, tr. Iskander, 2013: 71)

Like al-Sayyāb, Adūnīs approached Eliot through translation and was inspired by him as a modernist poet. Moreover, Adūnīs's role in the modernization of Arabic culture poetically and intellectually is often compared to Eliot's role in

Western culture. Both were pioneering poets, translators (mainly from French, as they both translated St. John Perse), critics and editors. Eliot was awarded the Nobel Prize in 1948 for his 'pioneer contribution'; Adūnīs has been a long-standing candidate for it for the same reason. Although Adūnīs rarely mentions his relationship to the Anglo-American poet, Eliot's impact on him is very clear, especially in the light of his translation (with al-Khāl) of *The Waste Land* in 1958. Since then, Adūnīs's poetry has become more complex. Interestingly, his *Qabr min Ajl New York* (Grave for New York), in which he addressed Walt Whitman, and not Eliot, is a good example of the influence of *The Waste Land*. *Qabr min Ajl New York* is also a multilayered poem, the central theme of which is the critique of Western civilization. The key to understanding Adūnīs's relationship with Eliot, however, lies in his collaboration with al-Khāl and the other *Shi'r* poets. They were all variously inspired by Pound's and Eliot's concept of modernity, as a collaborative endeavour. In his collaboration with al-Khāl, Adūnīs played Eliot's role while al-Khāl performed the role of Pound. Interestingly, al-Khāl claimed to have corresponded with Pound, and the latter agreed to be *Shi'r*'s correspondent. Indeed, al-Khāl started his famous collection *Al-Bi'r Al-Mahjūra* (*The Deserted Well*) (1958) with a dedication 'to Ezra Pound, the pioneer of the English modernity'.

سأَلناكَ ورْقة تينٍ
فإنَّا عراةٌ، عراةْ.
أثمْنا الى الشعر، فاغفرْ لنا
وردَّ إلينا الحياةْ.

(Al-Khāl, 1979: 197–8)

We asked you for a fig leaf
We are naked here, naked!
We've sinned against poetry, forgive us
Return our life to us

(Jayyusi, 1987: 17)

In the poem, Jayyusi opines that 'the subtle analogy' made 'between Pound and Christ' can also be applied to al-Khāl and 'Pound as a maligned and rejected literary pioneer'. Al-Khāl 'was determined to be a teacher and leader of poetic developments but foresaw the difficulties that would confront him, and his suspicion later proved right as his aesthetic attempts became mixed with his unpopular political ideas' (ibid.). By this, Jayyusi meant al-Khāl's (and Adūnīs's) siding with the Lebanese president Camille Chamoun during the civil war in 1958. Furthermore, when Pound was arrested by American troops in Italy in 1945 and charged as a traitor because of his support for the fascist Italian regime during the Second World War, al-Khāl joined a campaign set up by a group of prominent international writers to free him. On 6 January 1956, he wrote an article in support of Pound when the latter was admitted to a mental hospital in the United States. Adūnīs and al-Khāl appreciated the new concept of poetics which was based on Eliot's and Pound's approach. Eliot's poetics, in particular, encouraged them and their colleagues to challenge their own traditions and culture. Thus, it is little wonder they started their serial translations of Eliot whose writings so challenged English traditions.

Like Adūnīs and al-Khāl, Tawfīq Ṣāyigh began to tackle Eliot's poetic output in the 1950s, as the date of his translational manuscript (or draft) of *The Waste Land* clearly shows. As we have seen, however, he did not publish this translation. Instead, he published his translation of *Four Quartets* in 1970, possibly because he felt more 'affinity' to the latter than to the former. Ṣāyigh's poetic vision has often been compared to Eliot's religious vision in *Four Quartets*. Nevertheless, as a modernist, Ṣāyigh could not avoid or ignore the impact of *The Waste Land* on his own writing. This is exemplified in his use of 'free verse'. '[R]ight from the beginning' Ṣāyigh chose this form 'to express himself poetically' (Boullata, 1973: 74). In my opinion, his 'extreme kind of free verse', as Boullata described it, clearly resonates with Eliot's definition of this form, more than other Arab modernists' work does, and this is illustrated by his three collections of poetry: *Thalāthūn Qaṣīda* (Thirty Poems) (1954), *Al-Qaṣīda K* (1960) and *Mu'allaqat Tawfīq Ṣāyigh* (1963). Boullata adds, 'the poem for him was a completely free verbalization of human experience communicated aesthetically . . . in order to relieve the poet himself of an inner power that rose painfully in him like an electric charge' (Boullata, 1973: 75).

Ṣāyigh's poetic concepts such as the 'free verbalization', 'communicated aesthetics' the 'correlative and inner experiences' which Boullata described, not to mention the religious and mythological symbols, are first powerfully presented in Eliot's writings, notably *The Waste Land*. Like 'Abd al-Ṣabūr, Ṣāyigh was 'bold' in his use of spoken language. This is clearly in evidence in his second poem of *Thalāthūn Qaṣīda*:

قدمايَ نَطْنطا:
للباز يومُه

وللدودِة لا يخدشُ الصخرُ طراوتَها؛
يومُكُما أمرٌ
ساعاتُهُ دِنان
(لو تعي الشفاه)
. . . .
وتشحشطْتُما
الى تلّةِ المساكين والمنسحقي القلوب
ورفسْتُما الطوبى.

(Ṣāyigh, 1990: 31–2)

My feet are jumping:
The falcon has its day
And the worm, its softness is not scratched by the rock;
Your day is an order
Its hours are jugs
If only the lips would understand.
. . . .
You were dragged
To the hill of the poor and the heartbroken
And kicked the blessedness.

In the poem, Ṣāyigh used colloquial words such as 'نطْنطا' and 'تشحشطْتُما'. Jabrā, who admired Ṣāyigh's audacity, explained that these words added to his poetry's 'energy and liveliness' (Jabrā, 1982: 42). Like Eliot's 'goonight', these words cannot be replaced by standard 'equivalents', because they organically represented a certain voice in his poem – a voice which was typically ignored in classical Arabic poetry. Ṣāyigh rehabilitated this voice. The last line of this example 'رفسْتُما الطوبى' (you kicked the blessedness / beatitude) shows his rebellious side vis-à-vis religion. Although he was considered a 'Christian' poet, which he was, he did not hesitate to question his faith, again like Eliot. This explains the Arab response to *The Waste Land*, which was treated by many Arab modernists as a part of their heritage.

1.4 Concluding remarks

Each translator made his own choice when tackling *The Waste Land*. The richness of the poem, which is exemplified by the use of different languages and voices, as well as multiple layers and stanzas, indicates that a conventional approach to translation alone cannot address the complexity of the poem. Hence the present analysis of the Arabic translations of *The Waste Land* is designed to consider the poem in three contexts: situational, verbal and cognitive. The situational context has shown us that the innovative quality of *The Waste Land* was, for the Arab poets, the main motivation to translate Eliot's masterpiece. They were also motivated by the poem's central place in the global development of modern poetry at the beginning of the last century. It also helped that the poem's main theme, depicting the devastation of Europe in the wake of the First World War, resonated with Arab modernists in the aftermath of the Second World War. Some of them, like Adūnīs, al-Khāl and Ṣāyigh, responded positively to Eliot's modernizing approach from the beginning. Others, like the communist poet 'Awaḍ, criticized Eliot's political and social beliefs but admired his poetic contribution. When he was a member of ICP, al-Sayyāb initially adopted 'Awaḍ's view of Eliot, but he later changed his tune when he left the party and promptly adopted Eliot's poetic concepts and techniques. Al-Sayyāb's *Unshūdat al-Maṭar* is a fine example of his relationship with Eliot.

The verbal context has shown us how *The Waste Land* was reworked by Arab poet-translators to create seminal poems in the target culture. They used a verse into prose strategy, which is the modern standard. These modernists decoded the poem linguistically and translated it according to their lexical and stylistic choices. These choices are interpretively and/or literally reflected in the Arabic poems. The literal strategy is echoed by the closeness between the ST and TTs, as well as by the use of a single reading for the ST. The interpretive technique leads to a shift in approach when the literal translation produces nonsense and challenges the translator to create an authoritative version in the target culture. This strategy is also intended to address the inner and silent layers of the ST and to keep them alive poetically in the TT. It is not an explanatory style, as we have seen with 'Awaḍ's translation which often limited the 'potential' readings of the original to a single prosaic interpretation. His decision to localize the translation also produced restricted readings of the ST. Moreover, it disfigures the target poem by Islamizing Christian terms and injecting the source poem with alien terms. In addition, 'Awaḍ renders many poetic associations of the poem in ready-made forms, unchallenging colloquial words and clichés. And on a cognitive level, 'Awaḍ's decision to ignore the modernist qualities of *The Waste Land* contributed to a passive response to his

Al-ʿArḍ al-Kharāb in Arabic. At the same time, his critical writings about Eliot played an important role in introducing Eliot's work to the Arab modernists.

By contrast, Adūnīs–Khāl's translation was enthusiastically received, largely because their work goes beyond a purely verbal approach, and this proved their talents as pioneer poets. Their holistic approach enabled them to produce an authoritative and memorable poetic 'equivalent' to *The Waste Land*. They worked as a team to situationalize Eliot and Pound's collaborative modernity. They did not attempt to re-contextualize the original. On the contrary, they conveyed it simply but skilfully, and they let it 'sing' in the target culture. The range of the vocabulary and the way in which their words were syntactically shaped energized and poeticized the TT. As a result, many Arab modernists were inspired by Eliot's poetics. Ṣāyigh approached the task similarly, and his translations of Eliot have echoes in his own poetic output, from free verse form to the use of spoken language and to his poetic 'affinity' to *Four Quartets*. In sum, Adūnīs-Khāl and Ṣāyigh's translations were important in 'generalizing' and 'continuing' a new poetics in Arabic, and we can see why Arab modernists tackled Eliot's works before those of any other of the world modernists.

2

Translating Whitman's *Song of Myself* into Arabic

Walt Whitman (1819–92) published *Leaves of Grass* at the beginning of July 1855. In this, the first of nine editions, none of the twelve poems had titles, including his most popular poem, *Song of Myself*. In his introduction to the first edition of *Leaves of Grass*, Malcolm Cowley notes that even 'the names of the author and the publisher – actually the same person – are omitted from the title page' (Cowley, 1976: vii). However, Whitman's name appears twice in the first edition, 'but in different forms'. On the copyright page we read: 'entered according to Act of Congress in the year 1855, by WALTER WHITMAN.' On page 29, almost in the middle of the long first poem, we are introduced to 'Walt Whitman, an American, one of the roughs, a kosmos' (ibid: viii).

This self-published collection of poems was criticized by many writers at the time of its publication, in part because of its novel format and language. For example, in a review which appeared in *Putnam's Monthly*, New York, in September 1855, the first professor of the history of art at Harvard University, Charles Eliot Norton (1827–1908), described Whitman's book as

> a curious and lawless collection of poems, called *Leaves of Grass*, and issued in a thin quarto without the name of the publisher or author. The poems, twelve in number, are neither in rhyme nor blank verse, but in a sort of excited prose broken into lines without any attempt at measure or regularity, and, as many readers will perhaps think, without any idea of sense or reason.
>
> (Norton, 1971: 24)

In *A Reader's Guide to Walt Whitman*, Gay Wilson Allen mentions that the author of this review is Edward Everett Hale (Allen, 1997: 5). This confusion stems from the anonymity of its authorship. In 1856, a review in the *New York*

Daily Times described Whitman as follows: 'what Centaur have we here, half man, half beast, neighing defiance to all the world?' (Allen, 1997: 3).

The first positive reaction to *Leaves of Grass* was contained in a letter Ralph Waldo Emerson (1803–82) sent to Whitman on 21 July 1855, in which he expresses his admiration: 'I am not blind to the worth of the wonderful gift of "Leaves of Grass". I find it the most extraordinary piece of wit & wisdom that America has yet contributed . . . I greet you at the beginning of a great career, which yet must have had a long foreground somewhere for such a start' (Emerson, 1971: 21–2). By the beginning of the twentieth century, the major modernist poets were showing their admiration for Whitman's poetry, with the exception of Eliot. For his part, Ezra Pound claims that Whitman established American literature and opened the road to modernity. In his essay 'The Open Road', published first in 1909 under the title 'What I Feel about Walt Whitman', Pound described Whitman as 'America's poet. The only Poet before the artists of the Carman-Hovey period, or better, the only one of the conventionally recognized "American Poet" who is worth reading' (Pound, 1909/1962: 8).

By contrast, in his introduction to *Ezra Pound Selected Poems*, which was published first in 1928, T. S. Eliot rejects the idea that Whitman had a major impact on him or on Pound:

> I began to write, in 1908 or 1909, was directly drawn from the study of Laforgue together with the later Elizabethan drama; and I do not know anyone who started from exactly that point. I did not read Whitman until much later in life, and had to conquer an aversion to his form, as well as to much of his matter, in order to do so. I am equally certain – it is indeed obvious – that Pound owes nothing to Whitman. This is an elementary observation; but when dealing with popular conceptions of *vers libre* one must still be as simple and elementary as fifteen years ago.
>
> (Eliot, 1959: 8)

However, Eliot changed his view on Whitman later. In a lecture titled 'Walt Whitman and Modern Poetry' which was delivered first in 1944, Eliot says, 'There are two kinds of poet: one we may call traditional. . . . The other kind (as great and greater) find a way of saying hardly adaptable to anything else except what they themselves have to say. Whitman is in this class' (Eliot, 2017, V 6: 784).

For Harold Bloom, 'the authentic father' for Eliot's 'What the Thunder Said', the 'third who always walks beside you' and the 'Lilacs' is Whitman more than Dante, Baudelaire, Laforgue and Pound as Eliot claimed (Bloom, 2005: 15–16). In the last chapter entitled 'Whitman' in *Studies in Classic American Literature* (1924/1971), D.H. Lawrence explains the concept of 'the open road' formally and thematically. Formally, Whitman's contribution to world poetry was pronounced as 'the one pioneer. And only Whitman'. No one ahead of him. 'No English pioneers, no French. No European pioneer-poets . . . the same in America' (Lawrence, 1971: 179).

Thematically, the author of *Leaves of Grass* was, for Lawrence, the first poet who broke 'the mental allegiance. He was the first to smash the old moral conception that the soul of man is something "superior" and "above" the flesh' (ibid.: 180). In his introduction to the 1955 reprinting of the last edition of *Leaves of Grass*, which originally appeared in January 1892 and was known as 'Death-bed Edition', William Carlos Williams underlines the technical importance of Whitman's poetry:

> It was a challenge to the entire concept of poetic idea, and from a new viewpoint, a rebel viewpoint, an American viewpoint. In a word and at the beginning it enunciated a shocking truth, that the common ground is of itself a poetic source. . . . Whitman's so called 'free verse' was an assault on the very citadel of the poem itself; it constituted a direct challenge to all living poets to show cause why they should not do likewise.
>
> (Williams, 2001: xxiii)

This 'altered style' is too difficult to imitate, and according to Williams, in 'America, Whitman, and the Art of Poetry', first published in 1917, 'the only way to be like Whitman is to write *unlike* Whitman' (Williams, 1987: 2). What Williams 'had derived', in James E. B Breslin's words, was not Whitman's style, 'but a bold conception of his poetic task' (Breslin, 1985: 19).

The same Whitmanian 'bold conception' influenced Jorge Luis Borges. In a discussion about Whitman (1968) (published in 1975 under the title 'Walt Whitman: Man and Myth'), Borges suggests that Emerson found in Whitman the concept of the poet he was waiting for, and that *Leaves of Grass* is the book into whose pages 'the whole of America might find its way' (Borges, 1975: 710). 'The central problem' for Emerson was 'the problem of writing a democratic poem. For Walt Whitman, writing a poem to democracy did not mean saying, "Oh Democracy" and then going on. It meant working out a new pattern. Whitman thought of the past as being feudal. He thought of all previous poetry as mere feudalism' (ibid.). Borges admired Whitman to the point that he did not need to 'reread him because Walt Whitman ha[d] become a part of [him]'. In addition, the Argentinian writer knew that in Whitman's poems 'the words are less important than what lies behind the words' (ibid.: 711). In other words, what mattered to Borges was the 'bold conception' of Whitman's poetics. He goes on to quote the comparison that was made by the German writer Herman Bruetts between Whitman's words and the sea. Bruetts 'said that words followed after words as a wave follows a wave, and that the waves were not important, for the sea was behind them' (ibid.). Reading 'behind the words' and 'between the lines' is a distinctly translational job. In *Walt Whitman: The Making of the Poet*, Paul Zweig summarizes the sources of *Leaves of Grass* which shaped the style of Whitman's poetry:

> Much of his [poetry] was first written down as prose. [Whitman's] most influential models were not poems at all but Carlyle's gnarled prose, Emerson's essays, the King James Bible, Ruskin, maybe even Thoreau. There was far more great prose than poetry in Whitman's 'foreground'. His achievement was to incorporate the advantages of prose – its flexibility, its ability to mold itself freely to an actual speaking voice – into a new line that was subtly accented, yet never far from the extended rhythms of prose.
>
> (Zweig, 1984: 239)

These features are clearly present in *Song of Myself*, which most of Whitman's readers consider to be his masterpiece. For Allen, 'almost every critic will agree that "Song of Myself" is Whitman's supreme lyric. He would deserve the rank of major poet if he had written nothing else' (Allen, 1997: 126). Allen adds that this poem was 'more than the poet's desire to "sing himself," or to "put his life on record"' (ibid.). It 'is about the realization of the meaning of *self* or *selfhood*' (ibid.). The American poet Galway Kinnell claims that *Song of Myself* 'with each revision . . . became less representative and more exclusively autobiographical' (Kinnell, 2006: 6). In response, Frank D. Casale suggests that we 'should resist the urge to write about Whitman himself instead of writing about the fictional persona "Walt Whitman" (or, more generally, "Myself") who narrates the poem' (Casale, 2009: 83). In his view, 'the speaker of "Song of Myself" can also be viewed as a theatrical representation of Walt Whitman' (ibid.: 84). Indeed, this poem is considered to be, as Whitman himself posits, 'an attempt, from first to last, to put *a Person*, a human being (myself, in the later half of the Nineteenth Century, in America) freely, fully and truly on record' (Whitman, 1982: 671). No Whitman's poem accomplishes that feat more richly than *Song of Myself* (Greenspan, 2005: 9).

Whitman himself refers, sometimes openly and sometimes implicitly, to this poem as the core of his oeuvre. For instance, in an unsigned review published in *United States Review* in 1855 and in *Walt Whitman: The Critical Heritage* (1971), Whitman spoke about his first poem (which was then titled *Song of Myself*) for nearly half of his review, and in the second half he discussed all eleven other poems of *Leaves of Grass* (Whitman, 1971: 34–48). Speaking about himself in the third person, Whitman observes:

> Walt Whitman at first proceeds to put his own body and soul into the new versification:
>
> I celebrate myself,
>
> For what I assume you shall assume,
>
> For every atom belonging to me, as good belong to you.
>
> He leaves houses and their shuttered rooms, for the open air. He drops disguise and ceremony, and walks forth with the confidence and gayety of a child. For the old decorums of writing he substitutes his own decorums. . . . He will bring poems to fill the days and nights – fit for men and women with the attributes of throbbing blood and flesh. The body, he teaches, is beautiful. . . . To men and women he says, You can have healthy and powerful breeds of children on no less terms than these of mine. Follow me, and there shall be taller and richer crops of humanity.
>
> (ibid.: 37–8)

In the same review, Whitman remarks that the style of poems in *Leaves of Grass* 'is simply their own style, just born and red [*sic*]' (ibid.: 36). In the preface to the 1876 edition of *Leaves of Grass*, Whitman also reveals that his poetic form 'has strictly grown from purports and facts, and is the analogy of them' (cited in Allen, 1997: 156). In the introduction to the 1855 edition of *Leaves of Grass*, Malcolm Cowley argues that the poet 'was not working in terms of "therefore" and "however". He preferred to let one image suggest another image, which in turn suggests a new statement of mood or doctrine' (Cowley, 1976: xvi).

The novelty of Whitman is a result of 'consistent' elements that shaped his poems. In an unsigned review published by the *American Phrenological Journal* in 1856 and subsequently in *Walt Whitman: The Critical Heritage* (1971), Whitman asked,

> has not the time arrived for a school of live writing and tuition consistent with the principles of these poems? Consistent with the free spirit of this age and with the American truths of politics? Consistent with geology, and astronomy, and phrenology, and human physiology? Consistent with the sublimity of immortality and the directness of common sense?
>
> (Whitman, 1971: 40)

In the same review, Whitman made a comparison between *Leaves of Grass* and Tennyson's *Maud and Other Poems*. It seems as if his aim was to present a new concept of poetry, as well as to criticize English poetic and social traditions (ibid.: 43).

To Carl Sandburg, Whitman's poetry is 'the most peculiar and noteworthy monument amid the work of American literature' (Sandburg, 1921: iii). He attributes this to two features, the first of which is its style and this 'is regarded as the most original'. It is definitely the most 'individual' and the most 'sublimely personal' across American literature. The second feature is its 'controversial nature' which 'is the most highly praised and most deeply damned that ever came from an American printing press as the work of an American writer; no other book can compete with it' (ibid.: iii–iv). Indeed, as Allen explains, none of Whitman's critics could ignore his work as 'they either hated it or were fascinated by it (sometimes both at the same time), and either reviled or immoderately praised the poet. In this respect he was like the "revolutionary" leaders in American politics' (Allen, 1997: 4). This curiosity about Whitman can be attributed to the novelty of his poetry, thematically and technically.

The American poet Robert Hass describes the technical level of the poem as unexpectedly based on two 'realistic detail that was characteristic of journalism and the novel in his day, which was for him the idiom of the vivid present' (Hass, 2010: 4). Whitman believed that 'the poetry of a new democratic order had to have both these qualities if it was to embody new thoughts and have in it the feel of common life in cities' (ibid.).

In Hass's view *Song of Myself* belongs to everyone. Although it is an important document in America's history and culture, the poem 'escaped, almost immediately, the bonds of its fervent nationalism: it became a way forward in the twentieth century for poets all over the world – in Latin America and Russia and Portugal and China and India and North Africa (ibid.).

Hass mentions North Africa but not Arabic culture. Notwithstanding this, Whitman's poetry has been appreciated across the Arab world since the beginning of the twentieth century. *Song of Myself* has been translated in part into Arabic a number of times, including by the likes of Jabrā Ibrāhīm Jabrā in 1953/1982 and Yūsuf al-Khāl in 1958. The poem has also been translated in full by Saʿdī Yūsuf in 1976/2010, 'Ābid Ismāʿīl in 2006 and Rif'at Sallām in 2017.

2.1 The situational context

A number of Syrian and Lebanese writers immigrated to New York at the beginning of the last century where they established *al-Rābiṭah al-qalamiyyah* (the pen league) also known as *al-Mahjar* (the diaspora). Two members of that League, the Lebanese poets Jubrān Khalīl Jubrān (1883–1931) and Amīn al-Riḥānī (1876–1940), were the first to explore Whitman's poetry. In *Studies in Contemporary Arabic Poetry and Criticism*, Mounah A. Khouri explains that 'in his effort to modernize Arabic poetry and under the influence of Whitman's poetic theory, al-Riḥānī created the first consciously conceived model of prose poetry in Arabic'. In this experiment, the Lebanese poet tried to 'develop a new from, free from prosodic literary bonds and capable of expressing the ideas and feelings of the modern poet in a more suitable form and language' (Khouri, 1987: 103). In the preface to his first collection *Hutāf al-Awdiya* (Hymns of the valleys) written in 1910, al-Riḥānī attempts to define this 'new form' and Whitman's influence in shaping it:

> This type of new poetry is called *vers libre* in French and *free verse* in English, that is, free, or more properly, freed verse (*al-shiʿr al-ḥurr wa al-muṭlaq*). It is the most recent form achieved by poetic advances among the Westerners, in particular by the Americans and English. Milton and Shakespeare liberated English poetry from the bonds of rhyme; and the American Walt Whitman freed it from prosodic bonds such as the conventional rhythms and customary metres. But this freed verse has a new and particular rhythm, and a poem composed in it may follow numerous

> and varied metres. . . . Walt Whitman was the inventor of this method and its standard-bearer; after his death many contemporary European poets joined under this standard. . . . The distinctions of his poetry are not limited to its strange new form alone, but include philosophy and the depiction of that which is even more strange and new.
>
> (Translated by Khouri, 1987: 104)

Al-Rīḥānī made no clear distinction between free verse (الشعر الحر) and prose poetry (الشعر المنثور). As Khouri observes, 'a textual analysis of the structure of al-Rīḥānī's prose poems reveals that through his extensive use of rhyme, his declamatory language, oratorical tone and other devices, he was much less influenced by Whitman's style than by that of the Koran' (ibid.). Khouri later concludes that 'the apparent synthesis al-Rīḥānī endeavoured to achieve under the impact of both Arabic and Western sources has not fully succeeded in creating a truly free mode of artistic expression capable of providing modern Arabic poetry with the anticipated new directions' (ibid.).

Unlike al-Rīḥānī, Jubrān omitted mention of Whitman's influence, but many scholars highlight the similarity of their poetic experiences. Lin Fengmin is one such scholar, in her essay 'Walt Whitman and the Arabic Immigrant Poet Gibran Khalil Gibran': 'we can find in Gibran and Whitman's works that they shared a strong similarity in their poetics and thoughts' (Fengmin, 2006: 63). Artistically, 'Gibran's prose poetry . . . is of the same origin as Whitman's in his creative language. Both of them are adept at creating original images by ingenious combinations of words' (ibid.). Thematically, 'Gibran is as sharp as Whitman in his treacherous spirit. And their attitudes to sex are more similar. Both of them disregarded the traditional notion of sex and love, [and] boldly expressed their own opinions' (ibid.: 65). And in their poems, love is viewed as a part of their mystical experiences.

If this is so in the case of *al-Mahjar* poets who encountered Whitman's writings in the first three decades of the twentieth century, it is different with the modernist poets in the Arab world. The latter first approached Eliot in the wake of the Second World War at a time when his writings (prose and poetry) seemed to address their present plight. These same modernist poets did not find Whitman until a decade later (Jabrā's first translations of Whitman's poems appeared in 1953).

We face the question as to why Arabic modernists were influenced by Eliot rather than Whitman, although they knew the American poet through the writings of *al-Mahjar's* poets. To answer this question, I would like to raise a number of issues:

1. Although *al-Mahjar* poets began reading Whitman in the early twentieth century, they did not involve themselves in translating his poems into Arabic.
2. Al-Rīḥānī's attempt to introduce Whitman's ideas to an Arab audience was unsuccessful, as he failed to present a new poetic model for the modernists. That said, his attempt to change the course of Arabic poetry was one of the earliest.
3. Al-Rīḥānī wrote 'romantic' poems without metre and rhyme. He called it prose poetry (الشعر المنثور) which is different from a prose poem (قصيدة النثر), which is considered to be the most modernist form in Arabic poetry.
4. In the early twentieth century, this type of prose poetry failed to make its mark alongside the works of the major classical poets such as Aḥmad Shauqī, Ḥāfiẓ Ibrāhīm, Maʿrūf al-Rūṣāfī and Muhammad Mahdī al-Jawāhirī. Nor could prose poetry compete with the output of the romantic poets, who used classical poetic form.
5. Jubrān was part of the Romantic Movement which was seemingly reluctant to break with the traditions of the time. The conflict between the romantic and classical writers was not specifically about form, although it later became that. Rather, it concerned the new poetic language and themes which the romantic poets introduced.
6. Al-Rīḥānī limited himself to textual analysis of Whitman's poetry, and he ignored the situational and cognitive contexts.
7. After the Second World War, Arab poets were ready to break with the 'rigid' poetic form of the classical poem, and thus they began to scrutinize afresh Eliot's writings. Arab writers had studied Eliot's work in the 1940s from artistic and political perspectives. The later modernists went further in terms of employing Eliot's poetic and cultural concepts in Arabic, and thus they can be unreservedly described as Eliotian poets.

8. Finally, by the time the modernists translated Whitman in the second half of the twentieth century, Eliot had already been absorbed in the 1940s into Arabic culture and adopted as the pioneer of world poetic modernity. Thus, his ideas dominated the Arabic literary scene at that time, more than those of any other writer.

The last three points highlight the 'Whitmanian' Arab poets' failure to understand the situational context of *Song of Myself*. Their misunderstanding or ignorance of the background of the original significantly affects the other two discursive contexts: the verbal and cognitive. The poem was written against the background of the American Civil War (1861–5). In *Whitman the Political Poet*, Betsy Erkkila emphasizes that 'the drama of identity' in the first edition of *Song of Myself* 'is rooted in the political drama of a nation in crisis' (Erkkila, 1989: 94). This nation, as the American president at the time, Abraham Lincoln, said was 'living in the midst of alarms and anxiety in which "we expect some new disaster with each newspaper we read"' (ibid.). Erkkila adds that 'the poet's conflict between the separate person and the en masse, pride and sympathy, individualism and equality, nature and the city, the body and the soul symbolically enacts the larger political conflicts in the nation' (ibid.). This conflict

> grew out of the controversy over industrialization, wage labour, women's rights, finance, immigration, slavery, territorial expansion, technological progress, and the question of the relation of individual and state, state and nation. The self that emerges in 'Song of Myself' is united by the same constitutional system of checks and balances – between the one and the many, self and other, liberty and union, urban and agrarian, material and spiritual – that Whitman envisioned for the American republic.
>
> (ibid.)

The modern Arab poets did not consider these topics as major themes when they translated *Song of Myself*. Jabrā first tackled Whitman's poetry while he was a student at Harvard in the 1950s, and he repeated 'abstract' concepts such as the body and the soul, the self and the universe, I and the other and so on which some critics link to Whitman without explaining their circumstances. In addition, although Jabrā describes the form used in *Song of Myself* as *al-shi'r al-mursal* (blank verse), which is not dissimilar to al-Rīḥānī's '*al-shi'r al-mutlaq*', he fails to elaborate upon the significance of this issue:

> Whitman was not able to express all mankind but in an overpowering stream in which the words push each other profusely, to break the chains of poetry, to despise metre and rhyme, and to give *al-shi'r al-mursal* eventually a rank in Western literature when his imitators were not able to do the same.
>
> (Jabrā, 1982: 174)

Whitman began writing '*al-shi'r al-mursal*', because 'his emotional and intellectual overflow could not bear the cruelty of prosody' (ibid.: 177).

Jabrā dated his translations of some sections of *Song of Myself* to 1953, although it was not until 1982 that they were published in *Al-Ḥuriyya wa al-Ṭūfān* (Freedom and the flood). In this book, Jabrā discusses the impact of Western cultural issues on Arabic literature. For example, in the second chapter, he addresses the misinterpretation of Jean-Paul Sartre's concepts of freedom and commitment as existential terms in modern Arabic literature. In the eleventh chapter, entitled Ughniyyat *Nafsī* ('Song of Myself'), Jabrā discusses the importance of Whitman's poems:

> The poet spent about eight years composing, extending and truncating them in order to express a specious self, which extends to contain the whole universe. But what is easier than misunderstanding a poet who made himself a symbol for humanity, and went enumerating and singing his origins? This is because he sings the body of humanity itself.
>
> (ibid.: 173)

Jabrā describes *Song of Myself* as a 'long song which expresses that vast wide "self" in which generations of humanity, its core and garbage, mix in it' (ibid.: 177). He adds that 'undoubtedly, "Song of Myself" is the greatest poem produced in the American territory in the 19th century' (ibid.: 179).

As for al-Khāl, he translated five out of fifty-two sections of *Song of Myself*. These sections (6, 7, 18, 21 and 25) were published in his journal *Shi'r* (Poetry) in 1958 and also in his book *Dīwān al-Shi'r al-Amīrkī* (Divan of American poetry) in the same year. In 1963, al-Khāl translated several other poems from *Leaves of Grass*, including 'As I Ponder'd in Silence', 'As Adam Early in the Morning', 'In Paths Untrodden' and 'Scented Herbage of My Breast'. These translations were published in *Shi'r*, too. In his afterword to the sections of *Song of Myself*, al-Khāl explains the relationship between the Whitmanian poetic form and the themes in *Leaves of Grass*. Al-Khāl terms this new form *al-shi'r al-ḥurr* (free verse), and he attributes Whitman's stylistic experiments to his desire 'to be flexible, sweeping like the America which he wants to depict. Thus, *Awrāq al-'Ushb* [*Leaves of Grass*] came out in a free verse style' (al-Khāl, 1958b: 55). In the same afterword, al-Khāl summarizes the importance of Whitman's poetry as comprising five features:

> 1. Whitman's poetry is a personal one. The history of poetry rarely knew such personal writings. *Leaves of Grass* – the book that contains all Whitman's poems – is like an autobiography which shows frankly and clearly Whitman's ideas and opinions, and shows, in detail and comprehensively, the aspects of his personality. Thus, Whitman himself said about his book: 'when you touch it, you touch a human.'
> 2. Whitman's poetry had a huge impact on the development of world poetry, European in particular. His style, which escaped the common standards and regulations of prosody, was an indication of a renewed (تجديدية) poetic period.
> 3. Whitman's poetry is characterized by its epic nature. In this respect, some of Whitman's critics put him in the ranks of Shakespeare, Dante and Homer. As for his poetic content, some critics, like Emerson, put Whitman on a par with Socrates, Confucius, Laozi and other great teachers in history.
> 4. Whitman's poetry expresses, in a great genuineness, his generation's hopes, wishes, sorrows and struggles for life, and how people can 'win this life' in a virgin wild vast continent. Thus, he sang himself as he sang America.
> 5. Whitman's poetry has deep and manifold sources. Many world literary trends meet in his poems. The poet was familiar with the works of Homer, Shakespeare, Dante, Cervantes, Goethe, Hegel, Rousseau . . . and the English translation of the Torah. The Sufi tendency overcomes his poetry, as well as the nationalistic one.
>
> (ibid.: 54–6)

Regardless of his stylish description, al-Khāl omits to mention Whitman's importance for modernist Arab poets, although he does acknowledge, in his foreword to *Dīwān al-Shi'r al-Amīrkī*:

> The influence of Whitman's poetic revolution on the future of poetry wherever it was. By virtue of Whitman, the movement of free verse was launched . . . and by virtue of Whitman, Arabic literature knew this poetic

style through Amīn al-Rīḥānī and Jubrān. This poetic style has since then been called prose poetry, and Amīn al-Rīḥānī, especially, had his own attempts in it.

(Al-Khāl, 1958c: 9)

In fact, neither Whitman nor his Western critics described the new form of *Leaves of Grass* as 'prose poetry'. Rather, it was commonly described as 'free verse', although this does not mean 'prose verse', as some Arab writers thought. It is 'free' from the regulatory standards of the poetic metre.

Unlike Jabrā and al-KhāI, Sa'dī Yūsuf wrote a relatively long introduction to *Awrāq al-'Ushb* (*Leaves of Grass*) which was first published in Baghdad in 1976. In this edition, Yūsuf translates all fifty-two sections of *Song of Myself* and other poems from *Leaves of Grass* such as 'As I Ponder'd in Silence', 'Shut Not Your Doors', 'Thou Reader' and 'As Adam Early in the Morning'. In the introduction, Yūsuf rejects the idea of a mystic or Sufi tendency in *Leaves of Grass* and accuses Whitman's critics of having distorted his poetry on two occasions. For Yūsuf, the critics either focus on the poet's ideas or on the aesthetic aspect of *Leaves of Grass*, without consideration of Whitman's conceptual approach. To American and European writers, Whitman was a prophet or mystic (Yūsuf, 2010: 5). Like Jabrā, Sa'dī Yūsuf views Whitman's poetry as *shi'r mursal* (blank verse), albeit this type of verse is not without regulations, as the poet resorts to 'al-tajnīs', 'al-muṭābaqa' and euphony in order to give his poem a musical quality (ibid.: 21). Thematically, Yūsuf acknowledges the fact that 'the Civil War's poems occupy a huge space of *Leaves of Grass*. The poems depict the battles and pangs of the wounded, human massacres . . . but [these poems] are full of great hopes' which people seek at the end of the war (ibid.: 17). Yūsuf justifies his translation by saying that introducing Whitman to our readers and poets in this period is of great significance (ibid.: 22). This is because:

1. Whitman's poetry is a healthy breeze [compared with] so many poetries which have been translated to our language.
2. He is a poet of a nation in a state of renewal, who can offer to our poetry, which looks forward to being the voice of our renewal, a great example.
3. He is also a writer of a poetic revolution which extended to Europe and paid off. Hence, *qaṣīdat al-nathr* (prose poem) was not able to pave its European road without Whitman's great contribution.

4. Furthermore, Whitman is a poet of sensuality and reality and of living words. We, and our poetry, are in need of [those] sensual, real and living words.

(ibid.: 22–3)

If Whitman is considered to be the pioneer of English free verse, Yūsuf is one of the pioneers of Arabic free verse. Like Whitman, Yūsuf's 'sensual, real and living words' inspired the prose poem's poets as we will see in the cognitive context. In *Nineteenth-Century U.S. Literature in Middle Eastern Languages*, Jeffrey Einboden reveals the circumstances behind Yūsuf's translation of *Leaves of Grass*:

> It was during a critical intermission in these migrations – in 1976, intersecting with Youssef's 1972 return to Iraq from Algeria, and his final exile in 1978 – that he would publish his 'أوراق العشب' (*Awrāq al-'Ushb*): the first substantive translation of *Leaves of Grass* in the Arab world. Printed in Baghdad, this edition transplants a poetic icon of American democracy within the soil of the ancient Iraqi capital – an act that now seems laden with irony, raising questions for twenty-first-century readers that extend beyond the literary concerns of Youssef's own introductory query in 1976. In its uneasy fusion of national and literary identities, *Awrāq al-'Ushb* not only reflects the exilic 'trail' that envelops its production, however, but also the fraught future of its place of publication, predicting the upheavals and circulations that shape current prospects in the Arab world, reaching from revolution in Middle Eastern verse to revolutions in Taḥrīr Square.
>
> (Einboden, 2013: 157)

2.2 The verbal context

From *Song of Myself*, I selected sections 1, 5, 18, 21, 24, 43 and 52 to study along with their Arabic translations.

2.2.1 I celebrate myself

Many scholars have explored Whitman's relationship to European poetic traditions and how differently these traditions function in *Song of Myself*. For Casale, Whitman opens *Song of Myself* with lines that

> not only declare the subject of the poem but also its radical break from the poetry of the past. 'I celebrate myself', writes Whitman, simultaneously echoing the opening of Virgil's epic poem the Aeneid ('I sing of arms and the man') but also revising the epic poem's traditional emphasis on military heroism, the gods, and the history of great nations.
>
> (Casale, 2009: 87)

It was, in fact, Homer who started this tradition, as we read at the beginning of the *Iliad*: 'sing, goddess, of the anger Achilleus, son of Peleus' (Homer, 1987: 3). Later in his Aeneid, Virgil wrote: 'I sing of arms and of the man, fated to be an exile' (Virgil, 2003: 3). In any case, the hero of *Song of Myself*, as a modern epic, 'is "Myself": not a proud, aloof hero like Achilles or Aeneas but a universal figure corresponding to all people' (Casale: 87). In section 24 of this poem, Whitman names himself 'his own muse, singing himself' freely, and he confirms 'that the subject of his epic will be himself', instead of appealing to 'the muse to allow him to sing the epic song of war, rage, and distant journey' (Folsom, 2012). It seems that Whitman was well aware of this tradition, as he 'opens his poem with a conventional iambic pentameter line, as if to suggest the formal openings of the classic epics, before abandoning metrics for a free-flowing line with rhythms that shift and respond to the moment' (ibid.).

Yūsuf al-KhāI does not translate this section. Jabrā ignores the last stanza of this section, without offering any explanation. Moreover, he blends stanzas 2 and 3 together. Both translations interpret 'I' as 'إني'. Jabrā and Sa'dī Yūsuf use the accusative particle *inna* (حرف نصب) (إن) which is also a particle of emphasis (حرف توكيد). Yūsuf interprets 'celebrate' in Whitman's poem:

> I celebrate myself, and sing myself,
> And what I assume you shall assume,
> For every atom belonging to me as good belongs to you.
>
> (Whitman, 2001: 33)

as 'أحتفي' (honour/salute):

> إني أحتفي بنفسي، وأغني نفسي
> وما سآخذ به ستأخذون به
> وكل ذرة فيّ، هي ذرة فيكم
>
> (Whitman, tr. Yūsuf, 2010: 88)

The immediate Arabic equivalent of 'I celebrate' is 'أحتفل', as it appears in Jabrā's translation:

انى احتفل بنفسي، واتغنى بنفسي،
وكل ما ادعيه انا عليك انت ان تدعيه،
لان كل ذرة تنتمي إليّ تنتمي اليك ايضاً.

(Whitman, tr. Jabrā, 1982: 179)

Jabrā also interprets 'sing' as 'اتغنى' (praise), invoking an old epic style. In addition, he translates 'assume' as 'ادّعى' (claim) or even (pretend). In discussing, philosophically, the separate pronoun 'أنا' in the Arabic translations of Descartes's *Cogito, ergo sum* (*Je pense, donc je suis*; I think, therefore I exist; انا أفكر، إذن أنا موجود), Ṭāha Abd al-Raḥmān explains that this pronoun has three functions:

1. Emphasizing the self: I am someone who thinks.
2. Denial of the otherness: I am someone who thinks, not someone else who thinks.
3. Proving the singularity: I alone think, and there is no one else who thinks with me.

(Abd al-Raḥmān, 2013: 413–17)

These functions are equally important for translating poetry, especially Whitman's poetry. The given Arabic translations consider these functions in approaching *Song of Myself*. However, the Whitmanian 'I' is not synonymous with ego. In an unsigned review first published in the *Brooklyn Daily Times* in 1856, the poet, using the third-person pronoun, completely denied egotism in his poetry: '[w]hat good is to argue about egotism? There can be no two thoughts on Walt Whitman's egotism. That is avowedly what he steps out of the crowd and turns and faces them for' (Whitman, 1971: 46).

In the second line of stanza 1, Jabrā translates the second pronoun 'you' as 'أنت', but this is problematic. In English, there is one form 'you' for the masculine and feminine, singular, dual and plural, formal and informal. In Arabic, on the other hand, there is a specific form for each category of 'you'. Jabrā writes 'أنت' without a sign to know whether it is masculine (انتَ) or feminine (أنتِ). Nevertheless, poets sometimes use a masculine form of a pronoun as neutral; they also sometimes use a masculine pronoun but refer contextually to a feminine. This classical technique is still used in Arabic poetry. In addition, the Arabic language sometimes employs a masculine form of a pronoun to generalize its gender. It seems the last two points were in Jabrā's mind when he translated 'you'. The problems of translating 'you' in Arabic will be discussed further in the next section.

In a chapter entitled '"As if I Were with You" – The Performance of Whitman's Poetry', Stephen Railton notes that 'every reader has noticed how often Walt Whitman says *I*. There are few pages of *Leaves of Grass* without at least some form of the first-person pronoun – *I, me, mine, my, myself*' (Railton, 1995: 7). Railton adds, while Whitman does not mention 'you' as much as he mentions 'I', 'he uses the second-person pronoun more pervasively than any other major poet' (ibid.). Whitman uses this technique to engage his reader poetically and directly. He wants his reader to play not only an imaginative but an active role. On a deeper level, the ultimate purpose of his poetry is to 'fetch you whoever you are flush with myself', as the poet posits in section 42 of *Song of Myself*. This is because 'all I write I write to arouse in you a great personality', writes Whitman in *Notebooks and Unpublished Prose Manuscripts* (Whitman, 1984: 202; also cited in ibid.). Railton also explains that the shift 'from the first person to the second, from an apparent self-absorption to a real concern with another, is a very common pattern in Whitman's poetry' (Railton: 8). Railton notes too that 'the first word of "Song of Myself" . . . is *I*, but the last word is *you*' (ibid.). Furthermore, stanza 1 of the first section 'announces this larger pattern explicitly' (ibid.). For his part, Yūsuf chooses to interpret 'you' as 'أنتم' (in the plural form), by which he may refer to the poet's audience or readers; alternatively, it could refer to everyone as Whitman's poem suggests. Regardless of the legitimacy of his approach, Yūsuf interprets 'you' contextually, or even discursively, not as an isolated word. Like Jabrā, Yūsuf changes the shape of this section, as its four stanzas shrink into one in his translation. In fact, he uses this approach throughout his work, and he admits that there is no translational justification for this. In a footnote to his introduction, he says, 'in the Arabic text, I did not consider the original length of the verses; but I proceeded to a certain cutting' (Yūsuf, 2010: 21). In stanza 2 of the first section, Yūsuf translates 'loafe' as 'أطوف' (wander). Interestingly, he translates it with the same context as 'التسكع' in section 5. On this point, Yūsuf followed Jabrā in translating the same word in the first section.

Like 'you', the Whitmanian 'self' is expressed by several terms in *Song of Myself*. In *How to Read and Why*, Harold Bloom offers the explanation that there are three main categories of 'self': 'my soul', 'myself' and 'the real me', also called 'the me myself'. These categories have their own conceptual values in the poem '"I" is the "Myself" of *Song of Myself*, or Whitman's poetic personality. "The other I am" is the "me myself", inner personality. Whitman fears mutual abasement between his character and his real self, who seems capable only of a master-slave relationship, sadomasochistic and ultimately destructive to both' (Bloom, 2001: 91). According to Bloom, 'the Whitmanian soul is his unknown nature, ethos or character, and derives from the Emersonian Over-soul' (ibid.). In his essay 'the Over-soul' first published in 1841, Emerson defines this concept as referring to 'the Supreme Critic on the errors of the past and the present, and the only prophet of that which must be is that great nature in which we rest, as the earth lies in the soft arms of the atmosphere; that Unity, that Over-soul, within which every man's particular being is contained and made one with all other' (Emerson, 2010: 155–6).

The concept of 'oneness' dates back to the Neoplatonic philosophy of the infinite or 'eternal ONE', as its doctrine states. In this philosophy, according to Kamuran Godelek, there is only 'one exalted God, that is a supreme power, the final cause, the cosmic force. God is the highest spiritual, and creative Being' (Godelek, 1999). Godelek emphasizes that Muslim Sufis view *Allāh* (God) in the same way:

> In Sufism, the universe is just an appearance of God, and does not have an independent existence. To think of the universe and the God as being separate is to deny the 'Oneness' and to suggest a 'duality' between God and the universe. But in reality, the God and the universe are the 'One' and the same thing such that God reflects himself as the universe. It is not possible to think of God and the universe as separate entities because God is not something outside the universe as Islam favours, but rather something within the universe. . . . this belief was initially suggested by Neoplatonism. They both see the existence of the universe as an emanation from God.
>
> (ibid.)

Similarly, 'Ibn 'Arabī says that there is only one ultimate Reality in the whole of existence. This is certainly monistic, but not the same thing as pure monism, which maintains that there is only one entity' (ibid.). A. E. Affifi explains that Neoplatonism was one of Ibn 'Arabī's sources, alongside classical Sufism and Islamic theology (Baldick, 1989: 83). Ibn 'Arabī's concept is called *Wahdat al-Wujūd* (the Oneness of Being) or (the Unity of Existence), and he added *ḥubb* (love) to describe the relationship between the elements of existence. Whitman used the same concept.

2.2.2 I believe in you my soul

In *Varieties of Religious Experience*, William James cites section 5 of *Song of Myself* as 'a classical expression of this sporadic type of mystical experience' (James, 1902: 395; also cited in Allen, 1997: 127). In his introduction to the first edition of *Leaves of Grass*, Malcolm Cowley says 'Whitman transformed by new experience, so that he wonders among familairs objects and find that each of them has become a miracle' (Cowley, 1976: xxxvi). As a result of a conversion with Cowley, Allen suggests that the 'new experience' was a mystical one which enabled Whitman to compose *Song of Myself* (Allen, 1997: 118; also see 213 note 14). Ed Folsom observes that in this section:

> [Whitman] evokes the ancient tradition of poets imagining a conversation between the body and the soul: the difference is that instead of having the soul win the debate (as happens in virtually all the poetry before Whitman's), the body and soul in this poem join in an ecstatic embrace and give each other identity. Where poets before Whitman imagined the soul as the enduring part of the self, the part that transcended the body at the body's death, Whitman imagines a descendence (instead of a transcendence).
>
> (Folsom, 2012)

However, as Folsom himself postulates about the 'sexual' scene in the last two stanzas of this section, 'It is difficult to tell just what kind of sex act Whitman portrays as he evokes the sensual joining of his "I" with the "you". It is an act of intimacy that produces "voice", but a voice that does not speak in words, music, or rhyme, a voice that does not "lecture" but rather "hums"' (ibid.). The sexual allusion of this section was mostly inferred by Whitman's readers, who were described as conservative and lived in the poet's time. They 'tend to castigate' this section 'as sacrilegious' (Greenspan, 2005: 129). The controversy focuses on four stanzas in this section which have 'evoked an extraordinarily divergent array of interpretations ranging from devotional and pastoral to orgiastic' (ibid.). For the most part, however, Whitman's readers interpret this section 'in a religious context', because it can be read 'as pantheistic, with comparisons made with the thought and expression of Ralph Waldo Emerson and/or the Transcendentalists' (ibid.). Influenced by Neoplatonism, the concept of the human soul and its transcendent ability is a popular subject in Islamic philosophy and Sufism. For example, Mulla Sadra (d. 1050/1640) states that 'the human soul, during its perception of intelligibles, ascends towards the degree of the Active Intellect and becomes united with it in such a way that is known to those who are deeply rooted in knowledge (*al-rasikhun fī al-'ilm*)' (cited in Kuspinar, 2000: 54). In his article 'Perception: A Way to Perfection in Sadra', Bilal Kuspinar goes on to explain that 'according to Sadra, it is in the very nature of the human soul to perceive all the realities of creation and unite itself with them in an immaterial union' (ibid.).

Translating 'soul' as well as translating the second pronoun 'you' can be problematic. Here, the difficulty arises because of the requirement to translate the gender:

> I believe in you my soul, the other I am must not abase itself to you,
> And you must not be abased to the other.
>
> (Whitman: 38)

أؤْمن بكِ يا نفسي
لكن عليَّ ألّا أجعل الآخر أقلّ منكِ شأناً
وعليكِ أنت ألّا تكوني أقلّ من الآخر شأناً،

(Whitman, tr. Yūsuf: 95)

Yūsuf interprets the gender of the second pronoun as feminine. In my opinion, he does this because of the use of *nafs* as equivalent to 'soul' in the initial stanza. In Arabic, this word is feminine when it is used as 'soul' and masculine when it is used for a person. Stanza 1 'invokes the traditional Christian dichotomy of the soul and the body ("the other I am"), only to subvert it by declaring belief in both – and not just belief but equal belief, stated in rhythmically balanced verbal units' (Greenspan, 2005: 129). In his translation of the first line of this stanza, Yūsuf translates 'soul' as *nafs* (self). In Islamic philosophy where the target poem was generated, *nafs* and *ruḥ* have similar meanings. This explains why *nafs* is often rendered as 'soul' or 'self' in English. It also explains why Yūsuf chose to translate 'soul' as *nafs*. In the Qur'ānic context, *ruḥ* is normally translated as 'spirit'. For example, in 17:85:

وَيَسْأَلُونَكَ عَنِ الرُّوحِ قُلِ الرُّوحُ مِنْ أَمْرِ رَبِّي وَمَا أُوتِيتُم مِّن الْعِلْمِ إِلَّا قَلِيلًا

> They ask you concerning the Spirit. Say: 'the Spirit (comes) by command of my Lord: of knowledge it is only a little that is communicated to you, (O people!).'

This explains why Yūsuf uses 'روح الله' to translate 'spirit of God' in stanza 4 of this section. Unlike the first section where Yūsuf (and Jabrā) interprets 'I' as 'إنـي' (I do), he translates 'I believe' as 'أؤْمن' replacing the subject 'I' by the implied pronoun of the present tense 'أؤْمن', although both 'I's of the two sections appear in a similar context. The emphasis shifts from the subject which appears as a separated first pronoun 'أنا' (I) and is joined by the affixed one 'ي' in the first section, to the object 'نفسي' (my soul) which is joined by the quasi-sentence 'بكِ' (in you). Here, the translator clearly shows his ability to elucidate the differences between the original concepts and to clarify their philosophical and poetical functions in the target culture.

As for the mystical experience, Jabrā attributes Whitmanian mysticism to 'Emerson's teachings' which include 'the individuality and the Sufi unity with nature'. Whitman's poetry shows both, 'with a new consciousness – the consciousness of the masses' (Jabrā, 1982: 174). With this statement, Jabrā offers his own interpretation of stanza 3:

أذكر كيف اضطجعنا في الصبح الرقيق ذات صيف،
وكيف استقر رأسك على ردفيّ وانقلبت بلطف علي،
وكشفت القميص عن عظم صدري، واهويت لسانك الى قلبي المعرّى،
وامتدت يداك حتى مستا لحيتي، حتى مستا قدمي.

(Whitman, tr. Jabrā: 180)

Jabrā published his text without *tashkīl* (diacritics), but the context of the TT indicates the masculinity of the second pronoun. This stanza is the only one translated from the whole section. This approach alters the original by ignoring the other stanzas, especially the first one which refers to 'the mystical experience' as the main theme. Translating isolated lines or even stanzas from the original often produces a different text in the target culture. Although he does not translate this section, al-Khāl states that Whitman's poetry is dominated by two 'tendencies': 'Sufi' and 'national' (al-Khāl, 1958b: 56). By mentioning 'national', al-Khāl refers to the 'Americanism' of Whitman's poetics. Jabrā also refers to the importance of the 'national' side, but he includes 'equality' as a universal factor in Whitman's work: 'Whitman's poetry glorifies its country, but it also represents a trend toward the parity between the American life style and the equality between people in the world' (Jabrā, 1982: 191).

In his introduction to *Awrāq al-'Ushb* (*Leaves of Grass*), Yūsuf rejects what he calls 'attributing Sufism to Walt Whitman', because it carries an intentional denial of the whole heritage of the poet, poetically and politically: this denial 'is an attempt to root out the poet from his true land which is filled with the faces, stories and trees'. It is also an attempt to put Whitman in هلامية 'vagueness', the poet himself denied. Describing Whitman as a Sufi poet, Yūsuf claims, 'is not justifiable by any of his important texts'. As a communist poet, Yūsuf attributes these readings of the American poet to 'the reactionary thought' of some of his critics, for whom *Leaves of Grass* was 'a threat' from the moment of its first publication in 1855 (Yūsuf, 2010: 12–13). The translator does not explain why he considers them as 'reactionary'. To my mind, such readings may be abstract, but not 'reactionary'. That said, Yūsuf himself approaches *Song of Myself* in a mystical fashion. For example, in his translation of ST 14 'And that a keelson of the creation is love', he uses 'love' as a Sufi concept 'ان أصل الخليقة الحب' in TT 26 of this section.

The concept of love is a Sufi one, as it appears in Ibn 'Arabī's famous lines in the eleventh poem of *Tarjumān al-Ashwāq* (*Interpreter of Desires*):

أدين بدين الحب أنَّى توجهت ركائبه، فالحب ديني وإيماني

(Ibn 'Arabī, 2005: 62)

I believe in the religion of Love: whatever its caravans
may lead, for love is my religion and my faith.

(Translated by McAuley, 2012: 1)

In the last line of this section, Yūsuf translates 'wormfence', which comes as one word in most editions of *Leaves of Grass*, as 'السياج المهترئ' (mangled fence). Here, the translator uses the adjective 'المهترئ' to describe the state of the fence, while Whitman, by using 'worm', meant to describe the shape of the fence. Historically, this fence has also been known since the American Civil War as a zigzag, split-rail or snake fence, because of its meandering design.

2.2.3 With music strong I come

Section 18 of *Song of Myself* was translated in full into Arabic by all three poet-translators: Jabrā, al-Khāl and Yūsuf. As is apparent, the word 'strong' in the first line of this section is interpreted rather differently:

With music strong I come, with my cornets and my drums,
I play not marches for accepted victors only, I play marches for conquer'd and slain persons.

(Whitman: 56)

بصادح الموسيقى اجيء، بأبواقي وطبولي،
ولست اعزف للظافرين المعروفين فقط، بل اعزف للمغلوبين والقتلى ايضاً.

(Whitman, tr. Jabrā: 180)

انا آتي مع الموسيقى قوياً، مع مزاميري وطبولي
انا لا اعزف اناشيد للمنتصرين فقط، انا اعزف
للأشخاص المقهورين والقتلى.

(Whitman, tr. Al-Khāl, 1958b: 51)

مع الموسيقى الضّاجة أجيء
بأبواقي وطبولي.
إنني لا أعزف المارشات للمنتصرين، حسب...
إنما أعزفها للمهزومين والمذبوحين أيضاً.

(Whitman, tr. Yūsuf: 121)

Jabrā uses an operatic term 'صادح' (tenor), while Yūsuf uses 'ضاجة' (loud). Al-Khāl uses the immediate Arabic equivalent 'قوياً'. He reads 'strong' as an accusative (ḥāl) to describe 'I' 'انا آتي مع الموسيقى قوياً' (with music I come strong). Jabrā and Yūsuf translate 'cornets' as 'أبواق', which suits the use of 'marches' in the second line of this section. Al-Khāl translates the same word as 'مزامير' (flutes/clarinets). He also interprets 'marches' as 'أناشيد' (chants/hymns), while Jabrā totally ignores this word, and Yūsuf Arabized it into 'مارشات'. Yūsuf also translates 'slain persons' as 'المذبوحين' (the slaughtered), while the context of this stanza refers clearly to the aftermath of a battle. Hence this phrase was translated by Jabrā and al-Khāl as 'القتلى' (the slain). In stanza 2, al-Khāl literally renders 'fall' as 'السقوط'. In Arabic, the meaning of 'to fall in battle' is 'to get killed'. Meanwhile, Jabrā translates 'fall' as 'الخسران', and Yūsuf as 'أن تفشل'. Both translations suit the context of the original.

As we saw in the first section, Jabrā and Yūsuf usually interpret the Whitmanian 'I' as 'إني' (I do), for example, both translators replace 'I' by 'I do' in stanza 3. In translating this stanza, Jabrā almost applies a word for word approach. This approach produces an unstandardized Arabic sentence:

اني اضرب وأقرع للموتى

This usage, which is very common in spoken and written modern Arabic, shows the impact of the English language on the Arabic. In *fuṣḥa* (standard) Arabic, a verb is not joined to another verb. Therefore, this sentence should be:

إني أضربُ للموتى وأقرعُ لهم.

Jabrā uses an Arabic equivalent 'مزامير' (flutes) for 'embouchures'.

In translating the same stanza, Yūsuf adds نون الوقاية (*nūn* of protection) to the first-person pronoun. He also replaces the two words 'beat' and 'pound' with one word 'أدق' (pound), and he adds an object 'الطبول' (drums), which does not exist in the original. The original, here, is the 'death-bed edition':

إنني أدق الطبول للموتى
وأنفخ في آلاتي الموسيقية أعلى الأصوات وأبهجها...
من أجلهم.

Yūsuf uses suspension marks in translating this stanza, and as Einboden notes in a different context, he uses other punctuation which does not exist in this edition. However, if we return to the initial edition of *Song of Myself*, we will find that Whitman uses this punctuation and 'drums' as well:

> I sound triumphal drums for the dead. . . . I fling through my embouchures the loudest and gayest music to them.
>
> (Whitman, 1855/1976: 42)

Comparing different editions of the original enables the translator to interpret what is missing in the final version. Using this strategy also helps the translator to create a poetic equivalent in the target culture. However, Yūsuf uses a 'superordinate' strategy in translating 'embouchures' as 'آلاتي الموسيقية' (my musical instruments). He uses general words to replace a specific action used in a wind instrument. He did not justify his strategy. In *Thinking Arabic Translation*, James Dickins, Sandor Hervey and Ian Higgins argue that 'generalizing translation is not acceptable if the TL [target language] does offer suitable alternatives, or if the omitted details are important in the ST but not implied or compensated for in the TT context' (Dickins et al., 2002: 57).

Unlike Jabrā and Yūsuf, al-Khāl always tends to translate the Whitmanian 'I' as a separate first-person pronoun 'أنا':

انا ادق واقرع لاجل الاموات

Like Jabrā, he also joins a verb with another verb in the first line of this stanza, which usage linguistically creates a non-standard Arabic sentence, although it is able sometimes to function poetically in the TT. In the second line of the same stanza, al-Khāl strangely made up 'فوهات مدافعي' (muzzles of my guns) to replace 'my embouchures':

انا انفخ في فوهات مدافعي احلى انغامي وامرحها لاجلهم.

(I blow in my gun muzzles my sweetest and gayest tunes for them.)

This 'surrealist' image explains al-Khāl's attempt to interpret the situational context of this stanza, which is an atmosphere of war. In addition, Whitman himself uses 'I fling through my embouchures' in the first edition of his poem, which perhaps encouraged al-Khāl' to go that far in his interpretation of this stanza.

2.2.4 I am the poet of the body and I am the poet of the soul

In this section, Whitman strikingly depicts the 'central' theme of his poem. Jabrā translates stanzas 1–2, 6–8 of this section. He bypasses stanzas 3–5. Once again, there is no justification for his approach. Unlike Jabrā, al-Khāl and Yūsuf translate the whole section.

In the third line of stanza 1, Jabrā and al-Khāl translate 'I graft and increase upon myself' literally 'أُطعِّم الاولى على نفسي فأزيدها' in Jabrā's version, and 'أُطعّمُ الاولى وازيدها على نفسي' in al-Khāl's. In contrast, Yūsuf uses a one-word strategy in translating two words or more. He chooses 'أغدق' (lavish) as an equivalent for 'graft and increase'. This is a popular strategy in translating poetry. For instance, Ezra Pound did not hesitate to replace a stanza with one or two words in his Chinese translations.

Stanza 6 was translated differently by our poet-translators. Jabrā uses a similar layout to the original and literally translates most words, although he makes some changes in the TT:

Press close bare-bosom'd night – press close magnetic nourishing night!
Night of south winds – night of the large few stars!
Still nodding night – mad naked summer night.

(Whitman: 60–1)

اضغط، وزد ضغطاً، يا ليلا عاري الصدر – زد ضغطاً يا ليلا مغناطيسيا مغذيا!
يا ليل رياح الجنوب – ليلَ النجمات القلائل الكبار!
يا ليلًا يتمايل ابدا – يا ليلا عاريا مجنوناً من ليالي الصيف!

(Whitman, tr. Jabrā: 182)

As we saw in the above text, Jabrā changes the form of the word 'still' from an adjective in the original to an adverb 'ابدا' (ever/eternally). He also changes the word 'nodding' from its adjective form in the ST to a verb 'يتمايل' (sway/wobble). In addition, he replaces the full stop at the end of the stanza with an exclamation mark.

Al-Khāl's interprets the same stanza as:

شدّد حصارك ايها الليل العاري الصدر ــ شدّد حصارك ايها الليل المغناطيسي المغذّي!
يا ليل الرياح الجنوبية، ليل النجمات الكبيرة القليلة
الليل الذي ما زال راضياً، ليل الصيف العاري المجنون

(Whitman, tr. al-Khāl, 1958b: 2)

In so doing, al-Khāl interprets 'Press close' as 'شدّد حصارك' (intensify your siege). He also interprets 'still nodding night' as 'الليل الذي ما زال راضياً' (the night that is still pleased), presumably reflecting thereby the significance of 'nodding' as a gesture of acceptance and approbation. Like Jabrā, he translates 'magnetic nourishing night' literally as 'ايها الليل المغناطيسي المغذّي'. Unlike Jabrā, stanzas 3–6 of the original are published in the form of one long stanza in al-Khāl's translation.

Yūsuf also changes the shape of this stanza from three lines in the original to six in his translation, and he divides the first line into two:

لتلتحم بي أيها الليل العاري النهدين
لتلتحم بي أيها الليل الجاذب المنعش

(Whitman, tr.Yūsuf: 127)

(Weld with me O bare-bosom'd night
Weld with me O attracting fresh night)

He interprets 'press close' as 'لتلتحم بي'. The verb 'التحم' can be translated as 'cohere', and it can also be translated as 'unite', as in the Sufi concept of 'unity'. It seems that this concept and the situational context of Whitman's poem encourage Yūsuf subconsciously to use Sufi language in his translation, although he denies this. Furthermore, Yūsuf ignores 'the large few' in the second half of the second line when he merged it with the last line of the stanza.

In the final stanza, the keyword 'prodigal' is rendered literally by Jabrā as 'ايتها المسرفة' (O prodigal). Interestingly, al-Khāl changes its gender to masculine 'أيها الضال' (O stray). However, the contextual relationship in stanza 7 between 'prodigal' and 'earth', which is feminine in Arabic, is clear. Yūsuf translates the same word as 'أيتها الهتيكة' (O profligate), but these Arabic words are not associated with 'love', which is the other keyword in this section. The literal translations of 'prodigal' made the TTs sound alien. 'Ābid Ismā'īl interprets it as 'السخية' (generous) which ably suits the context (Whitman, tr. Ismā'īl, 2006: 55). Meanwhile, Yūsuf uses punctuation once again for the word and for the rest of this last stanza, neither of which exists in the 'death-bed edition'. They did exist in the first edition of *Leaves of Grass*, however:

> Prodigal! You have given me love!. . . . Therefore I to you give love!
> O unspeakable passionate love!
>
> (Whitman, 1855/1976: 45)

Unlike Jabrā and al-Khāl, Yūsuf interprets the last line of this section mystically: 'O unspeakable passionate love' as 'آه، أيها المتشهّي الذي لا يمكن البوح به الحب!'. Notwithstanding, Yūsuf's rejection of the Sufi impact on Whitman's poetry, he uses the word 'البوح' (revelation) in a Sufi context, as al-Suhrawardī did famously in these lines:

> وا حسرتا للعاشقين تحمَّلُوا سِرّ المحبّةِ والهوى فضّاحُ
> بالسرِّ إن باحُوا، تُباحُ دماؤهم وكذا دماء العاشقين تُباحُ
>
> (Al-Suhrawardī, 2005: 58)

> Alas! For lovers bear the secret of love, but their love is exposed
> Whenever they reveal the secret, their blood is shed.
> Thus, the blood of lovers is shed with impunity.

2.2.5 Walt Whitman, a kosmos, of Manhattan the son

Section 24 of *Song of Myself* is long. It is exemplified here in stanza 1, in which Whitman explicitly uses his name for the first time:

> Walt Whitman, a kosmos, of Manhattan the son,
> Turbulent, fleshy, sensual, eating, drinking and breeding,
> No sentimentalist, no stander above men and women or apart from them,
> No more modest than immodest.
>
> (Whitman: 64)

This stanza was translated by Jabrā and Yūsuf. Jabrā also translates stanzas 6–9 of this section, which contains seventeen in all. Al-Khāl did not translate this section although it is considered by many to be the key section of *Song of Myself*.

Jabrā translates stanza 1 as follows:

> ولت وتمن، كونٌ، ابنٌ لمنهاتن،
> ثائر، جسدي، شهواني، يأكل ويشرب ويتناسل،

لا مائع العواطف، ولا يعلو بنفسه على الرجال والنساء، ولا يتنكّب عنهم،
ولا يزيد تواضعه عن كبريائه.

(Whitman, tr. Jabrā: 183)

Yūsuf approaches the same stanza differently, in terms of both form and language:

والت ويتمان
مواطن العالم
ابن مانهاتن...
فائر، جسدي، شهواني
يأكل، ويشرب، وينجب.
إنه ليس عاطفياً
ليس متعالياً فوق الرجال والنساء
وليس بعيداً عنهم
ليس متواضعاً أو غير متواضع.

(Whitman, tr. Yūsuf: 132–3)

We can see in Jabrā's translation that he opts for a literal rendition of 'kosmos' as 'كونٌ', while Yūsuf interprets it as 'مواطن العالم'. The concept of 'مواطن العالم' (citizen of the world) was first coined by the German poet Goethe in a letter he sent from Switzerland to fellow poet Schiller on 14 October 1797. Goethe signed it *der Weltbürger*, alluding spiritually (and politically) to the notion of a free citizen of the world and poetically to 'world poetry', as Pound demonstrated in his translations. Jabrā renders 'sentimentalist' as 'مائع العواطف' literally (fluid emotions) which has negative connotations, while Yūsuf uses an immediate equivalent 'عاطفي'. Jabrā uses 'يتنكب عنهم' for 'apart from them'. In so doing, he changes the stylistic value of the original which comes here as an everyday language to a slightly archaic variation. Yūsuf, on the other hand, uses almost the same stylistic value of the original. The last line of this stanza is intended to confirm that the hero of this section, that is, Whitman, is like anybody else:

No more modest than immodest

This was translated by Jabrā as 'his modesty does not exceed his pride', while Yūsuf translates it as 'he is not modest or immodest'.

As expected, Yūsuf divides this stanza into two, while Jabrā keeps the same layout, save for the last line which is published as if it were part of the third line. In sum, the vision of section 24 is addressed to everyone, not merely the poet or his poetic persona. The other stanzas in this section show us that Whitman's poetic monologue is, as Octavio Paz points out, a 'universal chorus' (Paz, 1990: 8).

We will look at the 'universal chorus' as a 'kosmos' concept in the next section.

2.2.6 I do not despise you

In section 43, the poet 'learned to respect all religions, without accepting any one, and as a poet he seriously cherished the idea of extracting the best of every religion to form a new eclectic religion' (Allen, 1997: 20–1). However, the diversity of this 'religion' comes artistically from its poetic style and politically from its democratic vision. It is 'more a philosophy than a sect' where 'man would worship the divinity incarnated in himself' (ibid.: 21). This concept is manifested clearly in stanza 1 of section 43. Yūsuf is the only poet-translator who tackles this section.

In the first line of this stanza, Yūsuf translates 'all time, the world over' into 'كل العصوروكل العالم' (all ages, all the world):

> I do not despise you priests, all time, the world over,
>
> (Whitman: 100)

> لست أحتقركم، يا قساوسة كل العصور وكل العالم
>
> (Whitman, tr. Yūsuf: 179)

In Arabic, كل زمان ومكان is usually used in a neutral context. It appears in Ismā'il's translation of the same poem (Whitman, tr. Isma'il: 113). However, Whitman did not say 'all time and place', although he might want to mimic Emerson's 'Over-soul', albeit in his own way. Therefore, perhaps, Yūsuf chose to avoid replacing it with a ready-made expression. He also translates 'saluting the sun' as 'عابداً الشمس' (sun-worshipping), thereby changing the neutrality of the ST 'saluting', which can be translated as 'محييا', to a specific term 'عابداً'. In translating religious terms like 'gymnosophist', Yūsuf once again resorts to a superordinate strategy without offering any justification. He translates this term as 'متصوّفاً' (Sufi). According to the OED, gymnosophist is 'a member of an ancient Indian sect that wore very little clothing and was given to asceticism and contemplation'. In other words, religion and its associated terms were in Yūsuf's mind although he rejected a strict interpretation. He uses a similar strategy to interpret the Aztec temples 'teokallis' as what Muslim Sufis wear 'القباء الخشن' (coarse cloak). Yūsuf could have used *khirqa* (a Sufi cloak) to localize his translation further, but he is uneven and inconsistent in the application of his strategy. What is more, he sometimes omits to translate 'religious' terms. For example, he did not translate 'minding the Koran' in ST 9 although this phrase, especially 'minding' which can be translated as (تدبر / تدبروا), was used by Whitman in a Qur'ānic style. For example, in 4:82:

> أفلا يتدبرون القرآن ولو كان من عند غير الله لوجدوا فيه اختلافا كثيرا
>
> Do they not consider the Qur'an (with care)? Had it been from other than Allah, they would surely have found therein much discrepancy.

In '"Minding the Koran" in Civil War America: Islamic Revelation, US Reflections', Jeffrey Einboden notes that the poet 'voices a personal fragment in 1855 that has largely escaped our notice' (Einboden, 2014: 84). This fragment 'submerges Islamic scripture under US self-portrait, weaving together worldly biography and holy book, American secularity and Muslim sacred' (ibid.). Einboden adds that 'while it is surprising to find "America's poet" appealing to "the Koran", it is perhaps Whitman's active verb itself – his "minding" – that seems most intriguing, and, ultimately, most instructive' (ibid.). Einboden explains that the word 'minding' implies 'not only "consideration", but also "concern", not only "care", but "carefulness", "awareness", as well as "wariness"' (ibid.).

In the ST 12 of this stanza, Yūsuf utilizes another strategy when he Arabizes 'puritan' as 'البوريتانية' in TT 19. This contradicts his previous decision to transpose 'gymnosophist' as 'Sufi', since 'puritan' can be directly rendered by the mystical term تطهري أو طهراني. Yūsuf's varied approach may reflect his ideological beliefs as a communist poet. He was not always able to avoid translating Whitman's 'Sufi' allusions, as we shall see.

2.2.7 I too am not a bit tamed, I too am untranslatable

Section 52 is the last in *Song of Myself*. In his approach to this section, Jabrā declines to translate stanza 3. In addition, he blends stanza 4 with the second one. Although Yūsuf translates the whole section, he changes its layout. Al-Khāl did not translate this section.

In translating 'swoops by' in the first line:

> The spotted hawk swoops by and accuses me, he complains of my gab and my loitering.
>
> (Whitman: 114)

Jabrā uses the verb 'يُسفّ' which suits the movement of its subject, namely a 'hawk':

> يُسفّ الصقر الارقط ويمرّ بي متهماً اياي، متذمراً من ثرثرتي وتسعكي.
>
> (Whitman, tr. Jabrā: 187)

However, he adds 'يمر بي' ([it] passes by me) for the same word. Thus, he simultaneously uses contradictory strategies: 'subordinate: يُسفّ' and 'superordinate: يمر'. Accordingly, the Whitmanian line becomes in Jabrā's translation:

> (The spotted hawk swoops by and passes by me.)

Yūsuf uses the same superordinate strategy in translating 'swoops by' as 'يمر بي'. In the third line of this section, Jabrā chooses a subordinate strategy to translate 'yawp' as 'نعقتي' (my caw). Once again, this choice suits the comparison made between the hero of this section and the spotted hawk. Yūsuf uses a superordinate word 'صرختي' (my cry) for the same word. Jabrā translates:

> I too am not a bit tamed, I too am untranslatable
>
> (Whitman: 114)

as:

> ولكنني انا ايضاً لا أرَوَّض، وانا ايضاً لا أُترجم
>
> (Whitman, tr. Jabrā: 187)

(But I am too not tamed, I am too untranslatable.) As we can see, Jabrā ignores 'a bit', while Yūsuf translates it as 'ولو قليلًا':

> أنا أيضاً، لست مروّضاً، ولو قليلًا
> أنا أيضاً غير قابل للترجمة
>
> (Whitman, tr. Yūsuf: 198)

Interestingly, in the essay 'Jack Spicer's After Lorca: Translation as Decomposition', Daniel Katz remarks that

> The term 'translation' emerges at several key points in *Leaves of Grass*, and is one of Whitman's favourite words for examining two related issues: the relationship between author and reader, and the relationship between the singularity of the individual subject, and the traces and remainders which it is capable of producing: writing, footprints, and the green grass itself which grows out of corpses above their graves.
>
> (Katz, 2004: 93)

Katz suggests that the poet concentrates on the concept of translation in order to decode 'the mysterious writing of the "grass", whose proffered communication has given the title for his entire writing project' (ibid.). Hence, '*Leaves of Grass* is nothing other than a reflection on translation, "grass" signifying nothing but signification and mediation, or the world as foreign text' (ibid.).

In the same seminar 'Whitman in Translation' at the University of Iowa, the Chinese translator Huang reports that Zhao Luorui believes that 'it is hard to translate Whitman because he himself says so. . . . one of the important things about Whitman is his personality; he does not conform to rules or regulations. He says whatever he wants to whenever he wants to' (Huang, 1995: 15). Bloom attributes Whitman's irregularity to his genius in using 'figurative language' (Bloom, 2003: 1). In turn, Whitmanian 'figurative language' should be viewed by the translator as part of the whole discursive message; otherwise a deformed text will be reached in the target language. For example, the ninth line,

I bequeath myself to the dirt to grow from the grass I love,
was translated by Jabrā as:

واخلّف نفسي للزبل لأنمو من العشب الذي اعشقه.

Strangely, he uses 'الزبل' (garbage/rubbish) for 'dirt', which departs from the original. Yūsuf uses 'التراب' which, alongside the use of the verb 'أوحّد' (I unite), suits the Whitmanian theme (of the Unity of Existence) although Yūsuf denies it in Whitman's poetry.

Thus we have seen that there were differences between the various translations of *Song of Myself*. The differences do not occur only because the translators translated parts of Whitman's poem, as is the case with Jabrā and al-Khāl, or in full, as in the case of Yūsuf. A partial translation no doubt affects the work since it cannot produce the whole text in the target language. However, what affects the original the most is over-interpretation of the ST, as we have seen with al-Khāl's translation, or reshaping the ST in such a way that it alters the ST, as is the case with Jabrā's translation. Yūsuf's complete translation is the most popular, and it has been printed several times since the 1970s. Most importantly, he produced an 'equivalent' poetic text in the target language.

Yūsuf achieved this on the verbal level. However, on the cognitive level, the purposes of these translations are the same, because of the similarities in the poetic backgrounds of the translators; they all belong to the generation of pioneers who took it upon themselves to introduce a new language to modern Arabic poetry. The resonance of Whitman's style in Arabic modernity and how he was read by the pioneer Arab poets will be explored in the next context.

2.3 The cognitive context

As we have seen, Whitman has three poetic 'selves'. First, he is an American poet. Indeed, he is considered to be the first poet of what can be characterized as American poetry. Second, he is a universal poet, that is, his themes are of a 'kosmos' type. Third, he is a creator of a new poetic language, representing a break with the typical language of English poetry. In addition, his 'kosmos' poetic 'selves' taught world modernists including their Arab colleagues how to free themselves not only thematically and stylistically but also spiritually. Whitman summarizes these 'selves' or 'tasks' of the great poet:

> The greatest poet hardly knows pettiness or triviality. If he breathes into anything that was before thought small it dilates with the grandeur and life of the universe. He is a seer . . . he is individual . . . he is complete in himself . . . the others are as good as he, only he sees it and they do not. He is not one of the chorus . . . he does not stop for any regulation . . . he is the president of regulation. What the eyesight does to the rest he does to the rest.
>
> (Whitman, 1976: 9; ellipses in the original)

It is clear why Whitman's poetry was so admired by many leading world writers. His *Leaves of Grass* was translated into many languages. Equally important, Whitman was addressed poetically by a number of prominent modern poets, such as Fernando Pessoa, Federico Garcia Lorca, Pablo Neruda and Allen Ginsberg. He became almost a poetic icon in their poems. For example,

Pessoa wrote 'Salutation to Walt Whitman' in 1915 after he read an original version of *Leaves of Grass* in 1914. Roger Asselineau explains that Whitman's book was 'a revelation' to him '*Leaves* acted upon him more like a catalyst' (Asselineau, 1995: 148). It was, adds Asselineau, 'indeed a very strange and quite unexpected case of superposition of two dissimilar poets; the result was a cataclysm which changed the face of contemporary Portuguese poetry – and the face of Whitman, too, for he cannot be read quite in the same way after one has read Pessoas's modernist "Salutation" to him' (ibid.). Unlike Pessoa's poem which is a pure 'salute' to Whitman, Lorca addressed Whitman through his poetic account of New York, and his poem 'Ode to Walt Whitman' is a part of *Poeta en Nueua York* (Poet in New York). It was written in 1929 while he was staying at Columbia University in New York City during the Great Depression: 'it provides a complex vision of the city. While poverty, ruthless capitalism, and the lack of spiritual life fill Lorca with awe, the poet is also mesmerized by what Whitman was the first to sing: the rhythms of urban modernity, the shock of encounters with the crowds' (Rumeau, 2014: 419). More importantly, Lorca's poem established a tradition for the world poets to write about New York and Whitman, and to express their feelings (and mostly their anger) towards America more generally. Ginsberg's "A Supermarket in California", which was written in 1955, was stylistically inspired by Lorca's poem in terms of its 'surrealist' language, and thematically by its political subject matter (Ginsberg, 2009: 144).[1] But it seems that Neruda's poem 'Ode to Walt Whitman', which was written in 1956, is the more famous poem in this tradition. It 'is not only an address to Whitman but also a response to García Lorca. . . . Whitman is thus not only the addressee of the odes, but also a great mediator enabling García Lorca and Neruda's dialogue' (Rumeau: 418).

Lorca's poem and its responses create a Whitmanian (or a New Yorker) 'tone' in world poetry. Modernist Arab poets are a part of it. Thus, since the 1970s we have witnessed, mostly thematically, Arabic 'Whitmanian' poems where Whitman is addressed as a poetic icon. Likewise, we see, mostly stylistically, Eliotian Arabic poems of the 1950–60s. This 'generalization' alongside 'experientialism', 'stylistics' and 'continuity' can help us to capture the 'tone' of a phenomenon. Stockwell remarks that

> One of the most difficult aspects of literary experience to describe rigorously is the way in which reading a literary work can create a tone, an atmosphere in the mind that seems to persist long after the pages have been put down.

> Literature is valued because of this *resonance* which is difficult to articulate or define.
>
> (Stockwell, 2009: 17)

Indeed, as Jean Boase-Beier emphasizes '[r]eading is a cognitive process. It is also a major part of the translator's task. So how do translators read?' (Boase-Beier, 2006: 74). She adds, 'with all the freedom and involvement of the reader. We are still always trying, not just in literature, but in every type of communication, to find a reading which is more than merely personal' (ibid.).

Arabic readings of Whitman's poetry on a cognitive level have their own 'generalization', and *Song of Myself* establishes the modernist style on a world scale, while on a thematic level it reflects all humanity; at the same time, its individual side is very clear. But the Arab poets differ in the 'tone' that they produced according to their readings (or their interpretations) of *Song of Myself*, and in the ways in which they addressed Whitman poetically. Al-Rīhānī and Jubrān were the first to address Whitman's poetry at the beginning of the twentieth century. Although their approaches did not create a 'general' mode in Arabic poetics, they did introduce new techniques, the most important of which was prose poetry. The technique was adopted in the mid-twentieth century by a number of Arab poets, and it is this form which dominates Arabic poetics now. Thus, there is no doubting the impact of the prose poem on the works of the classical and free-verse poets. In his book *Studies in Modern Arabic Prose and Poetry*, S. Moreh observes that 'like Walt Whitman, both al-Rīḥānī and Gibran used this type of verse in order to express their pantheism and democratic emotions' (Moreh, 1988:10). 'Like Whitman, they argued that poetry does not lie in metre, rhyme and memorizing classical verse' (ibid.). Nevertheless, 'while Whitman and Gibran adopted the Biblical style based upon symmetry and balance in thought and phrases, al-Riḥānī adopted . . . the Qur'ānic style based upon the same technique' (ibid.: 11). These developments notwithstanding, these two styles (biblical and Qur'ānic) did not lead the young Arab poets of the first half of the twentieth century to form a new poetic school. What did inspire them, however, especially during the 1970s are the Whitmanian techniques which were thematically a mixture of sources and stylistically a combination of techniques. Unlike Jubrān and al-Rīḥānī, modernist poet-translators approached Whitman's poetry differently in their translations and in their use of his techniques in their own compositions.

There are three famous Arabic poems offering different readings of Whitman as an American and as a 'kosmos' poetic figure. They each address him through his country and his city New York. These poems are

1. Adūnīs's 'قبر من أجل نيويورك' (1971) which was translated into English by Samuel Hazo in 1994 as 'The Funeral of New York' and by Shawkat M. Toorawa as 'A Grave for New York' in 2004;
2. Al-Bayātī's 'قداس جنائزي إلى نيويورك' (1971) (A Mass for New York) which has seemingly not been translated into English;
3. Sa'dī Yūsuf's 'America, America' (1995). The title of this poem is in English, and thus Khaled Mattawa's translation in 2002 keeps it as it is.

In 'A Grave for New York', Adūnīs starts his poem by criticizing American civilization and the iconic Statue of Liberty in New York:

نيويورك،
جسدٌ بلون الإسفلت، حول خاصرتها زنّارٌ رطب، وجهها
شبّاك مغلق . . . قلت: يفتحه وولت ويتمان – "أقول
كلمة السر الاصلية" – لكن لم يسمعها غير الهٍ لم يعد في
مكانه. السجناء، العبيد، (اليائسون)، اللصوص، المرضى
يتدفقون من حنجرته، ولا فتحة لا طريق. وقلت:
جسر بروكلين! لكنه الجسر الذي يصل ويتمان ووول
ستريت، بين الورقة – العشب والورقة— الدولار.

New York,
A body the color of asphalt. Around her waist is a damp girdle, her face
Is a closed window . . . I said: Walt Whitman will open it – 'I speak
the password primeval' – but no one hears it except an unreturning
god. The prisoners, the slaves, the despairing, the thieves, the
diseased spew from his throat. There is no outlet, no path. And I
said: 'The Brooklyn Bridge!' But it's the bridge that connects Whitman
to Walt Street, that connects leaves-grass to paper-dollars.

(Adūnīs, tr. Toorawa, 2004: 124–7)

Adūnīs addresses Whitman using his concepts and techniques. But the relationship which Adūnīs portrays between the American poet and his city is not the optimistic Whitmanian image but a pessimistic one. The Brooklyn Bridge 'connects Whitman to Walt Street' and 'leaves-grass to paper-dollars'. As Toorawa mentioned in his notices and in the afterword to his translation of Adūnīs's *A Time between Ashes and Roses* (2004), 'A Grave for New York' echoes *Song of Myself* in several places. For example:

'I speak the password primeval' is Whitman's *Song of Myself*, in section 24 'I speak the pass-word primeval' and the list of 'the prisoners, the slaves, despairing and thieves' is also from the same poem. In section 24, Whitman says:

Voices of the interminable generations of prisoners and slaves,
Voices of the diseas'd and despairing and of thieves and dwarfs.

(Whitman, 2001: 65)

Adūnīs's 'every moment is a shovel or a pick' is from section 33: 'I heard the distant click of their picks and shovels.' It seems that the Portuguese poet Fernando Pessoa was the first to incorporate Whitman's key concepts in his poem 'Salute to Walt Whitman':

Open all the doors!
Because I have to go in!
My password? Walt Whitman!

(Translated by Brown, 1995: 151)

In 'A Grave for New York', Adūnīs also echoes Eliot's *The Waste Land* formally and stylistically when he suddenly introduces, in a fantastic way, a character to the poetic narrative. Adūnīs's 'Mrs. Brewing' reminds us of Eliot's 'Madame Sosostris'. Moreover, Adūnīs uses Eliot's 'prophetic visionary' of *The Waste Land* as well as his poetic techniques. It seems that Arab poets were not the only ones to approach Eliot before Whitman. For example, the Polish poet, Czeslaw Milosz, who is known for translating Whitman into Polish, was influenced by Eliot first. Eliot 'was the most important of Milosz's poetic masters' (Skwara, 2008: 12). The reason is perhaps that Eliot's writings provide their readers with modernist tools to approach not only his own poems but also the works of other major poets, among them Whitman. Evidently, Eliot's writings became a guide for other writers.

Like Adūnīs, al-Bayātī's 'A Mass for New York' criticizes America and New York by describing its Statue of Liberty as a 'stony beast':

وحش حجري يتربع فوق الفولاذ المسنون، بعين واحدة يرنو لليل المثقوب بطلقات رصاص، ينفث،
في وجه الفجر دخانا
ينشب في لحم الساعات مخالبه، يتمطى فوق رغاء الأصوات المسحوقة، تغلي في داخله أوساخ
الطوفان البشري المهزوم، بعين أعماها النور يحدق في طقس الروتين اليومي

(Al-Bayātī, 1998: 144)

A stone monster sits on top of the pointy steel, with one eye watching the night pierced by bullets, sputtering smoke into the face of dawn, he thrusts his claws in the flesh of the clocks, and stretches over the rumble of defeated voices. Inside of him, boils the dirt of the human flood, with an eye blinded by light he stares at the daily routine.

Whitman also appears in al-Bayātī's poem like a 'drop of light' which quickly disappears:

في نقطة ضوء "والت ويتمن"
يبحث عن أمريكا في أمريكا
من يبكى بين مخالب هذا الوحش الضاري، من؟

(ibid.: 145)

In a point of light 'Walt Whitman'
Looks for America in America
Who weeps between the claws of this brutal beast, Who?

Al-Bayātī's 'vision' in this poem is close to Adūnīs's 'A Grave for New York', albeit it is stylistically distinct.

In 'America, America', which was written in 1995 after the first Gulf War, Yūsuf approached the subject differently, almost in a surrealist style:

أميركا !
لنستبدلْ هداياكِ
خذي سجائركِ المهرّبة
وأعطينا البطاطا.
خذي مسدس جيمس بوند الذهب
وأعطينا كركرةَ مارلين مونرو.
....
خذي اللحية الأفغانية
'وأعطينا' لحيةَ والت ويتمان الملأى بالفراشات.
خذي صدّام حسين
وأعطينا ابراهام لنكولن!
أو لا تعطينا أحداً.

(Yūsuf, V 4, 2014a: 117–18)

America:
Let's exchange gifts.
Take your smuggled cigarettes
and give us potatoes.
Take James Bond's golden pistol
and give us Marilyn Monroe's giggle.
....

Take the Afghani mujahideen beard
and give us Walt Whitman's beard filled with butterflies.
Take Saddam Hussein
and give us Abraham Lincoln
or give us no one.

(Yūsuf, tr. Mattawa, 2002: 174–5)

Although Yūsuf here addresses America and Whitman, his poem, with all its lyricality and use of surrealist images, belongs to Lorca's tradition as he was the first to tread this path. Lorca's style clearly resonates in Yūsuf's poem:

Walt Whitman, lovely old man,
Have I failed to see your beard full of butterflies.

(Lorca, 1990: 157)

Like Whitman, Yūsuf's sources were not primarily poems but prose writings. Although he is considered one of the free-verse poets, his 'prose' techniques greatly inspired Arab prose poets. In his editorial *Sa ʿdī Yūsuf fī al-Sabʿīn* (Saʿdī Yūsuf at seventy) to the literary Journal *al-Karmal* in Autumn 2004, the Palestinian poet Maḥmūd Darwīsh highlights the impact of Yūsuf's poetry on him and modern Arabic poetry as a whole:

> Ever since I began reading Saʿdī Yūsuf he became the one who appealed the most to my poetic taste. In his transparent poem, one finds the purity of aquarelle and in its subdued tone – the rhythm of everyday life. [Although he does not write a prose poem] . . . it moves in the expressionist climate that Saʿdī Yūsuf's poetry has established within the aesthetic taste, ever since he mastered the art of fusion between lyric and narrative. He is one of our greatest poets.
>
> (Translated by Huri, 2006: 320; see also Darwīsh, 2004: 1)

Indeed, we can trace the impact of Whitman, through Yūsuf's translation, on many poets. Fāḍil al-ʿAzzāwī's 'أغنية نفسي' (Song of myself) (1994) is a good example of this. Al-ʿAzzāwī borrowed not merely the title directly from Whitman, but also the 'prose' autobiographical style:

عندما بلغتُ العاشرة من عمري
قلتُ: كل شيء سيكون على ما يرام يا فاضل
. . . .
عندما بلغت العشرين من عمري
لم أكن في حديقة أو مقهى

وإنما في سجن ببغداد

. . . .

عندما بلغت الخمسين من عمري

رأيتُ شجرتنا تُقطع بالفأس

وبيتنا تقطنه الجرذان

وكتبي مطمورة في بئر.

(Al-'Azzāwī, V 2, 2007: 43–6)

When I reached ten
I said to myself:
Everything will be right, Fadhil,

. . . .

When I turned twenty
I wasn't in a park or a café,
But in Baghdad Prison

. . . .

And when I turned fifty
I saw our old tree cut down with an axe,
our house infested with rats,
and my books thrown into the well.

(Al-'Azzāwī, tr. Mattawa, 2003: 82–4)

As we can see in the above lines, al-'Azzāwī not only localized but also individualized Whitman's poetic concepts. Nevertheless, this example shows how *Song of Myself* resonated powerfully not only among the pioneer poets but also among the poets of subsequent generations.

2.4 Concluding remarks

Whitman's *Song of Myself* functions in modern Arabic poetics on three levels:

1. Formally: the new poetic form of Whitman's poem encouraged the modernist Arab poets to experiment with a new form: the 'prose poem'. This form is more flexible than 'free verse', which Arab poets had experimented with in the wake of Eliot.
2. Thematically: Whitman's poem motivated them to use different sources, even some that are not typically classified as poetic. Hence, we witnessed for the first time such 'social-political' poems as were highlighted in the cognitive context.

3. Stylistically: *Song of Myself* taught Arab poets to free themselves by using 'new' poetic language. Thus, the 'classical language' retreated in the face of 'the public language' which was now considered the 'modern' one.

The extent of the influence of *Song of Myself* owed much to the works of the three modernist poets: Jabrā, al-Khāl and Yūsuf. These poet-translators were already acquainted with the poetic modernity of Eliot. They learnt from Eliot how to view *Song of Myself* as a 'world' and not merely as a linguistic text. Hence the importance of reading Eliot before any other poet. Although Eliot did not speak about poetry in the light of discourse analysis, his poetic vision was a discursive one. This also explains why al-Rīḥānī and his colleagues failed to establish a new poetic school in Arabic culture in the first half of the twentieth century. They lacked the Eliotian modernist tools to achieve this. From the 1940s onwards, Eliot's techniques helped modernist poets to form a new school of 'free verse', and then to go further, inspired by Whitman and French poets (directly or via English translations), to establish 'prose poem' as a new school in modern Arabic culture.

The discursive approach used by the Arabic translators of *Song of Myself*, especially Yūsuf, allowed them to introduce an influential text to an Arab readership. This text and its translations and responses created a new 'fixed' mode in Arabic poetry as well as a cognitive poetics – a poetics of a dialogic type which can creatively function across different cultures. In *Translating Literature*, Lefevere states that 'because the study of translations and the rewriting inevitably uncover the mechanisms of canonization, integration, exclusion, and manipulation that are at work on many levels – . . . of literature, but of society – it acquires relevance beyond the realm of literary studies' (Lefevere, 1992: 3).

3

Al-Sayyāb's translational contribution

As we discussed in the Introduction, Arabic poetic modernity, like the Western one, is based on translation. Hence, all modernist Arab poets are effectively translators. Some of these poets practice 'proper' translation by conveying Western writings directly in their native tongue. Others do this indirectly by introducing Western poetic techniques in their poems. The Iraqi poet Badr Shākir al-Sayyāb (1926–64) was a pioneer in approaching Western poetry in both ways – as a poet and as a translator. The interaction between translation and poetry shapes modern Arabic literature, in particular al-Sayyāb's work. To this end, I have chosen his translations of Eliot's 'Journey of the Magi', Pound's 'The River-Merchant's Wife: A Letter' and Sitwell's *The Shadow of Cain*. The last poet and her central symbol 'Cain' had a momentous influence on al-Sayyāb's writings on textual and cultural levels. This chapter will be divided into three. In the first part, we will look at situational context and will review al-Sayyāb's engagement with English poetry. In the second part, we will analyse the texts of the Arabic translations of these three poems. And in the final part, we will review the cognitive context and will trace the impact of these translations on the poet-translator himself and on modern Arabic poetry more generally.

3.1 The situational context: al-Sayyāb's engagement with English poetry

In the search for new styles, forms and themes, translation has been central to the efforts of modernist Arab poets. It is rooted in their poetry as one of their sources, if not their primary source. A review of al-Sayyāb's translations will demonstrate his commitment to this activity. Translation for al-Sayyāb was not merely a 'technical' challenge but also an inspiration and a motivation.

What follows is a summary of his translational achievements, which owes much to ʿAbd al-Jabbār Dāūd al-Baṣrī:

i. Al-Sayyāb's poetic translations:
   1. In 1951, he published his translation of ʿUyūn Ilzā (*Les Yeux d'Elsa)* by the French poet Louis Aragon.
   2. Also in 1951, he published unsigned translations of several poems by the Turkish poet Nāẓim Ḥikmat.
   3. In 1953, he published his translation of *Al-Shāʿir wa-al-Mukhtariʿ wa-al-Kulūnīl* (The poet, inventor and colonel) by the playwright Peter Ustinov.
   4. In (1955?), al-Sayyāb published his translation of a selection of world poetry *Qaṣā'id Mukhtāra min al-Shiʿr al-ʿĀlamī al-Ḥadīth* (Selected poems from modern world poetry). In this book, he translated, directly from the English language, poems such as Eliot's 'Journey of the Magi', Pound's 'The River-Merchant's Wife: A Letter' and Sitwell's 'A Mother to Her Dead Child'. He also translated, from English translations, poets from other languages such as Neruda, Lorca, Rimbaud, Rilke, Nāẓim Ḥikmat and Tagore.
   5. In 1960, he published under the name *Abū Ghailān* (*Ghailān* is his son) *Three Poems of the Atomic Age* by Sitwell. We will study the second poem in this trilogy *The Shadow of Cain* in the verbal context.

ii. His cultural and political translations which were mostly published unsigned:

   1. In 1959, al-Sayyāb published his translations, in sequence, of some chapters from *The God that Failed* in the Baʿath Party newspaper *al-Ḥuriyya*. This book is about six ex-communist writers discussing their experience of Communism. The writers are Richard Wright, Arthur Koestler, Inacio Celloni, Lewis Fisher, Stephen Spender and Andre Gide.
   2. In 1961, he translated two books: *The Birth of Freedom* (1959) by Virginia Eifert and *The Black Stallion* (1941) by Walter Farley.
   3. In 1965, al-Sayyāb's name appeared as one of the translators of the first volume of *American Poetry and Prose*, which was edited by Norman Forester. The Arabic translation of this volume was directed

by Jabrā and published under the title *Thalāthat Qurūn min al-Adab* (Three centuries of literature) in Beirut.

(Al-Baṣrī, 1966: 83–4)

However, al-Sayyāb's engagement with English poetry started in the early 1940s. Therefore, I will review here his involvement with English poetry through his translations and as a source of inspiration. In a letter to his friend Muḥammad 'Alī Ismā'īl dated 24 December 1943, al-Sayyāb told him that he had translated 'To Summer' by the English poet William Blake (1757–1827). Here, it is worth quoting al-Sayyāb's Arabic translation of Blake's 'To Summer' (Blake, 1988: 121–2), which was possibly his first such effort:

'الى الصيف'
أيهذا الذي مرَّ بودياننا
إكبح بعزمك خيولَكَ الشرسة وأُخمد حرارتكَ،
فذلك السعير من مناخرها .. أيُّهذا الصيف.
**
مراراً ما ضربتَ خيامَكَ الذهبيةَ هنا
ونمت تحت أشجار الصفصاف ونحن نشاهد – بسرور – أطراف الورديّةَ وشَعْركَ الزاهر.
**
وكثيراً ما سمعنا صَوْتَكَ تحت الظلال الكثيفة (والظهيرةُ في عَرَبتها المتوقّدة) ؟؟!!
وكثيراً ما ركبتَ السماء العميقة عند الربيع.
فأقمْ في ودياننا الخضراء على ضفة نهرٍ رائق، واخلعْ ثيابك الحريرية والقِ بنفسك في الجدول..
فودياننا تحبَّ الصَّيْفَ في عُجّبه.
**
شُعراؤنا شهيرة بضرب السلاسل الفضيّة.
شبابنا أشجع من ريفييّ الجنوب.
خرائدنا أجمل ما يمكن في رقصة الطرب.
فلا يعوزنا، أناشيدُ وآلاتُ الطرب، ولا أصداء حلوةٌ وماءٌ صافٍ
كالسماء ولا أكاليل من الزهور، امام الحرارة اللافحة.

(Al-Sayyāb, 1994: 71–2)

In this translation, al-Sayyāb changes the form of the original from three to four stanzas. He also uses a prose language in his Arabic version, and this significantly affects the poetics of the source poem. However, this translation, which al-Sayyāb did as a seventeen-year-old, reflects his serious engagement with one of the fathers of the English Romantic Movement.

When only eighteen years old, al-Sayyāb read poems by the English romantic poet Percy Bysshe Shelley (1792–1822) 'in their original English', as he told his friend the Iraqi poet and playwright Khālid al-Shawwāf in a letter dated on 11 July 1944 (ibid.: 79). Approaching Shelley's poems, especially 'Follow Me', led al-Sayyāb to write his poem *Itba*'īnī ('Follow Me'). Luwīs 'Awaḍ, as Nājī 'Allūsh notes in his introduction to al-Sayyāb's Dīwān, regards *Itba*'īnī as 'a variation on Shelley's "Follow me"' ('Allūsh, 2005: 62). In addition to Blake and Shelley, al-Sayyāb approached the English romantic poet John Keats (1795–1821). In his poem *Ḍikrā Liqā'* (Memory of a date), al-Sayyāb translates some lines from Keats's last poem 'Bright Star' and uses them in his own:

وتمتد يمناك نحو الكتا ب كمن يَنشُد السلوة الضائعة
فتبكي مع العبقري المريض وقد خاطب النجمة الساطعة:
'تمنيت يا كوكب
ثباتا كهذا – أنام
على صدرها في الظلام
وأفنى كما تغرب'

(Al-Sayyāb, 2005: 331)

Your right hand stretches towards the book like someone seeking lost consolation
You cry with the sick genius who addressed the bright star:
'I wish for you, O planet
Stability like this – to sleep
On her breast in the dark
And to die like you set.'

In a note to *Ḍikrā Liqā'*, al-Sayyāb mentions that 'العبقري المريض' (the sick genius) 'is the English poet John Keats who died at the age of twenty five by having been affected with tuberculosis' (ibid.). Keats's lines fit his poem thematically and prosodically. His selection also reflects al-Sayyāb's skill in reading and borrowing from other poets. It seems that the Iraqi poet learnt this from Eliot who had himself theorized and practised borrowing lines from others. There is another reason for approaching 'the sick genius', which is al-Sayyāb's sympathy for the English poet who died very young through illness. Al-Sayyāb is viewed similarly within modern Arabic poetry circles, since he also died at the premature age of thirty-eight, due to illness. Prosodically, this is al-Sayyāb's first metrical translation attempt. As we will see in the next context, he developed this strategy in his translations.

In 1944, al-Sayyāb changed course at Baghdad College of Teachers and moved from the Arabic department which he entered in 1943 to the English one. However, this early connection with English romantic poets, especially Shelley, signifies, as Iḥsān 'Abbās states in *Badr Shākir al-Sayyāb: Dirāsa fi Ḥayātih wa-Shi'rih* (Badr Shākir al-Sayyāb: A study in his life and poetry), 'the seed of the transformation' which underlies al-Sayyāb's poetry (Abbās, 1992: 50). In an article published in *Badr Shākir al-Sayyāb: al-Rajul wa-al-Shā'ir* (Badr Shākir al-Sayyāb: The man and the poet), al-Sayyāb describes what he studied in the College of Teachers' English programme:

> I studied Shakespeare, Milton, and the Victorian and Romantic poets, and during my last two years at the Teachers College I approached – for the first time – the English poet T. S. Eliot, and my admiration for the English poet John Keats was not less than my admiration for Eliot.
>
> (Cited in ibid.: 88)

Shortly afterwards, as DeYoung notes, al-Sayyāb 'would begin to place the now-canonically-decertified poetry of Edith Sitwell on level equal to or perhaps even higher than Eliot's" (DeYoung, 1998: 148). In a note, DeYoung reminds us, following Geoffrey Elborn's *Edith Sitwell: A Biography*, that 'at the end of World War II Edith Sitwell's reputation was much higher than it is today. She also recorded many of poems on LP's [long-playing records], a format that seems to have held much appeal for Sayyāb' (ibid.: 294). Some of Sitwell's recorded poems were brought to Iraq in the 1940s, and al-Sayyāb's colleagues point out that he listened to some of these records. In an article published in *Badr Shākir al-Sayyāb: al-Rajul wa-al-Shā'ir*, Bulānd al-Ḥaidarī says:

> We had not even reached the age of twenty. At that time the world was exhausted from the aftermath of wars. Through Europe's rubble, screaming seeped to us as poetry and prose in a revolutionary and angry [tone]. [It was] strikingly unusual and exciting. . . . we sometimes escape from our silence to a friend's house to listen to [recorded poems] by Eliot, Sitwell and Dylan Thomas till late into the night. Badr [al-Sayyāb] refuses to let us go before we listen to Sitwell again. Hence, the record plays again for more than half an hour. And [when we were leaving our friend's house] we stumbled many times into the door . . . [listening] to the calm and withered voice of Sitwell playing on the record.
>
> (Cited in al-Baṭal, 1984: 71; brackets added)

Al-Ḥaidarī did not reveal their friend's name. However, the Iraqi architect Qaḥtān al-Madfa'ī, in an interview published in 2008/2015, states that he brought with him from England some recordings of English poetry readings.

It is possible that al-Ḥaidarī meant another friend because of the difference between his date (around 1946) and that of al-Madfa'ī:

> In 1954 or 1955, when I was studying in England I brought with me records of Edith Sitwell's poems. He [al-Sayyāb] was influenced by this poetess, and at the same time he was writing his famous poem [*Unshūdat al-Maṭar*]. Edith wrote her poem during the bombing of London in 1940. Al-Sayyāb [listened] to her [recorded] poems including her poem 'Still Falls the Rain'. The rain here was the bombs which were falling on London like rain. I think Badr translated this poem, and his poem *Unshūdat al-Maṭar* was influenced by Sitwell's poem, and therefore we read in his poem 'rain . . . rain/ and falls the rain'.
>
> (Al-Madfa'ī, 2015: 9; brackets added)

It is notable that al-Madfa'ī also mentions al-Sayyāb's strong relationship with Sitwell's poetry. However, there is no evidence that al-Sayyāb translated Sitwell's poem 'Still Falls the Rain'. There is also no evidence that he translated Eliot's *The Waste Land*, as the *Shi'r* journal announced in its third issue in 1957 by saying the Iraqi poet 'dedicates his time to translating Eliot's "The Waste Land"' (*Shi'r*, 1957: 117). Nevertheless, these statements indicate al-Sayyāb's engagement with the most influential English poets of the twentieth century.

In 1944, al-Sayyāb wrote five poems dedicated to the English romantic poet William Wordsworth (1770–1850), but he did not publish them in his lifetime. They were found later and published in 1974 in *Qīthārat al-Rīḥ* (The lyre of wind). As far as prosody is concerned, the poems are written in a classical form, and thematically they mostly celebrate nature through descriptions of the poet's village. In the same year, influenced by Baudelaire's *Fleurs du Mal* (Flowers of evil), al-Sayyāb wrote *Bayn al-Rūḥ wa-al-Jasad* (Between the soul and the body). This poem was not published in the poet's life, either. Subsequently, 120 lines of it were published in *Qīthārat al-Rīḥ*. It is worth noting that the title of al-Sayyāb's first poetic collection *Azhār Dhābila* (Withered flowers) has a Baudelairian resonance. In a letter to Sāliḥ Jawād al-Ṭu'ma on 7 May 1947, al-Sayyāb reminds him to tell the Iraqi poetess Lamī'a Abbās 'Umārah to bring back his copy of a poetry book by the English poet Rupert Brooke (1887–1915), 'because I have an urgent desire to read it nowadays' (al-Sayyāb, 1994: 101). In this same letter, the Iraqi poet refers to his health, which had started to decline. Al-Sayyāb also told his friend that he liked the poem 'To C. L. M.' by the English poet John Masefield (1878–1967), which was dedicated to his mother (Masefield, 1978: 289–90). In addition, al-Sayyāb informs his friend that he is 'translating the first stanza of it, then I will summarize the content of the other stanzas' (al-Sayyāb, 1994: 102).

In fact, al-Sayyāb also translated the last stanza of Masefield's poem in a prose style. This is perhaps his second translational attempt on a textual level:

> في الرحم المظلم، حيث وجدتُ اول مرة، جعلتني حياة امي بشراً سوياً، وكان جمالها يغذي ارضي القاحلة ويرويها خلال اشهر الحمل التسعة الطوال: فلم أكُ قادراً على ان أرى، او اتنفس، أو أتحرك إلّا بموت بعض منها.
>
> بأي شيء وَفّى دَيْن هذه المرأة عنده، وما الذي صنع جزاء هذه المرأة الحبيبة المتوفاة؟ ان الرجال لا يزالون يطأون حقوق النساء بالاقدام، وان بعضاً منهم ما يزال يدّعي ويتبجح ببطولاته امام النساء، وان البعض الآخر يكاد يغرق الكون في شهواته؟ فما الذي صنع هو جزاء لتلك المرأة العظيمة؟ ايها القبر – لتبقَ موصداً لئلّا اخجل!!
>
> (ibid.: 102–3)

As with Keats, sympathy underlies al-Sayyāb's choice of poem. Al-Sayyāb lost his mother when he was very young. In ST 2:

> In the dark womb where I began
> My mother's life made me a man.
>
> (Masefield, 1978: 289)

'a man' was interpreted by al-Sayyāb, in TT 1, in a Qur'ānic usage 'بشراً سوياً' (a man in all respects) as in 19:17:

> فَاتَّخَذَتْ مِن دُونِهِمْ حِجَابًا فَأَرْسَلْنَا إِلَيْهَا رُوحَنَا فَتَمَثَّلَ لَهَا بَشَرًا سَوِيًّا
>
> She placed a screen (to screen herself) from them; then We sent to her our angel, and he appeared before her as a man in all respects.

Here, the relationship between mother and child in the original inspired al-Sayyāb to use the Qur'ānic story of Maryam and her child (Jesus) as a source for his translation. He developed this strategy further in his 'mature' translations, as will be demonstrated in the next context.

In the early 1950s, al-Sayyāb worked as a translator for several newspapers and magazines. For example, as Maḥmūd al-'Abṭa mentions, the Iraqi poet Muḥammad Mahdī al-Jawāhrī (1899–1997) gave him a job as an editor and translator in his newspaper *al-Thabāt* (Persistence) (cited in Bullāṭa, 1981: 63). It seems that al-Jawāhrī's sympathy for al-Sayyāb was, alongside his poetic talent, a result of their common political backgrounds as communist poets. For the same reason perhaps, al-Sayyāb translated poems by the Turkish communist poet Nāẓim Ḥikmat. Ḥikmat's poetic and political experiences were admired by many Arab left-wing poets and writers such as al-Bayātī, who met him in Moscow in the late 1950s and became a friend. Al-Bayātī wrote about, and, via English versions, translated some of Ḥikmat's poems into Arabic. Furthermore, al-Sayyāb translated, probably in the early 1950s, the French communist poet Louis Aragon's poem *Les yeux d'Elsa* (The eyes of Elsa) from an English translation (al-Baṣrī, 1966: 83). These translations show al-Sayyāb's engagement with 'world poetry'. Indeed, his involvement with Western, in particular English, poetry was, as DeYoung notices, extensive 'during the 1940s as whole, while his work never ceases to engage with the Arabic literary tradition, [al-Sayyāb] grows increasingly aware of, and appropriative of, Western literature, especially English (DeYoung, 1998: 147). As we have mentioned, al-Sayyāb studied Arabic literature before moving to the English Department at Teacher Training College in Baghdad. In his book *Badr Shākir al-Sayyāb: Ḥayātuh wa-Shi'ruh* (Badr Shākir al-Sayyāb: His life and poetry), 'Īsa Bullāṭa explains that the Iraqi poet 'felt that this change could secure his future. This is because the need for teachers of English was greater than for those who teach Arabic. On other hand, his readings of English literature had increased his desire to study Western thinking more widely' (Bullāṭa, 1981: 38). Tackling Western writers was like 'a new horizon has been opened to him' and al-Sayyāb 'wanted to make that horizon a part of his [poetic] vision':

> He was not seen in his spare time with Abī Tammām, al-Buḥturī or al-Mutanabbī['s poems] but with Shakespeare's plays, and with the Romantic [poetry books] of Wordsworth, Byron, Shelley and Keats in particular. And four poems have been found in his unpublished writings, written in 1944, dedicated 'For the Spirt of the Poet Wordsworth', and another one 'For the Spirit of the Poet of Nature Wordsworth'.
>
> (ibid.)

However, as Bullāṭa himself points out, al-Sayyāb 'did not totally break with his favourite Arab poets, and he never lost his interest in the current poetic movement in the Arabic world' (ibid.).

In the same introduction to *Dīwān al-Sayyāb*, 'Allūsh tries to find an answer to al-Sayyāb's move from the Arabic department to the English. 'Allūsh says that there are many reasons, but the most important one is that 'he wants to master the English language in order to extend his knowledge of foreign literature' ('Allūsh, 2005: 26). He adds that, at that time, al-Sayyāb's readings 'went beyond Shelley and Keats to Stephen Spender, Rupert Brooke, William Henry Davies and Edgar Allan Poe during 1948-1950. Then he went on to T. S. Eliot and Edith Sitwell' (ibid.: 65). At the same time, al-Sayyāb, as a communist poet, 'was imbibing from the communist culture, and struggling with the Iraqi Communist Party (ICP) against the tyranny and the colonial conspiracies' (ibid.).

'Abbās also considers the cultural sources of al-Sayyāb's poetic experience in his study of the Iraqi poet. In a chapter called *al-Yanābī' al-Thaqāfiyya* (The cultural sources) which focuses in the main on al-Sayyāb's famous work *Unshūdat al-Maṭar*, 'Abbās notes that 'in his search for a poetic source that suits his nature and method', al-Sayyāb was influenced by Edith Sitwell alongside other poets such as Lorca and Eliot ('Abbās, 1992: 184). Al-Sayyāb's admiration of the Spanish poet owed much to 'his deep expression of violence and death, and his great ability to portray reality' (ibid.). However, Lorca's impact on al-Sayyāb was not as profound as Sitwell's, and al-Sayyāb felt alienated by Lorca's poetic images which use 'surrealist features. And al-Sayyāb could not stay away too much from clarity in terms of imagery' (ibid.). To my mind, Lorca's poetry influenced modern Arabic poetry on a thematic level. For instance, some of al-Sayyāb's and al-Bayātī's major poems are about (or inspired by) Lorca. Moreover, a number of Lorca's poems were translated by al-Sayyāb himself, al-Bayātī and 'Abd al-Ṣabūr, who also translated Lorca's play *Yerma* (with Waḥīd al-Naqāsh). Sa'dī Yūsuf was another poet who translated a selection of Lorca's poems. Alongside Lorca, English poets, including Eliot and Sitwell, influenced Arab poets artistically and thematically. According to 'Abbās, there are many reasons to explain al-Sayyāb's 'attraction' to Sitwell's poetry, but the most important is that 'al-Sayyāb wanted another source for his poetry'. After all, Eliot's 'poetic symbols were imitated by al-Bayātī. Despite the acknowledgement of Eliot's greatness, al-Sayyāb wanted to deny [the impact of Eliot on him] in order not to use the same source as al-Bayātī' (ibid.: 186). This may be a superficial view of al-Sayyāb's poetic relationship with Sitwell. Interestingly, 'Abbās was aware of al-Sayyāb's interview, in which he puts the impact of Sitwell on his poetry on the same level as Abū Tammām (d. 845):

> When I review this long history of the [poetic] influence, I have found that [the impact of] Abū Tammām and Edith Sitwell is dominant . . . and

> therefore the way that I write most of my poems now is a mixture of Abū Tammām and Edith Sitwell. [They both use] cultural aspects, myths and history in writing poetry.
>
> (Cited in al-Baṭal: 73; see also 'Abbas: 184)

In fact, al-Sayyāb admired her 'nuclear' poems, which describe the aftermath of the bombing of Hiroshima and Nagasaki in Japan at the end of the Second World War. He especially admired 'Three Poems of the Atomic Age', which he translated into Arabic, and he was impressed by the techniques Sitwell used in these poems to poetize (and actualize) the biblical character 'Cain'. He also admired her poem 'Still Falls the Rain' and the way in which she uses 'rain' as a symbol for the bombing of England during the Second World War. In sum, al-Sayyāb benefited hugely from these two symbols: Cain and rain.

In 1957, al-Sayyāb worked as an editor and a translator for the Baghdad newspaper *al-Sha'b* (The people) which was known for its openness to Western ideas and culture (Bullāṭa, 1981: 96). It suited him well since he was himself open to Western poets, especially those who were 'contemporaries and innovators in their poetries, and dispensed with old forms and inherited traditions' (al-Baṣrī: 84). In his translations of these poets, 'al-Sayyāb was searching for himself' (ibid.). Indeed, for al-Sayyāb, free verse was more than a prosodic break from the classical poetic form. In an interview, al-Sayyāb states that

> Free verse is more than using a different number of similar feet between one line and another; it is a new artistic structure, a new realistic tone, which has come to crash the soft flaccidity of romanticism, the literature of the ivory towers, and the rigidity of Classicism. Likewise, it has come to crush the platform poetry that politicians and social reformers have been accustomed to write.
>
> (Translated by DeYoung, 1998: 195)

Al-Baṣrī argues that al-Sayyāb translated communist poets during his Marxist period and 'other poets' after he had broken away from the ICP (al-Baṣrī: 84). This is not entirely true because al-Sayyāb published his main body of translations in 1955, and they included various communist poets such as Neruda and Ḥikmat. This was after he left the ICP in 1954. Al-Sayyāb also translated a number of Soviet poets, but only, he claimed, because he wanted to show that 'communism and poetry are opposite, and therefore they cannot meet in any way' (al-Sayyāb, 2007: 123). In particular, he mocks the poetry of Konstantin Simonov (1915–79) by translating a long part of his poem *Al-Mutawaḥḥishūn* (The savages) (ibid.: 135). His translation of Simonov appears in one of a sequence of articles which were published in *al-Ḥuriyya* (Freedom) newspaper in 1959. Al-Sayyāb entitled the articles *Kuntu Shuyūʿiyyan* (I used to be a communist), and they were later published in book form in 2007:

> There you have comrade Simonov's poem. Any sixth grader could compose rote lines about a trip to the sea and it would be better than this poem. But as a communist, you are compelled to live it, and forced to consider it a treasure.
>
> (Translated by Colla, 2015: 257; also see al-Sayyāb, 2007: 135)

In *Al-Mutawaḥḥishūn*, Simonov criticizes the Marshall Plan which was an American initiative to help Western European countries after the end of the Second World War. The Soviet Union and the Eastern Bloc rejected the plan, and the following lines reflect that:

هذه ليست أوربا
ولا هي التي دافعت
عن الحرية في ميدان قتال
وآثرت أن تموت، على أن
تستسلم
أما هذه التي على سطح السفينة
فقد فضلت أن تبقى لمدة
سنوات سبع
في الولايات المتحدة الأمريكية
لتدير آلة موسيقية في
الطريق،
ولتلمع أحذية النخبة،
ولتنحي وتذل، وتستجدي عطفهم
وتكون كلبهم الحارس
وعبدهم
. . .
الآن،
مع مشروع مارشال (أم إنها خطة!)
الشيخ الشاحب . . .
المتدثر بلحاف محرق الحافة
سيعود بعد الآن بأشهر
قليلة
الى حلمه القديم،

ويحصل على منصب وزير
ويبيع فرنسا الجميلة، ثانية.

(Translated by al-Sayyāb, 2007: 131–3)

This isn't Europe . . .
This isn't the one who defended
Freedom on a battlefield
This isn't the one who preferred to die rather than surrender
And as for the one on board the ship
She preferred to stay for
Seven years
In the United States of America
To play a musical instrument
In the road,
To polish the elite's shoes,
To kneel and be humiliated, and to beg their sympathy
And to be their guard dog
And their slave
. . . .
Now,
With the Marshall Project (or rather, plan!)
The pale old man
Who was wrapped in a quilt with a burnt edge
Will be back in a few months
To his old dream,
And he'll become a minister
And he will sell beautiful France, once more.

As we can see from this back translation, the poem is not as bad as al-Sayyāb's description of it, although it is not one of Simonov's best. Simonov is known internationally for his poem 'Wait for Me', which he wrote in 1941 when he left home to work as a correspondent during the Second World War.

More significantly, these writings criticized Western civilization generally and American policies in particular, and they influenced al-Sayyāb and his generation to censure America, especially for its interventions in the Arab world. Indeed, translating writings from the four corners of the world enriched al-Sayyāb's writings thematically and stylistically. In short, his translations, to use al-Baṣrī's words, 'complete his poetics'. Before he embarked on the translation of other poets, al-Sayyāb's own verse had no 'brackets, myths, parentheses, and hymns'. It also refrained from 'criticising the new civilization, imagery, expression and so on which are considered the features of Western poetry'. Thus, 'he resorted to translation' in order to develop his poetics by embracing these features. Once he had mastered them, al-Sayyāb 'stopped translating poetry because he was able to achieve in his own poetry what he had been searching for' (al-Baṣrī, 1966: 84). Al-Baṣrī claims, moreover, that al-Sayyāb actually stopped translating poetry after the publication of his book *Unshūdat al-Maṭar* in 1960. After that, his health declined and al-Sayyāb died in 1964.

In his preface to Bullāṭa's book about al-Sayyāb's life and poetry, Yūsuf al-Khāl underlines al-Sayyāb's admiration of 'world poetry', courtesy of the translations in English:

> When pages of good poetry in English fall into his hands, he focuses on resolving their problems and diving into their deep meanings. He often uses a dictionary. Thus, the page margins are filled by vocabulary and annotations. When he finds beautiful and wonderful poetry he would be happy, and complains at the same time. I heard him saying: 'How far we are from this [great] poetry!'. He had a great talent, and he was great in evaluating the other [poets]. And he was sincerely passionate about knowledge and he was honest in his appreciation [for other poets].
>
> (Al-Khāl, 1981: 13)

In addition, Bullāṭa informs us that in the middle of the 1950s, al-Sayyāb was 'preoccupied with translations more than writing poetry. It is true that he translated a number of progressive world poets. However, it seems that he did not want to declare his position [as an opposition poet in order not to clash] with the authorities when he writes [his own] new poems' (Bullāta, 1981: 84).

However, al-Sayyāb's translations, in particular his book *Qaṣā'id Mukhtāra*, would increase suspicion by security men in Iraq. Therefore, he was detained for seven days in al-Kāẓimiyya Police Station.

Abbās claims that there are some 'problems' in al-Sayyāb's *Qaṣā'id Mukhtāra*:

> It was right that these translated poems should be studied by comparing the originals and their Arabic translations, but such study requires an investigation which this research cannot deal with. I made some comparisons here and there, and I have found [the translator] sometimes does not understand the originals. In addition, [his translations] are lacking in poetic style.
>
> (Abbās, 1992: 173)

Abbās's generalization is not helpful here since he fails to specify what these 'problems' are. Abbās adds that *Qaṣā'id Mukhtāra* was also attacked by the Lebanese magazine *al-Thaqāfa al-Waṭaniyya* (The national culture) in its November 1955 issue. According to al-Sayyāb, the magazine accused him of translating 'some fascist and Nazi poets such as Pound and some spies of the Intelligence Service like Stephen Spender'. Al-Sayyāb defended the 'humanist content' of the poems (ibid.: 174).

We have seen in this review that al-Sayyāb's own works and his translations interacted with each other poetically. His personal circumstances and his political involvement shaped his choice of which poems to translate, especially in his romantic and communist phases. In his final phase, al-Sayyāb tackled modernist English poets to assist in the process of renewal of Arabic poetry. We will now consider the impact of English poetry on al-Sayyāb and his generation in the verbal and cognitive contexts.

3.2 The verbal context

In this context, we will study al-Sayyāb's translations of three poems: Eliot's 'Journey of the Magi', Pound's 'The River-Merchant's Wife: A Letter' and Sitwell's *The Shadow of Cain*. I have chosen these three poems because of their impact on al-Sayyāb's own poetics as well as on Arabic modernity more generally. These poems have not been translated by another pioneer poet, as far as I am aware. That said, 'Journey of the Magi' was translated by Māhir Shafīq Farīd (2013). In addition, there are several translations of Eliot's and Pound's poems by less experienced translators which have been published on the internet. Sitwell's poem was also translated into Arabic by 'Alī al-Baṭal (1984) and Nadhīr al-'Aẓamah (2004).

3.2.1 'Journey of the Magi'

Eliot uses three sources for this poem. The first is the biblical story which regards this journey as one of the most important events in the history of Christianity. It is described in The Visit of Magi (Mt. 2.1-12):

> After Jesus was born in Bethlehem in Judea, during the time of King Herod, Magi from the east came to Jerusalem and asked, 'Where is the one who has

> been born king of the Jews? We saw his star when it rose and have come to worship him.'
>
> (Holy Bible, New International Version: 1423)

The second source of this poem, which in turn was influenced by the biblical story, is the Bishop of Winchester Lancelot Andrewes (d. 1626). Eliot borrows the first five lines from Andrewes's nativity sermon of 1622, although he does not refer to the original source of these lines in the poem. He does, however, mention Andrewes's sermon in his essay 'Lancelot Andrews', in which he analyses this account of the journey of 'the wise men come from the East' to witness Jesus's birth. In his essay, Eliot shows his admiration for the bishop's sermons in general: Andrewes 'takes a word and derives the world from it; squeezing the word until it yields a full juice of meaning which we should never have supposed any word to possess' (Eliot, 1936: 21). Here is Andrewes's description of the mission:

> It was no summer progress. A cold coming they had of it at this time of the year, just the worst time of the year to take a journey, and specially a long journey in. The ways deep, the weather sharp, the days short, the sun farthest off, in *solstitio brunall*, 'the very dead of winter'.
>
> (Cited in ibid.: 24)

The third source for the 'Journey of the Magi' is the poet's own experience. Published in 1927, it was his first poem after his conversion to the Anglo-Catholic Church. It was during this time that he began his sequence of poems 'Arial', which contain, alongside 'Journey of the Magi', 'A Song for Simeon' (1928) and 'Animula' (1929). 'Journey of the Magi', as Grover Smith points out, 'is the monologue of a man who has made his own choice, who has achieved belief in the Incarnation, but who is still part of that life which the Redeemer came to sweep away' (Smith, 1956: 122). Smith adds that the 'man' in Eliot's writings 'cannot break loose from the past. Oppressed by a sense of death-in-life . . . he is content to submit to "another death" for his final deliverance from the world of old desires and gods, the world of "the silken girls"' (ibid.).

These sources mostly influenced 'Journey of the Magi' on a thematic level. Stylistically, some scholars argue that the poem has a fourth source. According to them, the narrative technique of 'Journey of the Magi' 'contains more descriptive elements than is customary with Eliot; to some extent, general rather than specific', and they attribute this 'to the stimulus of St. John Perse's

Anabase' (Pinion, 1989: 172). Eliot embarked on his translation of Perse's poem in 1926, although he did not publish it until 1930.[1] Meanwhile, 'Journey of the Magi' was published in 1927. In 1949, in a letter to Jean Paulham, Eliot confirmed that the impact of the French poet on him 'is seen in several of the poems that I wrote after having completed the translations: the influence of images and also perhaps of rhythm. Students of my later works will perhaps find that this influence always persists' (cited in Southam, 1996: 236). When he was invited to 'write down a more detailed motivation' for nominating Perse for a Nobel Prize in 1960, Eliot responded with great admiration:

> My interest in the work of St-John Perse began many years ago when I translated his *Anabase* into English. This task gave me an intimacy with his style and idiom which I could not have acquired in any other way . . . with Perse, I have felt rather an influence which is visible in some of my poems written after I had translated *Anabase*.
>
> (Eliot, 2011: 909–10)

In his essay 'The Influence of St.-John Perse on T. S. Eliot', Richard Abel explains that 'Journey of the Magi' 'provides the clearest introduction . . . to the kind of influence St.John Perse had on Eliot's poetry' (Abel, 1973: 217). The narrator of 'Journey of the Magi' 'lives in an ancient kingdom or barbaric civilization, uneasy in the midst of transition. The narrator of *Anabase* . . . inhabits a similar barbaric world' (ibid.). Moreover, both narrators have 'to enter and cross the desert on a journey of spiritual, as well as physical, fulfillment' (ibid.).

The title of Eliot's poem 'Journey of the Magi' is replaced by *Riḥlat al-Majūs* in al-Sayyāb's translation. As in English, the Arabic *Riḥlat*, although its immediate equivalent is a 'journey', also means (mission) *mahamma*. If the wording of the first five lines is derived from Bishop Andrewes, the lines appear in a condensed form in the ST. In this way, Eliot has poetized Andrewes's prose. He thereby shows his skill in reading and choosing particular lines and words to fit or to be developed, and which thereafter are regarded as an organic part of his poem:

> A cold coming we had of it,
> Just the worst time of the year
> For a journey, and such a long journey:
> The ways deep and the weather sharp,
> The very dead of winter.
>
> (Eliot, 1972: 65)

This perhaps justifies these lines appearing in the TT without quotation marks:

في البرد القارس جئناها،
في شر وقت من العام
لأن تزمع فيه رحلة، ومثل هذه الرحلة الطويلة،
الدروب عميقة، والطقس حديد،
كان الشتاء في منتهاه

(Eliot, tr. al-Sayyāb, n.d. (1955?): 10)

In his book *Thomas Stearns Eliot: Poet*, A. David Moody claims that stanza 1 of 'Journey of the Magi' 'presents the detail of the journey in a manner which arrives at no vision of experience' (Moody, 1994: 133). This is because 'the present participles and the paratactic syntax, presenting one thing after another in a simple narrative, hold us to the banalities of romantic travellers' (ibid.). In my opinion, the subordinating types of adjectives used in this stanza, which ratchet up from 'cold' to 'worst time' to 'sharp' to 'the very dead of winter', intensify the image of the poem's opening. And the interaction between these 'strong' adjectives through their 'paratactic syntax' creates a type of 'inner' rhythm. Al-Sayyāb adopts a similar 'paratactic syntax' in his translation. Both the English and Arabic texts are dominated by short and simple sentences, clauses and phrases. The conjunctive tools, which link them together, are used in a coordinated manner to present a clear cohesive narrative. The use of the additive tool 'and' in English and 'wa' in Arabic dominates these conjunctions. After all, the 'historical' narrative requires a 'clear' setting to depict the background of the event. Moreover, this type of narrative usually shows a logical relationship between the linguistic items of its verbal context. This is particularly evident in stanzas 1–2 of the English and Arabic texts. This means the poet-translator was aware of the stylistic technique of the source poem, as was he aware of the biblical story of the Magi and their mission. In an accompanying note, he adds:

> Just before the birth of Christ, a group of Magi travelled to explore the matter of the new baby – Christ – for whom their sacred books had prophesied his birth. They witnessed the star, whose story is known, and then they knew Christ was born.
>
> (Al-Sayyāb, n.d. (1955?): 100)

Inspired by Eliot's poem, al-Sayyāb used the same note for his own poem *Qāfilat al-Ḍayā'* (The convoy of loss), as Ḥasan Tawfīq mentions in his introduction to *Badr Shākir al-Sayyāb: Aṣwāt al-Shā'ir al-Mutarjim* (Badr Shākir al-Sayyāb: The voices of the poet-translator). Tawfīq explains that this note had appeared when the poem was initially published in the Beirut literary magazine *al-Ādāb* in 1956 (Tawfīq, 2012: 23). The impact of 'Journey of the Magi' on al-Sayyāb's poetry will be highlighted in the next context.

In ST 1, al-Sayyāb changes the adjective 'cold' to a noun 'البرد' (the cold), and he uses the adjective 'القارس' (sharp) to describe the weather. He replaces the noun 'coming' and the verb 'had' by the past verb 'جاء' (came) in 'جئناها' (we came to it):

في البرد القارس جئناها

In the sharp cold we came to it

The TT also replaces the indefinite 'a cold' by a definite article 'البرد' (the cold).

In ST 2, al-Sayyāb translates 'the worst time' as 'شر وقت' (the most evil time). This expression is sometimes used in Arabic to describe the hardest time. In ST 4, he interprets 'sharp' as a metaphor with 'حديد' (iron). It is used by the Qur'ān with the same meaning in 50:22:

لَّقَدْ كُنتَ فِي غَفْلَةٍ مِّنْ هَٰذَا فَكَشَفْنَا عَنكَ غِطَاءَكَ فَبَصَرُكَ الْيَوْمَ حَدِيدٌ

(It will be said:) 'Thou were heedless of this; now have We removed your veil, and sharp is your sight this Day!'

In this context, the Qur'ānic usage of the TT resonates with the biblical story of the ST. This technique was increasingly used in al-Sayyāb's translational works.

Al-Sayyāb did not use the usual Arabic equivalent 'قارس' for 'sharp' in order to avoid repetition, as he had used it already in TT1. In ST 5, the Iraqi poet translates 'the very dead of winter' as 'كان الشتاء في منتهاه' (the winter was at its peak). One of the meanings of 'منتهى' is (peak) (قمة). 'منتهى' also means 'end' and 'aim' in Arabic. In ST 6, al-Sayyāb changes the passive structure of 'the camels galled' to active 'والجمال نال منها الجرب'. He translates 'gall' disease as 'الجرب' (mange), which is normally associated with 'camels'. There are classical poems which describe this terrible condition for people and animals alike in pre-Islamic Arabia. In the same context, al-Sayyāb replaces the adjective 'sore-footed' by a nominal sentence 'كلمى مناسمها' (their hoofs are wounded), which is a rather classical usage. For example, in line 62 of the *Qaṣidat* by al-A'shā:

إنّـي لَعَمْرُ الَّذي خَطَّتْ مَـنـاسِمُـها   لـه وَسِـيـقَ إلَـيْـهِ الـبَـاقِـرُ الـغُـيُـلُ
لَـئِـنْ قَـتَـلْـتُمْ عَمِـيداً لَمْ يَكُنْ صَدَداً   لَـنَـقْـتُلَـنْ مِـثْـلَـهُ مِـنْـكُمْ فَنَمتَثِلْ

(Al-A'shā (n.d): 304)

I swear by the life of her whose hoofs
Dig through the sandy desert that if you
Kill our master without a reason, we'll
Kill one like him and be even with you

(Translated by Nouryeh, 1993: 218)

In modern Arabic, *aqdām* (feet) is used more than *manāsim* for hoofs. In the same line, al-Sayyāb also replaces the adjective 'refractory' with a verbal sentence 'أصابها الحران'. Here, he could simply replace 'refractory' by حرون, but it seems that he uses that rendition to dramatize the theme. This strategy also helps him to syntactically harmonize his decision to translate this line as it is dominated by sentence forms. For the subject 'الجمال', he has chosen to use four predicates: two verbal sentences 'نال منها الجرب' and 'أصابها الحران', one nominal sentence 'كلمى مناسمها' and one noun 'باركات' which is attached to its preposition phrase 'في ذائب الثلج'. The last one is called a semi-sentence in Arabic grammar. In ST 17, applying the same 'classical' strategy, al-Sayyāb interprets 'we preferred to travel all night' as 'آثرنا الإدلاج' in TT 19. The Arabic word إدلاج means 'travelling/setting out at dusk'.

The strategy used in the TT helps to echo the ancientness of the original mission illustrated in the ST. Moreover, it does not affect the 'modernity' of the TT as it is formally produced as a prose poem. Hence, it shows the ability of a 'modern' poetic form to comprise 'classical' language, and it reflects al-Sayyāb's poetic skill as he practised both classicism and modernity in his short lifetime.

Al-Sayyāb uses a 'local' language as well. In his 'unsystematic' but 'poetic' approach, he wanted to reflect the variety of voices in the ST: modernity of the form (free verse in the ST, prose poem in the TT), classical content (the journey), locality of places in the poem. In discursive terms to use Baker's words, al-Sayyāb covers all register variation: field, in terms of the poetic 'speaker's choice of linguistic items', tenor in 'the relationship between the people taking part in the discourse' and mode in 'the role that the language is playing' (Baker, 1992: 15–6). In ST 10, for example, al-Sayyāb replaces 'sherbet', which originally comes from the Arabic *sharāb* (drink), with the transliterated form 'الشربت' in TT 11. This coinage is widely used in Iraqi dialect as a superordinate word for most types of juice. In the same context, in ST 11, the translator standardizes and localizes 'the men' as 'the camel men', and it is replaced by 'حداة الجمال وسواقها' (lit. Camelleers of camels and their drivers) in TT 12. In so doing, al-Sayyāb unnecessarily translates one word as two, since the standard 'حداة' is still used in most Arabic dialects. In addition, in TT 16, he uses 'دساكر', a Persian word used in Iraq, to translate 'towns' in ST 14. The choice of the Persian word enables al-Sayyāb to cover two levels: the originality of the 'Magi' and the locality of the 'towns'. In this context, *baldāt* is the Arabic equivalent of 'towns', while *mudin* is the equivalent of 'cities'. In Iraq, *mudin* is used for towns (big or small) and cities. He also avoids repetition by using 'دساكر' instead of 'مدن', which has already been employed to replace 'cities' in the same line. In ST 15, 'charging high prices' is rendered as 'تسومنا عالي الاسعار' (impose high prices upon us). The usual Arabic equivalent for 'charging' (a price) is يقاضي ثمناً, but in this context the 'charging' is not neutral (يقاضي). Rather, it is, as al-Sayyāb suggests, يفرض (imposes). The hidden adversative conjunction in this line could be decoded as:

> And the villages dirty and (yet, however etc.) charging high prices and made obvious in the TT:
>
> والقرى قذرة (مع ذلك) تسومنا غالي الأسعار

To harmonize the narrative of stanza 1, al-Sayyāb uses regular feminine plurals, such as 'الصبايات الناعمات والشرفات وجافيات', to translate 'silken girls, the terraces, unfriendly'. He also uses the present imperfect in its third-person plural masculine form 'يلعنون ويدمدمون ويولون ويصرخون' to translate 'cursing, grumbling, running, wanting', which serve to create a kind of an 'inner' rhythm in the TT.

In translating stanza 2, al-Sayyāb utilizes a rhyming strategy this time to 'versify' the descriptive narration of the ST. Thus, he has chosen 'الظلماء' in TT 25 instead of, for instance, 'ظلام', to replace 'the darkness' in ST 23 in order to rhyme with 'المساء' in TT 34. Furthermore, al-Sayyāb sometimes affixes extra words to the original in order to achieve a rhyme and thus to enhance the harmonic structure of the TT. For example, he adds to the end of TT 26 'بثراه' (in its soil). Hence ST 24:

> And three trees on the low sky is interpreted as:
>
> وشجرات ثلاث عند ملتقى سمائه الخفيضة بثراه،
>
> (And three trees where its soil meets the low sky)

'بثراه' rhymes with 'مرعاه' (in its meadow), and he uses this to replace 'in the meadow' in ST 25. He also adds 'مقامرات' (gamblers) in TT 30 as a second predicate to the subject 'ست أيد' (six hands) in the previous line in order to rhyme with 'الفارغات' in TT 32 ('the empty' in ST 28). The additional strategy helps to clarify the semantic level of the TT. In translating ST 25, al-Sayyāb uses two different strategies. The first is to exchange one word, 'galloped', by a sentence 'يعدو خبباً' ([the horse] racing at a fast trot) in TT 27. This is justified here since the poet-translator wanted to convey not just the meaning of 'galloped' but also its musicality, albeit *Riḥlat al-Majūs* is a prose poem. To do so, he uses variations *fa'lun* and *fa'ilun* of *al-Mutadārak's* foot *fā'ilun*:

يَعْدُو خَبَبَاً: فَعْلُن فَعِلُن

(fa'lun, fa'ilun)

This metre is also called *al-khabab* (trot) and *rakḍ al-khayl* (horse trot), because it is supposedly similar to the sounds of horses' hooves. This resonates with the 'temperate' atmosphere in the first half of stanza 2 as this metre 'has been exploited by the dancing Sufis' and 'can produce a kind of hilarious music' (Jayyusi, 1977: 611). The second strategy is to refrain from translating the adjective 'white', but this is unjustifiable since it does not develop the TT.

In (last) stanza 3, the 'voice' of the poem's narrator changes from an external objective account to an inner subjective one. Hence the stanza is overshadowed by uncertain questions of 'Birth and Death', which Eliot wrote when he was in a transitional phase. The poetic 'subject' changes from the plural 'we' to 'I'. The poem also changes from the 'realistic' and 'concrete' details of stanzas 1–2 to the internal philosophical questions in this stanza. Al-Sayyāb and his generation alighted on Eliot in the 1940s and 1950s at a time when the Arabic world was changing: culturally from classicism to modernism, and politically from colonialism to nationalism. It was in this atmosphere that the Tammūzī movement developed in Arabic poetry. The movement, of which al-Sayyyāb was part, took its name from the Mesopotamian religion in which Tammūz was a god of fertility. This movement was influenced by Eliot's mythological method in modernizing ancient legends, especially those of birth, death and resurrection. And these concepts overshadowed the poems of al-Sayyāb, Adūnīs, al-Khāl and Jabrā in the 1950s. It was Jabrā who coined the name of this movement in an article about al-Khāl's poetry.

In his translation, al-Sayyāb was aware of these concepts which puzzlingly dominate this central intricate stanza of 'Journey of the Magi'. Unlike stanzas 1–2, the last one is voiced by an individual 'Magus' who has just left his tribe and religion and now lives in limbo. Here, the poet-translator decoded the key phrase of this stanza 'but set down', in ST 33, as 'لو حللت' (if I resolved) in TT 38. The use of a conditional in the TT explains the 'uncertain' feeling towards their new religion.

In the same line, the TT utilizes two emphatic devices 'إنّ' and 'اللام' to translate ST 33:

And I would do it again as:

وإني لمعيد الكرّة

(And I will definitely do it again)

However, this sureness is conditional upon resolving the questions or understanding the differences between Birth and Death, and between the old and new dispensations. This dilemma makes the Magi (and perhaps all converts) alien not only to their past:

We return to our places . . .
But no longer at ease here.

But also to the 'bitter agony' of the Birth:

We had evidence and no doubt I had seen birth and death.

However, the Birth they were 'certain' about it could be another Death!
In translating 'Birth' and 'Death' with capital letters in ST 36, 38 and 39, the TT uses quotation marks to highlight the fact that these concepts are under consideration. They differ from 'birth' and 'death' with small letters in ST 37 and 43. Arabic has no such devices. The strategy, which is used commonly in translating English into Arabic, conveys the semantic level of this stanza. Stylistically, in ST 37 'evidence' was replaced by a Qur'ānic word 'آية' in TT 43 and 'dispensation' in ST 41 by 'الناموس'.

Although *Riḥlat al-Majūs* is formally considered a prose poem, al-Sayyāb has used metrical features such as rhymes and 'inner' rhythms. In short, this poem is an experiment. This strategy of mixing 'classical' language with a new form perhaps helped Arab modernists, in that transitional period of the 1950s, to work out novel techniques in their own writings.

3.2.2 'The River-Merchant's Wife: A Letter'

This poem was originally written by the Chinese poet Li Po (AD 702–762). Pound translated it via a Japanese translation (*Rihaku* is the Japanese name of Li Po) he had found in the notes of the Japanese scholar Ernest Fenollosa (1853–1908). From these notes, Pound published a pamphlet of his Chinese translations *Cathay* in 1915 which includes 'The River-Merchant's Wife: A Letter'. *Cathay* had an impact on modern English poetry, especially on the Imagist Movement. In his book *After Babel Aspects of Language and Translation*, George Steiner states that

> [*Cathay*] is . . . not only the best inspired work in Pound's uneven canon, but the achievement which comes nearest to justifying the whole 'imagist' programme. The 'Song of the Bowmen of Shu', 'The Beautiful Toilet', 'The River Merchant's Wife: A Letter', 'The Jewel Stairs', 'Grievance', the 'Lament of the Frontier Guard', 'Taking Leave of a Friend' are masterpieces. They have altered the feel of the language and set the pattern of cadence for modern verse.
>
> (Steiner, 1975: 358)

Interestingly, *Cathay* appears in *Ezra Pound: Selected Poems*, as his own poetry. In his introduction to Pound's selection, Eliot explains that

> As for *Cathay*, it must be pointed out that Pound is the inventor of Chinese poetry for our time. I suspect that every age has had, and will have, the same illusion concerning translations, an illusion which is not altogether an illusion either. When a foreign poet is successfully done into the idiom of our own language and our own time, we believe that he has been 'translated'; we believe that through this translation we really at last get the original.
>
> (Eliot, 1959: 14–15)

The description of Pound as 'the inventor of Chinese poetry for our time' is surely valid; even now many readers think that the poems of *Cathay* were indeed composed by him. The history of translation shows us that some translations are regarded as 'originals' in their target cultures. This is due to their influential roles in shaping those cultures. For example, many English readers regard The King James Version of the Bible as 'original'. *One Thousand and One Nights*, *Kalīla wa-Dimna* and some of Jubrān's writings are also regarded as 'originals' by their target readers. Similarly, many readers view Adūnīs's translations as 'Arabic' texts. Some scholars describe Pound's translations as 'creative adaptations' (Sullivan, 1961: 465). Steiner praises Pound's translation of Li Po's poem. In a comparison between Pound's translation and Arthur Waley's of the same poem, Steiner says that Waley's 'The Song of Ch'ang-kan' was greatly influenced by Pound's 'The River-Merchant's Wife: A Letter'.

The title of Pound's poem 'The River-Merchant's Wife: A Letter' is modified in al-Sayyāb's translation by *Risāla min Zawjat Tājir al-Nahr* (A letter from the wife of the river merchant). Here, *Risāla* (letter) heads the title to clarify its meaning, and therefore the main theme. Unlike 'Journey of the Magi', which is translated into Arabic as prose, 'The River-Merchant's Wife: A Letter' is translated by al-Sayyāb 'as poetry'. In a note to his translation, al-Sayyāb mentions that he produces 'this poetic translation because it is so close to the original'. He adds that 'the metre or rather the rhyme forced [him] to use "عذبات زان" instead of "قصب البامبو"' for 'bamboo stilts' in the third line of the poem (al-Sayyāb, n.d. (1955?): 100). Prosodically, al-Sayyāb uses *al-Kāmil* metre which is formed, in classical Arabic poetry, by three feet of *mutafā'ilun* in each hemistich. But in free verse, the poet is allowed to change the number of those feet, and al-Sayyāb does this in his 'free verse' translation.

Al-Sayyāb was aware of the differences and similarities between the Arabic and English metrical systems. In the preface to his collection *Asāṭīr* (Myths) (1950), al-Sayyāb notes from his readings of English poetry that it is controlled musically by 'the stress which is equivalent to the foot in [Arabic poetry] with the consideration of the difference between the two poetries' (al-Sayyāb, 1986: 11–12). He also notes that the English poetic line or *al-bayt* consists of stresses of one type 'but they are different in their number in some poems' (ibid.). In the same preface, al-Sayyāb emphasizes that

> It is possible to keep the musical harmony in the poem despite the difference in the musical lines by using the metres of the complete feet, provided that the number of these feet has to be different in each line. The first attempt of this kind for me was in the poem *Hal kān Ḥubban*? (Was It Love?) [published] in my first *Dīwān Azhār Dhābila* (Withered Flowers). This type of [poetic] music has been accepted by many of our young poets, one of whom is the inventor poet Miss Nāzik al-Malā'ika.
>
> (ibid.: 12)

In ST 1, 'while . . . was' is translated by 'قد كان' (it has been) in TT 1, which covers grammatically and semantically the past tense of 'played' in ST 2. This meaning is also supported by using 'أيام ذاك' (those days) in TT 3:

While my hair was still cut straight across my forehead
I played about the front gate, pulling flowers.
You came by on bamboo stilts, playing horse,
You walked about my seat, playing with blue plums.

(Pound, 1959: 129)

قد كان شَعْري ما يزال
يقص خطاً يستقيم على الجبين
- أيام ذاك- وكنت عند الباب ألعب بالزهور
وكنت تأتي راكباً عذبات زان
الوهم صيرها حصان.
قد كنت تنتظر حيث أجلس ، أو تدور
حول المكان وكان بين يديك من ريش الطيور
زرق لعبت بها كثار.

(Pound, tr. al-Sayyāb, n.d. (1955?): 14)

In fact, the past tense dominates the poem because the narrator is describing the past events of her life chronologically. As the translator explains, the target prosodic system, although in free verse, forces him to replace 'bamboo stilts' in ST 3 with 'عذبات زان' (beech stilts) in TT 4. This does not affect the imagery level since the TT covers the keyword 'playing' in the previous line, but the rather different image does function more rhythmically than the original one. In the same context, al-Sayyāb interprets 'plums', in ST 4 as 'ريش الطيور' (plumage) in TT 7, although the difference between these two words is greater than that of 'beech' and 'bamboo'. In addition, 'ريش الطيور' is used to meet the rhyme (راء) in 'الزهور', 'الطيور', in ST 2, and 'تدور' in TT 3 and 6 respectively. This last Arabic word replaces 'walked about' in ST 4. In TT 7, 'بين يديك' (in your hands) is added to clarify the image of this line; it also serves to achieve the four feet of *al-kāmil mutafa*'ilun, as can be seen in this prosodic script:

حوللْمكا/ نوكانبيْ/ نيديكمن/ ريشطْطيور

in:

حول المكان وكان بين يديك من ريش الطيور

This additional strategy is used in TT 8 by inserting 'كثار' (many) to meet the rhyme of 'كبار' (adults) which is added in TT 10. In the same prosodic context, the poet-translator interprets 'and we went on living' in ST 5 as 'كخير ما عاش الورى' (people never had it so good) in TT 9. This interpretation allows him to complete four feet of *al-kāmil*:

كُنْنانعي/ شكخيْرما/ عاشلْورى/ في شوْوكان

in:

كنّا نعيش كخير ماعاش الورى في شو - وكان

Here, al-Sayyāb has slightly changed the name of the village 'Chokan' to two words 'شو - وكان' (Cho wa-kan) to be metrically rendered (with 'في') into *mustaf*ilun (- - u -).

His interpretation of ST 6 'Two small people, without dislike or suspicion' 'as adults' is justifiable since it reflects the 'nostalgic' images of the speaker's childhood in this stanza. Thus, al-Sayyāb's additional strategy functions both metrically and semantically in the TT as it has helped to 'localize' the 'foreign' text. Furthermore, it 'personalizes' the ST. For example, the target stanza 4 is dominated by al-Sayyāb's 'late style', and it resonates with his 1962 poem *Raḥal al-Nahār* (The day has gone) on several levels, as we shall see in the next context.

3.2.3 *The Shadow of Cain*

The Shadow of Cain is the second of Sitwell's *Three Poems of Atomic Age* which also contains 'Dirge for the New Sunrise' and 'The Canticle of the Rose'. They appear in Sitwell's *Later Poems (from 1940 onward)* which consist of her best-known poems in the Arab world. In addition to *Three Poems of Atomic Age*, Sitwell's *Later Poems* include 'Still Falls the Rain', 'Lullaby', 'The Night Wind', 'Street Song', 'The April Rain' and 'A Mother to Her Dead Child'. Al-Sayyāb translated and found inspiration in these poems in the 1940s and 1950s. It was al-Sayyāb who introduced Sitwell's poetry to an Arab audience. He admired her 'human' approach to the world's catastrophes and wars. He was, in particular, inspired by her technique of symbolizing and modernizing biblical figures such as 'Cain' in her poems. Sitwell's *The Shadow of Cain* was written to depict the aftermath of the bombing of Hiroshima and Nagasaki in 1945. In 'Some Notes on my Own Poetry' to her *Collected Poems* (1961), Sitwell states that

> On the 10th September 1945, nearly five weeks after the fall of the first atom bomb, my brother Sir Osbert Sitwell and I were in the train going to Brighton, where we were to give a reading. He pointed out to me a paragraph in *The Times*, a description by an eye-witness of the immediate effect of atomic bomb upon Hiroshima. That witness saw a totem pole of dust arise to the sun as a witness against the murder of mankind.
>
> (Sitwell, 1961: xlii)

In the same 'Notes', she informs us that 'from that moment the poem began, although it was not actually written until April of the next year' (ibid.), and published in June 1947 (Sitwell, 1998: 483).

Although religious terms and names dominate *The Shadow of Cain*, the poem is interpreted in different ways. For example, it was, as John Pearson notes, viewed as a leftist poem by the Marxist critic Jack Lindsay when he analysed 'the poem in elaborate Freudian-Marxist terms, and then comparing Edith and her work with the development in France of such major left-wing poets as Tzara, Eluard and Aragon' (Pearson, 1989: 395). According to Lindsay, Sitwell was one of 'the poets who stand at the pivotal points of a vast and decisive spiritual change in man, bound up with social, political and economic revolutions' (ibid.). On the other hand, Mark S. Morrisson, in his essay 'Edith Sitwell's Atomic Bomb Poems: Alchemy and Scientific Reintegration', criticizes those scholars who interpret the 'scientific terms', which the poet uses widely in 'Three Poems of Atomic Age' 'as symbols for religious concepts' (Morrisson, 2002: 606). He explains that these three poems were possibly the most powerful ones of Sitwell's 'last phase of her career, although the most sustained discussion of them has primarily focused on their religious implications'. Undoubtedly, the poet 'would have approved of the perceptive religious readings of the nature of guilt in her poems, but the tight focus on theology seems not to have permitted these scholars to consider the vast array of scientific concepts invoked in the poems *as science*' (ibid.: 605–6).

It is true that Sitwell uses many scientific terms in 'Three Poems of Atomic Age', especially in *The Shadow of Cain*, but the terms function spiritually in the poem. She herself explains that

> This poem is about the fission of the world into warring particles, destroying and self-destructive. It is about the gradual migration of mankind, after the second Fall of Man that took the form of separation of brother and brother, of Cain and Abel, of nation and nation, of the rich and the poor – the spiritual migration of those into the desert of the Cold, towards the final disaster, the first symbol of which fell on Hiroshima.
>
> (Sitwell, 1961: xlii)

Here, it is helpful to see how al-Sayyāb approached *The Shadow of Cain* on a verbal level. I have chosen lines 1–51 of the 172-line poem for two reasons. First, these lines reflect 'Cain' as Sitwell's central symbol, and second, they highlight the main translational issues in al-Sayyāb's work. I conclude with a couple of examples from the closing lines of the poem.

As we noted earlier, al-Sayyāb published this translation under the name Abū Ghaylān in 1960 in the Iraqi magazine *al-Taḍāmun* (Solidarity). In 2013, Khālid 'Alī Muṣṭafā edited and published most of al-Sayyāb's translational works in *Min Nuṣūṣ al-Sayyāb al-Adabiyyah al-Mutarjamah* (From al-Sayyāb's translational literary texts). In this edition, which I rely on, al-Sayyāb's translation appears as a single stanza! Therefore, I have reshaped the Arabic text according to the layout of the original, which should help when we compare the two texts.

The title *The Shadow of Cain* is translated by al-Sayyāb as *Shabaḥ Qābīl* (Ghost of Qābīl). The immediate English equivalent of *Shabaḥ* is 'ghost'. 'Shadow' can be replaced by the Arabic *ẓill* which also means 'shade'. In this context, al-Sayyāb's 'ghost' is more than *ẓill*, as this Bible-based poem is, to use the poet's words, about 'false brotherhood' and being 'destroying and self-destructive'. The Qur'ān also mentions the story of Adam's sons in 5:31, but it does not mention their names, albeit they are known in Arabic-Islamic culture as *Qābīl* (Cain) and *Hābīl* (Abel). The poet-translator ignores the dedication of the original 'To C. M. Bowra'. Cecil Maurice Bowra (1898–1971) was an English classical scholar and literary critic who studied Sitwell's poetry.

In ST 1 the adjective 'great' which describes the plural nouns 'flags and banners' is translated as 'كبار' (an Arabic plural form of big, great, etc.) in TT 1:

> Under great yellow flags and banners of the ancient Cold
> Began the huge migrations

From some primeval disaster in the heart of Man.
There were great oscillations
Of temperature. . . . You knew there had once been warmth;

(Sitwell, 1961: 370)

تحت بيارق صفر كبار، بيارق البرد القديم،
بدأت الهجرات الهائلة
من فاجعة أولى في قلب الإنسان
كانت ذبذبات عظيمة في الحرارة
تدعك تعرف انه كان ثمة دفءٌ في يوم من الأيام.

(Sitwell, tr. al-Sayyāb, 2013: 95)

However, in Arabic we usually use a feminine singular adjective for any plural denoting inanimate objects. Therefore, al-Sayyāb should use 'كبيرة', but it seems he chooses 'كبار' to intensify the image of the opening stanza. In the same line, he translates 'flags' and 'banners' by a single word 'بيارق'. As a stylistic device, repetition is applied in the original to emphasize these two objects. 'Banners' can also be translated into Arabic as 'رايات'. In ST 4, 'oscillations' is rendered literally as 'ذبذبات' in TT 4, although it can be translated as 'تغييرات' (changes), which is how al-Sayyāb translated the same word in ST 17. In the same line, al-Sayyāb replaces 'great' by 'كبيرة', while in TT 4 he translates the same word as 'عظيمة'. In this strategy, the superordinate adjective 'great' in the ST is translated by means of subordinate adjectives such as 'كبيرة' and 'عظيمة' in the TT. The technique is also used to avoid repetition which could stylistically affect the poetics of the target poem. Here, the poet-translator is applying the opposite device to that of TT 1. In ST 8, 'variation' is translated by 'أفانين' in TT 7. This word is a synonym of words such as أعاجيب (miracles), فنون (arts) and so on. In this particular context, al-Sayyāb's suggestion suits the significance of stanza 3, where 'Zero/The Nothing' emerges from 'All Being and all variation'. In a note on his translation of this stanza, al-Sayyāb offers this interpretation:

> Man stripped of . . . [his] emotions, feelings and heritage. Nothing left for him but the body which the poetess described as 'Zero'. She ridicules the philosophers who believe that man will build, through experiments, his city from that 'Zero'.
>
> (Al-Sayyāb, 2013: 95; brackets added)

In ST 7, 'Nothing', in its philosophical context, is often translated by the classical term عدم *'adam*. However, al-Sayyāb replaces it by 'لا شيء' in TT 7, and he does the same in TT 10. The translator's choice is probably used more than عدم in modern Arabic, but he sometimes applies the opposite strategy. For example, the neutral word 'changed' in ST 12 is translated by the classical (and philosophical) 'آضَ' (became) in TT 12. In the same line, he replaces 'space' with two words 'مدىً ومكان' (space in time and place). As an astronomical term, the equivalent of 'space' is *faḍā'* and sometimes 'مدى'. In its more common usage, 'space' can be translated as 'مكان', but it may be that he uses 'مكان' in order to harmonize it with 'ألوان الأرجوان' (the purple colours) as a translation of 'purple perfumes' in ST 14. This also explains the reason behind translating 'perfumes' as 'ألوان' rather than the usual equivalent 'عطور'. Moreover, he changes the adjective 'purple' into a noun 'الأرجوان', as opposed to the adjective 'الأرجواني', notwithstanding the fact that 'الأرجوان' is associated with a colour more than with a 'perfume' in Arabic culture. These experimental strategies help the target readership to decode such a complex multilayered poem and therefore to find answers to Sitwell's questions. ST 22 was reshaped into two lines in TT 22 and 23, but this linguistic division does not affect the imagery level of the poem. In ST 23, 'the Antarctic Pole' is erroneously rendered as 'القطب المنجمد الشمالي' (the North Icy Pole) in TT 24. Similarly, 'atonic' in ST 24 is replaced by 'الذري' (the atomic). Unlike in the case of ST22, ST 25 and 26 appear as one line in TT 26. Here, the translator perhaps wanted to put the main statement of this stanza in a single sentence. In the same line, he translates the explicit cohesive device 'of' as 'لِـ'. Al-Sayyāb also translates 'the trace' in ST 25 and 27 as 'أثر'. This repetition, which was used in the ST to enrich and clarify the meaning, has a similar function in the TT. In ST 30, 'the Pampean mud'[2] is interpreted as 'الطين اللازب' (sticky clay). Here, al-Sayyāb applies a Qur'ānic usage to echo the 'religious' aspect of the ST. This usage appears in the Qur'ān in 37:11:

فَاسْتَفْتِهِمْ أَهُمْ أَشَدُّ خَلْقًا أَم مَّنْ خَلَقْنَا إِنَّا خَلَقْنَاهُم مِّن طِينٍ لَّازِب

> Just ask their opinion: are they the more difficult to create, or (other) beings We have created? Them have We created out of a sticky clay!

This reference serves to intensify the fragility of 'Man' and the 'subsidence' of his 'Race' which are mentioned in most religious books. This theme is maintained by translating 'was formed' in the same line into another classical word 'جُبِلَ',

rather than a modern one such as شُكِّل. In the same context, 'cloven in two' in ST 33 is translated as 'فلقتين' (a dual form of *falaq* (crack/split) in TT 34. *Al-falaq* is also the name of the penultimate chapter in the Qur'ān. In ST 34, 'glacial period' is imaginatively rendered as 'ثلاجات الجليد' (refrigerators of ice) in TT 35. Here, mistranslating the original affects not only its meaning but also the poetics of the TT. The Arabic equivalent for this period in prehistory is 'العصر الجليدي'.

Sitwell continually depicts the darker 'periods' of man. In the closing lines of *The Shadow of Cain*, she attributes this darkness to the fact that our world is still ruled by an evil combination of the killer 'Cain' and the rich and greedy 'Dives':

> we cry
> To Dives: 'You are the shadow of Cain. Your shade is the primal Hunger'
> (Sitwell, 1961: 376)

This biblical figure 'Dives' is, once more, replaced by a *Qur'ānic* figure, '*Qārūn*':

> 'نصرخ بقارون: 'أنت شبح قابيل، وإن ظِلَّك لهو الجوع الأول.
> (Sitwell, tr. al-Sayyāb, 2013: 103)

However, this is not a systematic strategy as al-Sayyāb sometimes uses Christian terms. For example, he replaces 'Judgment Day' by the biblical 'يوم الدينونة', rather than by an Islamic term such as يوم الحساب أو القيامة:

> To be our Fires upon the Judgment Day!
> (Sitwell: 376)

> لتكون لنا ناراً يوم الدينونة،
> (Sitwell, tr. al-Sayyāb: 104)

The 'unsystematic', but 'creative', approach applied in '*Shabaḥ Qābīl*', alongside *Riḥlat al-Majūs* and '*Risāla min Zawjat Tājiri al-Nahr*', reflects al-Sayyāb's translations of these poems. He employs every potential poetic feature of the target language in order to produce a 'powerful' poem in the received culture. To achieve this, he did not shy away from producing echoes of the 'classical' sources of these poems in modern forms. He also experimented with an Arabic metre in his translation of a Chinese poem into English. This latter strategy demonstrates the possibility of using the target prosodic system in poetry translations. Al-Sayyāb's translational work influenced his own writings and inspired the Arabic poetic scene from the 1940s onwards.

3.3 The cognitive context

As we have seen, al-Sayyāb was one of the first Arab poets to introduce modern English poetry to Arabic culture. Sitwell's poetry became known to Arabic readers solely through al-Sayyāb's translations. He developed (and Arabized) English techniques to fit into the Arabic system. Cognitively, al-Sayyāb's translational contribution created a new atmosphere among poets. The 'free verse' poets were the first to benefit from his contribution. Eliot's poems had a particularly significant impact on al-Sayyāb's modernity on various levels. For example, *The Waste Land*, although not translated by al-Sayyāb himself, inspired him to use its key features such as the mythical and multilayered forms.

I would like here to explore another aspect of Eliot's impact on al-Sayyāb and his colleagues, namely the use of the Christian symbols in modern Arabic poetry, which came about through al-Sayyāb's influence by Eliot's writings. At first, al-Sayyāb developed and adapted these symbols in his own poems, but they reverberate around Arabic modernity. We previously considered the principles of cognitive poetics, that is, adaptability, continuity, generalization and resonance. One of the aims is to understand those adaptations which the target culture continues to allow (Stockwell, 2009: 5). Eliot inspired al-Sayyāb to adopt and adapt foreign symbols alongside his pre-Islamic heritage in his poetry. In a letter to Suhayl Adrīs, al-Sayyāb underlined this issue:

> There is no condition that says that we must use symbols and myths that are connected to us by environment (*muḥīṭ*) or religion, to the exclusion of symbols and myths that are not linked to us by any of those close ties. Anyone who refers to Eliot's great poem *The Waste Land* will find that he uses Eastern pagan myths to express Christian ideas and Western cultural values.
>
> (Translated by DeYoung, 1998: 93)

Indeed, al-Sayyāb often localized (or even personalized) these Christian legends and symbols. Iḥsān Abbās points out that al-Sayyāb and his colleagues 'developed the habit of quoting extensively from western literature' (Goher, 2008: 9). They use 'Christianity as a basis for their poetic discourse', and they appropriated 'western narratives to fit into domestic cultural contexts' (ibid.). For example, al-Sayyāb's *Qāfilat al-Ḍayā'* (The convoy of loss), although inspired by Eliot's 'Journey of the Magi' in many ways (the difficulties of the journey and Christ as a symbol of destination), also differs in many ways.

Al-Sayyāb's poem depicts a contemporaneous and 'real' gloomy image of the aftermath of Palestine's Nakba in 1948 and the 1956 war during which many more Palestinians were dispossessed:

أرأيت قافلة الضَّياع ؟ أما رأيت النازحين؟
الحاملين على الكواهل ، من مجاعات السنين
آثامَ كلّ الخاطئين
النازفين بلا دماءْ
السائرين إلى وراءْ

(Al-Sayyāb, 2005: 39)

Do you see the convoy of loss? Did you see the displaced?
Who carry on their backs, from the famine of the years,
The sins of all sinners
Who are bleeding without blood
Who are walking backwards

Both 'The Journey of the Magi' and *Qāfilat al-Ḍayā'* depict the difficulties of these missions for the people who undertake them. For example, in al-Sayyāb's poem, Christ appears as a Palestinian victim displaced from his homeland:

النار تتبعنا، كأنَّ مدى اللصوص وكل قطّاع الطريقْ
يلهثن فيها بالوباء، كأنَّ ألسنةَ الكلاب
تلتزُّ منها كالمبارد وهي تحفر في جدار النور بابْ
تتصبّب الظلماء كالطوفان منه؛ فلا ترابْ
لِيُعادَ منه الخلق، وانجرف المسيح مع العبابْ
كأنَّ المسيح بجنبه الدامي ومئزره العتيقِ
يسدّ ما حفرته ألسنة الكلاب
فاجتاحه الطوفان: حتى ليس ينزف منه جنبٌ أو جبين
إلا دجىً كالطين تبنى منه دورُ اللاجئين.

(ibid.: 40–1)

The fire follows us, as if all thieves and highway robbers
Breathlessly supply it with pestilence,
As if the tongues of dogs
Stuck to it, like rasps carving a door in the wall of light
From which darkness surges in like a deluge;
There is no soil to restore creation, the Messiah was swept away with the
  torrent
As if his bloody waist and his old apron
Had plugged what the dogs' tongues had dug

And then was overtaken by the flood: so that no side or forehead of his would bleed
Except for darkness like clay from which to build the houses of refugees.

Meanwhile, the Magi interchange with the other Palestinian refugees:

سنظل نضرب كالمجوس نجسّ ميلاد النهار
كم ليلةٍ ظلماء كالرّحم انتظرنا في دجاها
نتلمس الدم في جوانبها ونعصر من قواها
شعّ الوميض على رتاج سمائها مفتاحَ نار
حتى حسبنا أن باب الصبح يفرج – ثم غارَ
وغادر الحرسُ الحدود.

(ibid.: 43)

We will continue to touch the birth of the day like the Magi
How many dark nights, like the uterus we waited in its darkness,
We touch the blood in its sides and squeeze from its strength
The gleam beamed on the sky gate of the nights like a key of fire.
Till we thought that the door of dawn will be released – and then it vanished
And the guards left the border.

This poem is also influenced by Sitwell's central symbol 'Cain', who crucifies and displaces his brother 'Abel' in the manner of 'Christ':

كي يدفنوا 'هابيل' وهو على الصليب ركامُ طين؟
'قابيل أين اخُوك؟ أين اخُوك؟'
جمّعت السّماء
آمادها لتصيح، كوّرت النجوم إلى نداء
'قابيل، أين اخُوك؟'
- يرقدُ في خيام اللاجئين

(ibid.: 39)

In order to bury 'Abel', who is on the cross like rubble of mud?
'Cain, where is your brother? Where is your brother?'
The sky wrapped up its duration
To shout, the stars were wrapped up to a call
'Cain, where is your brother?'
– He sleeps in refugee tents.

Al-Sayyāb keeps the 'biblical background' of this stanza, but he localizes its symbol by using the Qur'ānic phrase 'كوّرت النجوم' and the tents of refugee camps. Thus, 'Cain' becomes a central symbol in al-Sayyāb's poetry, too. Steiner states that there has always been a translational impact on the poet-translator's own work. For example, 'Ted Hughes's adaptation of Seneca's Oedipus in 1968 closely prefigures the idiom of *Crow* published two years later. Through translation of this order the past of other languages and literatures is made native to one's own and radical' (Steiner, 1975: 352). This is very much the case with the poetic and translational interaction between al-Sayyāb and Sitwell; Sitwell's 'Cain' 'prefigures' that of al-Sayyāb. In his book *Shabaḥ Qāyīn Baīn Idith Sītwal wa-Badr Shākir al-Sayyāb* (The shadow of Cain between Edith Sitwell and Badr Shākir al-Sayyāb), 'Alī al-Baṭal argues that the impact of Sitwell on al-Sayyāb started in 1951 when he wrote his long poem *Fajr al-Salām* (Dawn of peace) (al-Baṭal, 1984: 73). In particular, al-Baṭal refers to stanza 8 of this poem:

ظل لقابيل ألقى عبء ظلمته: فحماً يسود البرايا حوله القلقُ
فحماً تصدى له الباغي بمقلته يذكيه منها لظى يخبو ويأتلقُ

. . . .

وانقض- من حيث تهوى الشمس غاربة- ليل من القاصفات السود أو شفقُ
جن الرضيع الذي يحبو وهبَّ على رجليه يعدو ويلوي جسمه العنقُ
من فرط ما طال واسترخى وقد صهرت أعراقه الزرق ناراً فيه تختنقُ

(Al-Sayyāb, 2005: 375–6)

A shadow of Cain threw his burden of darkness: like coal dominates the world with fear.
Coal which the oppresser accosts with his eye, to inflame its blaze which fades and glow

. . . .

. . . .

A night of black bombers or twilight swooped down from where the sun sets
The infant, who crawls, became insane and raised his legs to run but his body is twisted by his neck.
Because he innocently stayed for a long time, therefore the fire which suffocates him has melted his blue veins

In a note to these last three lines, al-Sayyāb, after depicting a terrifying image of the atomic bombings of Hiroshima and Nagasaki, informs us that they describe 'a child whose body was disfigured by the explosion of the atomic bomb' (ibid.: 376). According to al-Baṭal, al-Sayyāb's relationship to Sitwell began with him quoting some of her lines in *Fajr al-Salām*, from there to 'scattering' some of her images in *Al-Asliḥa wa al-Aṭfāl* (The weapons and children) and *Al-Mūmis al-'Amyā* (The blind whore), and later to him 'transmigrating of her soul' in

*Qāfilat al-Ḍayā*ʿ (al-Baṭal: 73). Indeed, as we have just seen, al-Sayyāb develops her symbol 'Cain' to the extent that it almost becomes his own.

Another poem which carries the impact of Sitwell is his *al-Asliḥa wa-al-Aṭfāl* which contains the following:

ومن يُفْهِمُ الأرض أن الصغار
يضيقون بالحفرة الباردة؟

(Al-Sayyāb, 2005: 194)

Who can make the earth understand
That children are restless in the cold holes?

Al-Sayyāb refers here to Sitwell's lines in her 'A Mother to Her Dead Child':

The earth: she is too old for your little body,
. . . .
The earth is so old
She can only think of darkness and sleep, forgetting
That children are restless like the small spring shadows

(Sitwell, 1961: 286)

The stanza, which inspires al-Sayyāb's *al-Asliḥa wa-al- Aṭfāl*, appears in his 1955 translation:

الأرض شمطاء شاخت فما تستطيع
أن تفكر إلا في الظلام والرقاد،
ناسية أن الأطفال
حركون كظلال الربيع الصغيرة

(Translated by al-Sayyāb, n. d. (1955?): 50)

Like 'Cain', 'rain' is a central symbol in the poetics of Sitwell. The English poet extensively symbolizes 'rain' in many poems such as 'Rain', 'The April Rain' and 'Still Falls the Rain'. The last poem, in particular, greatly influenced al-Sayyāb's 'rain' poems. In Sitwell's poem, 'rain' is a metaphor for the bombing raids by Hitler's air force on Britain during the Second World War in which 'Christ' is still crucified and 'Cain' kills his brother 'Abel':

Still falls the Rain –
Dark as the world of man, black as our loss –
Blind as the nineteen hundred and forty nails
Upon the Cross.
. . . .

In the Field of Blood where the small hopes breed and the human brain
Nurtures its greed, that worm with the brow of Cain.

(Sitwell, 1961: 272–3)

In his introduction to *Selected Letters of Edith Sitwell*, Richard Greene regards the bombings in her masterpiece poem, 'Still Falls the Rain' 'as an assault on the body of Christ. The moral extremities of wartime, combined with the still-raw experience of [her friend Hellen] Rootham's death, had led to redefine the centre of her poetry as Christian mystery of redemption (Greene, 1998: xvii).

The extent to which al-Sayyāb developed Sitwell's 'rain' can be seen in the fact that, in Arabic poetry, he became known as 'the poet of rain' especially through his poem *Unshūdat al-Maṭar* (Hymn of the rain). Sayyāb's poem reflects the Iraqi political and social life of the 1950s, and he exhorts his fellow Iraqis to change their miserable situation. Thus, unlike in Sitwell's poem, al-Sayyāb's 'rain' is regarded as a 'revolutionary':

في كل قطرة من المطرْ
حمراء أو صفراء من أجنّةِ الزهر
وكل دمعة من الجياع والعراة
وكل قطرة تراق من دم العبيد
فهي ابتسامٌ في انتظار مبسم جديد
أو حلْمةٌ تورَّدت على فم الوليد
في عالم الغد الفتيّ واهب الحياة!
مطر . . .
مطر . . .
مطر . . .
سيُعشبُ العراق بالمطر

(Al-Sayyāb, 2005: 122–3)

Every drop of rain
whether red or yellow flowers bloomed
and every tear from the hungry and the naked
and every drop spilled from the blood of slaves
Is a smile awaiting fresh lips
Or a rosy nipple on the mouth of the new-born
In tomorrow's young world, life-giver
Rain . . .
Rain . . .

Rain . . .
Iraq will be green with rain.

(Al-Sayyāb, tr. Iskander: 69–70)

In her essay 'A new Reading of Badr Shākir al-Sayyāb's 'Hymn of the Rain'', Terri DeYoung explains that *Unshūdat al-Maṭar* 'is considered to be the first poem in which [al-Sayyāb] successfully integrates political statement with personal experience' (DeYoung, 1993: 39). This poem 'combines Sayyāb's nostalgic longing for his idealized homeland, while in hiding in Kuwait from the Iraqi police, with longing of the people of Iraq for an idealized post-revolutionary future after the fall of the hated Nuri Said regime' (ibid.).

In his essay 'Al-Sayyāb wa-al-Shi'r al-Ṣīnī' (Al-Sayyāb and the Chinese poetry), the Palestinian-Iraqi poet Khālid 'Alī Muṣṭafā suggests that al-Sayyāb's 'rain' was influenced by the Chinese 'rain', via Pound's translations. According to Muṣṭafā, the Chinese poem 'To-En-Mei's "the Unmoving Cloud"' by Tao Yuan Ming (AD 365–427) influences al-Sayyāb's *Unshūdat al-Maṭar* more than Sitwell's 'Still Falls the Rain'. He explains that 'al-Sayyāb 'invests the magical energy of repeating rain' by the Chinese poet in *Unshūdat al-Maṭar*' (Muṣṭafā, 2010: 8–11). Muṣṭafā compares Tao Yuan Ming's poem:

The clouds have gathered, and gathered, and the rain falls and falls,
The eight ply of the heavens are all folded into one darkness,
. . . .
The birds flutter to rest in my tree,
and I think I have heard them saying,
. . . .
He cannot know of our sorrow.

(Pound, 1959: 139–40)

With al-Sayyāb's *Unshūdat al-Maṭar*:

كأنَّ أقواسَ السحابِ تشربُ الغيومْ
وقطرةً فقطرةً تذوبُ في المطر. . .
وكركرَ الأطفالُ في عرائش الكروم،
ودغدغت صمتَ العصافيرِ على الشجر
أنشودةُ المطر
مطر. . .
مطر. . .
مطر. . .

تثاءبَ المساءُ والغيومُ ما تزال
تسحُّ ما تسحّ من دموعها الثقالْ.

(Al-Sayyāb, 2005: 119–20)

Like the bows of mist drinking the clouds
drop by drop melt into rain

And the children babbled among the vine trellises
while the hymn of rain

Tickled the silence of the birds upon the trees

Rain . . .
Rain . . .
Rain . . .

The evening yawned while the clouds remained
pouring what they pour of their heavy tears.

(Al-Sayyāb, tr. Iskander: 66–7)

In the same essay, Muṣṭafā adds that the link between the rain and sadness in *Unshūdat al-Maṭar*, and in other poems by al-Sayyāb such as *al-Nahr wa-al-Mawt* (The river and death), is also attributable to the impact of Chinese poetry (through Pound's translation) (Muṣṭafā, 2010: 5). For example, the gloomy personal image depicted in Li Po's 'Lament of Frontier Guard':

And sorrow, sorrow like rain.
Sorrow to go, and sorrow, sorrow returning,
. . . .
And no children of warfare upon them,
No longer the men for offence and defence.

(Pound, 1959: 132)

Strongly resonates in this stanza of *Unshūdat al-Maṭar*:

أتعلمين أيَّ حزنٍ يبعثُ المطر؟
وكيف تنشجُ المزاريبُ إذا انهمر؟
وكيف يشعرُ الوحيدُ فيه بالضياع؟
بلا انتهاء- كالدمِ المُراق، كالجياع كالحبّ كالأطفالِ كالموتى-
هو المطر

(Al-Sayyāb, 2005: 120–1)

Do you know what sadness the rain brings?
How the gutters weep when it pours?
How the lonely man feels lost?

Without end – like bloodshed, love, children, and the dead –
So is the rain

(Al-Sayyāb, tr. Iskander: 67)

Similarly, al-Sayyāb's translation of 'The River-Merchant's Wife: A Letter' inspired his poem *Raḥal al-Nahār* (The day has gone), which was published in *Manzil al-Aqnān* (The house of slaves) in 1963. We may therefore infer that he wrote it eight years after translating 'The River-Merchant's Wife' in 1955. Both al-Sayyāb's poem and his translation *Risāla min Zawjat Tājiri al-Nahr* are based rhythmically on *al-Kāmil* metre and dominated by the rhyme 'راء rā'. Furthermore, these poems take non-arrival as a primary theme, as we saw previously. The following lines from al-Sayyāb's *Raḥal al-Nahār* reveal the similarities with his translation of stanza 4 of Li Po/Pound's poem:

خصلات شعرك لم يصنها سندباد من الدمار
شربت أجاج الماء حتى شاب أشقرها وغار
ورسائل الحب الكثار
مبتلة بالماءء منطمس بها ألق الوعود
وجلست تنتظرين هائمة الخواطر في دوار
سيعود لا غرق السفين من المحيط الى القرار
سيعود لا حجزته صارخة العواصف في إسار
يا سندباد متى تعود؟

(Al-Sayyāb, 2005: 284)

The curls of your hair were not protected from destruction by Sinbad
They drank water till the blond hairs went grey and sank
And the countless love letters,
Are drenched in water, and the glow of promises wiped out
You sat waiting with your thoughts floating around dizzily
He'll return; the ship won't sink in the seabed
He'll return; the stark storms won't capture him
O, Sinbad, when will you return?

In his essay 'Philip Massinger', Eliot states that 'a good poet will usually borrow from authors remote in time, or alien in language, or diverse in interest' (Eliot, 1960: 125). In my opinion, this applies equally to the poet-translator. As Steiner observes, such a translator 'can modernize not only to induce a feeling of immediacy but in order to advance his own cause as a writer. He will import from abroad convention, models of sensibility, expressive genres which his own language and culture have not yet reached' (Steiner, 1975: 351). His observation also stands as an answer to Saʿdī Yūsuf's question 'Kayfa Tasalla Lī Bū al-Shāʿir Ilaynā?' (How did the poet Li Po slip into us?). In his article, Yūsuf mentions al-Sayyāb's publication in the mid-1950s of his translational works, one of which is Ezra Pound's '*Risāla min Zawjat Tājir al-Nahr*' ('The River-Merchant's Wife: A letter'). At first, Yūsuf (and maybe others) thought this poem belonged to Pound, and then they realized that it was not his own

> but it is Pound's translation from the Japanese language of Li Po's poem which was conveyed in this language [Japanese] from its original. Pound had acted freely, as he pleased, and then he produced a beautiful and moving text. However, there are serious [problems] in this translation. One of them is that the addressee in the original is not a merchant, a merchant of a river, but he is, as we say in Basra and the Gulf, a *nawkhdha*, a river captain of the Yangtze River.
>
> (Yūsuf, 2014c)

Yūsuf underlines the importance of al-Sayyāb's translation of this poem, and how it inspired him to use its themes in his own poetry. In Yūsuf's view, al-Sayyāb's translation 'is luxurious. He complied with the metre, as the more accurate and professional translators usually do. Has anyone noticed the importance of al-Sayyāb's work?' (ibid.). Yūsuf adds that he learnt the poem by rote, and his most well-known poem *Yā Sālim al-Marzūq* (O *Sālim al-Marzūq*) is inspired by Li Po's poem:

يا سالم المرزوق، خذني في السفينةِ، في السفينةْ
خُذْ مقلتي ثمناً، سأفعلُ ما تشاء
إلّا حكاياتِ النساء

(ibid.)

Salim Marzouq, take me on a ship on a ship.
Take my eyes for ransom . . . I'll do what you wish
except what women are supposed to.

(Yūsuf, tr. by Mattawa, 2002: 8)

The above stanza comes from Yūsuf's poem *Ilḥāḥ* (Insistence). In his article 'Skyping with Saadi, Channeling Li Po', Khaled Mattawa opines that Yūsuf 'offers the persona of a young river merchant who is filled with longing for his wife, matching that of Li Po's female speaker'. The poetic 'speaker implores the captain, Salim Marzouq, to take him on his ship' (Mattawa, 2014: 53). According to Mattawa, Yūsuf told him that al-Sayyāb approached 'The River-Merchant's Wife' as if it were Pound's own poem (ibid.: 51). This also underlines the importance of literary translation in, to use Pound's term, 'world poetry'. Li Po's poems with their English and Arabic translations are 'a powerful poetic cocktail that mixed Chinese classicism with Anglophone and Arabic modernist poetics' (ibid.: 52). Yūsuf, through Pound and al-Sayyāb's translations, 'takes the modernist appropriation of Li Po to its logical conclusion. He localizes the tender feelings of Li Po's female speaker and responds to them with a local male voice rising from the marshlands of Basra' (ibid.: 53). The resonance of the ST, first in the poet-translator's own works and then in modern Arabic poetry, creates the most significant cognitive principles of generalization, reflection and contentiousness in the target poetics.

3.4 Concluding remarks

Although al-Sayyāb may not himself have used the term 'discursive' about his translations of Eliot's 'Journey of the Magi', Pound's 'The River-Merchant's Wife: A Letter' and Sitwell's *The Shadow of Cain*, this is precisely how he approached them. In short, al-Sayyāb covers the three contexts of the discourse: situational, verbal and cognitive in his Arabic translations. Situationally, his early involvement with modern world poetry enabled him to establish a new phenomenon in Arabic poetry. The phenomenon goes well beyond merely changing the classical Arabic metrical system to one of 'free verse'. Although the new system is important artistically, it is not enough discursively to establish a new movement. Many Arab poets who preceded al-Sayyāb changed that system, but their work did not create a new poetic school. The explanation for this is that those poets like al-Rīḥānī approached 'world poetry', especially English language poetry, as separate texts, not as discursive works. On the other hand, al-Sayyāb was inspired by the textual richness of the given poems to employ different stylistic techniques in order to translate them on a semantic and linguistic level.

Furthermore, al-Sayyāb substituted the symbols and 'historical' sources of the original poems for parallel 'Arabic' memes in his translations. He was not afraid to transfer (and transform) what is thought to be a 'foreign' discourse.

By translating 'foreign' poems, the Iraqi poet also gave voice to certain 'local' political and social issues which he could not discuss openly in his own poems. Cognitively, al-Sayyāb's translations of these three poems function thematically and stylistically across Arabic modernity from the middle of the twentieth century onwards. In other words, these translations inspired al-Sayyāb and his generation to 'modernize' the 'classical' sources in their poems. Hence we witnessed 'Abel' and 'Christ' as Arab refugees or victims in a 'social-political' context. Moreover, Chinese classical themes, including about 'non-arrival', as in the example of Li Po's poem, found echoes in modern Arabic poetry as a result of Pound's translation. Moreover, using an Arabic metre in a translation is evidence of the capacity of the target prosodic system in translating poetry.

Al-Sayyāb approached these three poets with a clear resolve to breathe fresh air into Arabic poetry. Understanding the techniques of English poetry and comparing them with traditional conventions of Arabic poetry was a key part of al-Sayyāb's contribution to the production of TTs with their own poetic qualities. Another part of his motivation in Arabizing the ST's features was in order to make important world poets more accessible to an Arab readership. 'Domesticizing' the 'foreigner' is a popular strategy in translating poetry. However, al-Sayyāb does not adhere to this or any other strategy consistently, because his approach derives organically from the original rather than being imposed upon it from outside. Thus, his translations are simultaneously classical and modern, local and foreign, often in the one poem. This 'poetic' approach, which was adopted by most of the other Arab poet-translators, reflects the 'organic' relationship between translation and modern poetry.

Conclusion

This study has shown that the translation from English into Arabic of certain modern poems, such as Eliot's *The Waste Land*, Whitman's *Song of Myself*, Pound's "The River-Merchant's Wife: A Letter" and Sitwell's *The Shadow of Cain* contributed greatly to the cause of modernity in Arabic poetry. These poems were translated by the leading Arab poet-translators of their day, namely Adūnīs, al-Khāl, Ṣāyigh, Jabrā, Yūsuf and al-Sayyāb. This study argues, moreover, that the poetic 'affinities' to the works of those Anglo-American poets were the primary reason for selecting them for translation. These 'affinities' occur not only on a textual level but on a sociocultural one. Hence, this study proposes that the Arab modernists approached these American and English poems in a comprehensive manner, rather than as 'divorced' texts. Consequently, this study operated as a discursive analysis. To this end, we decided to analyse the selected translations in three discursive contexts – situational, verbal and cognitive. This approach allowed me to articulate each of the translations in its pre- and post-linguistic contexts, as well as in its linguistic one. In this way, we can contextualize the originals and their Arabic translations within their sociocultural structures. Discourse analysis is recognized today as a valuable means of analysing poetry and studying the relationship between literature as a text and its wider relevance. In addition, by scrutinizing these contexts I have been able to tell a more complete story of Arabic modernity in its translational and its comparative aspects.

These translations led Arab poets to explore beyond the 'rigidity' of the classical Arabic cadenced system, which had lasted for some fifteen centuries. This in turn led to the establishment in the 1940s and 1950s of new schools of modern Arabic poetry, namely free verse and the prose poem. Translation opened Arab modernists' eyes to new poetic possibilities at both stylistic and thematic levels. Thematically, the environment these poets faced in the aftermath of the Second World War encouraged them stylistically to search for a 'flexible' form which could reflect their realities. Like their Western counterparts, Arab poets saw translating poetry as a creative process, and thus they resolved to do it themselves. This resulted in the spread of the phenomenon of poet-translators in modern Arabic literature. Indeed, almost all of the Arab modernist poets who emerged in the middle of the twentieth century were translators. Translation for Arab modernists was not, to use Yao's words, a 'minor mode of literary production or an exercise of apprenticeship . . . it also has its fundamental part of the modernist movement' (Yao, 2002: 6). Thus, this study is a first step on a new path for studies of Arabic poetic modernity in both a translational and a comparative sense.

The debate between classical and modernist writers ran for almost the entire second half of the twentieth century, and translation was at the heart of that discussion. Classical writers resisted translations as they saw them as a threat to their tradition and identity, while modernists welcomed them as a tool to facilitate interaction with the non-Arabic-speaking world and, thereby, to revive and enrich Arabic culture more generally. In the end this debate paved the way for the establishment of a modernist movement in Arabic poetry, and the first two free-verse poems were al-Sayyāb's *Hal Kān Ḥubban*? (Was it love?) and al-Malā'ika's *Al-Kūlīra* (Cholera).

This movement did not stop at free verse, but it opened the door to other formal experiments, including prose poems. From the 1960s onwards, this form became the most popular in poetic and translational Arabic works, in part because of its flexibility, and in part because of the difficulty of rendering the metrical system of the original in another metrical form of the target language. Indeed, rendition of the same cadenced system of the original in a translated poem is impossible, especially between different languages such as Arabic and English. That said, an 'untranslatable' system can be partially manipulated and used as a 'mimetic strategy' by keeping some of the original in the translated text. Moreover, Arab modernists used their metrical system in their translations, but in free verse form. Questions surrounding the acceptability of these translational strategies have always created a valuable dialogue about the creative freedom of translators, and in particular of poet-translators.

As a globally known poet-translator, Pound's works were at the heart of this dialogue. His approach emphasized that translation can be as creative as poetry itself. Furthermore, his Chinese translations demonstrated that he used not only the linguistic text but also the wider cultural potential of the verse when conveying such poems in English. Thus, his approach dealt equally with both the textual and non-textual features, and therein lies the reason for the impact of Pound's translational works on other cultures.

In the Introduction, I highlighted the importance of the translational and intercultural exchange in both West and East. The reaction of some classic Arab scholars towards translation was also included here. The relationship between modernity and translation was discussed in both systems: Western and Arabic. The Introduction also considered the phenomenon of the 'poetic affinity' among world poets. This phenomenon is one of the main motives that poets translate other poets or sometimes translate each other.

In Chapter 1, we showed the importance of the translations into Arabic of T. S. Eliot's writings, most notably his poem *The Waste Land*. This poem was translated three times by the modernist poet-translators: Adūnīs-Khāl, 'Awaḍ and Ṣāyigh. These translations played a crucial role in shaping the free-verse school in Arabic culture in the 1940s and 1950s. In sum, modern Arabic poetry is inconceivable without these translations. Situationally, modernity was the common motivation for those Arab poet-translators in tackling Eliot's poem, because of its unconventional form and language. The form adopted by Eliot allowed for multiple techniques to reflect and unify fragmented subjects into a single central theme and this was what attracted Arab modernists to it. There are other analogical elements between *The Waste Land* and major Arabic poems. The 'fall' of Western civilization in the aftermath of the First World War was thematically and stylistically developed by Arab modernists to depict the catastrophes of Palestine and the Second World War.

Verbally, the Arabic translations of *The Waste Land* differ in their outcomes. 'Awaḍ's explanatory approach tended to make the original seem more distant by adding words. His approach also led him into 'unpoetic' lexical choices, as he used archaic and classical words to render a modern poem. 'Awaḍ tried to be interpretive, but interpretation should not permit us to amend the original without good reason. The interpretive approach requires a systematic decoding of the original in order to reveal its full content in the received culture. As this study argues, the 'invisible' possibilities of the original are beyond the linguistic level of the text. They are encapsulated in the non-textual features. By ignoring this discursive fact, 'Awaḍ applied a 'dangerous' method that threatened the poetics of the translated text. Thus, he produced an old-fashioned text with ready-made phrases, and this not only affected the modernity of the original but also failed cognitively to create modern poetic generalization and continuity in Arabic culture.

On the other hand, Adūnīs-Khāl's translation demonstrated that they were well aware of Eliot's modernist agenda and hence it functions poetically on its own in Arabic. Forcing the source poem to say something that is not in its own texture would have resulted in a disfigured poem in the target culture. Therefore, Adūnīs-Khāl mostly maintained the original features of *The Waste Land* in their *Al-'Arḍ al-Kharāb*. They conveyed the beauty of the ST verbally and stayed 'close' to its poetics in their lexical and stylistic choices. These new choices were widely copied in modern Arabic poetry. Adūnīs-Khāl's translation set this English poem firmly in the realm of Arabic poetry. In their *Al-'Arḍ al-Kharāb*, Adūnīs-Khāl sought to preserve the original and to protect Eliot's work from interpretations which they deemed irrelevant. Their strategy, to use Borges's words, 'created a beauty all its own' (Borges, 2000: 71).

Like Adūnīs-Khāl, Ṣāyigh recognized the importance of introducing Eliot's modernity to Arabic culture. His *Al-'Arḍ al-Kharāb* followed *The Waste Land* rather closely and tried to convey Eliot's poetics in Arabic. Eliot's poetics are also exemplified in Ṣāyigh's own writings: his use of free verse, and his 'boldness' in including different linguistic levels in a single poem. The new features soon appeared in the works of other Arab poets. Al-Sayyāb is a great (if not the greatest) proponent of Eliot's techniques in his own poetry, in particular in *Unshūdat al-Maṭar*, which is considered to be the Arabic equivalent of *The Waste Land*.

Chapter 2 explored other Arabic translational adventures, notably the Arabic translations of Whitman's *Song of Myself* which were made by Jabrā, al-Khāl and Yūsuf. Situationally, as in the case of Eliot's *The Waste Land*, modernity was the main but not the only reason for tackling this poem. Its novel form and language encouraged Arab poets to further stylistic experiments such as the prose poem. Over and beyond this, Yūsuf viewed the poem as a manifesto for justice and humanity. In his translational notes, he acknowledged that he was influenced by the poem's 'human' themes rather than its stylistic features. Nevertheless, in practice, he succeeded in conveying Whitman's language in all its variations, including the Sufi style, which dominates almost the entire poem. In sum, the experimental styles and themes of *Song of Myself* with their Arabic responses inspired Arab modernists to adopt new techniques, even including some features not typically regarded as literary.

In Chapter 2, we also focused on the reasons why Arab modernists were inspired by Eliot's writings first, and only later by Whitman's poems, even though the latter preceded the former by half a century. More surprisingly perhaps, some Arab romantic writers of the *al-Mahjar* school had first alighted on Whitman's work at the beginning of the twentieth century. It is our contention that their approach to his writings was not discursive. Al-Rīḥānī, for instance, who introduced some of Whitman's poetic concepts to Arabic culture at that time, opted not to utilize them in practice. Moreover, Eliot's critiques taught these Arab modernists how to approach and benefit from the greats of world poetry. Eliot provided the means for them (and many other world poets) to appreciate their own heritage, and he showed them how to modernize that heritage using and developing the techniques of leading poets, including Whitman, Baudelaire and Pound.

In Chapter 3, we selected al-Sayyāb's translational works as a case study. Translation was for him at the heart of his poetics, as it was for many other world modernists, and it was closely interrelated with his own creative output. He translated into Arabic poems from a host of different languages via English translations. Moreover, in the mid-1950s, al-Sayyāb used translation rather than his own poetry to express himself, as a 'mask' from behind which to criticize the Iraqi government of the day. In his translations of Eliot's 'Journey of the Magi', Pound's "The River-Merchant's Wife: A Letter" and Sitwell's *The Shadow of Cain*, al-Sayyāb experimented with different strategies and forms. As the 'first' pioneer of free verse in Arabic poetry, he applied it with the *al-Kāmil* metre when he translated Pound's text. It was a demonstration of the translational capability of Arabic prosody. The aim of these free-verse pioneers was to shake the sociocultural structure of Arabic society by challenging what had been considered a 'sacred' poetic form, namely the *qaṣīda*. In his translations of Eliot's and Sitwell's texts, which were translated as prose poems, al-Sayyāb localized many of the 'foreign' symbols of the originals in order to relate them to Arab life. He wanted to integrate them into the target culture. In other words, he applied this strategy not only for translational reasons but also for creative and cultural ends. Thus, 'Christ', 'Magi', 'Abel' and 'Cain' were utilized cognitively alongside Islamic and ancient Iraqi myths. In the poems of the Arab modernists, such symbols were updated and domesticated to represent ordinary Arabs in the twentieth century suffering from the likes of 'Cain' and the greedy 'Dives'.

To conclude, this study demonstrated that on a cultural level 'modernity' was the main reason why Arab poets opted to translate these modern poems into Arabic. On a creative level too, they felt 'affinity' for these poems. The resulting translations are verbally varied owing to the different approaches and strategies adopted by the various poet-translators. Inevitably, too, the translations reflect the abilities and talents of the poet-translators. Cognitively, these translations shaped Arabic modernity; they posed questions of the target poetic heritage; and they produced novel poetic languages, forms and themes. Most importantly the new features became more commonly utilized and echoed in Arabic poetry. This explains why certain poems and translations have influenced modern Arabic poetry more than others. It also answers my research question in its three principles: why and how Arab modernists translated the selected poems, and their impact on modern Arabic poetry. In addition to these 'main' translational principles, there are others which can be summarized in the following propositions:

1. These Arabic translations revealed the 'centrality' of these poems within their own system, and they conveyed this 'centrality' to Arabic culture. However, they would not have 'occupied', to use Lefevere's terms, 'the same position in the target culture', had they been tackled by non-modernist poets, as we saw in the case of al-Riḥānī with Whitman.
2. Arab poet-translators were aware of the prestige to be gained by linking themselves to the world's leading modernist poets such as Eliot, Pound and Whitman.
3. They were also able to canonize what until then had not been canonized in their own system. A translation offered a means to make something which was at first unnoticeable function powerfully in the target culture, as we saw with al-Sayyāb's translation of Sitwell.
4. As well as using these translations to enrich their own poetics, Arab modernists also viewed them, to use Birsanu's words, 'as a means to express the aesthetic agenda' of the new school (Birsanu, 2011: 179).
5. Translating these English poems encouraged Arab modernists to become actively involved in the source culture, alongside their own. They used these translations to critique both cultures, as we saw in particular with 'Awaḍ, al-Sayyāb and Yūsuf.
6. Translating the selected poems helped Arab modernists to establish a new poetic system in Arabic culture. Translating Eliot, in particular,

provided them with new techniques by which they could widen their sources, not only for textual material but also for inspiration.

7. Indeed, Arab modernists were empowered to move beyond conventional Arabic literary practice to explore new territories which had not already been mapped by their tradition. This expanded not only their own poems but the very stylistic dimensions of the Arabic literary scene as a whole.
8. For some Arab modernists, translation was, to use Pound's terms, an 'elaborate mask' to express themselves through other world poets. For others, it was an 'aesthetic search' which enabled them to fulfil and complete their own poetics. These two concepts, in particular, are reflected in al-Sayyāb's translational works.
9. The translational experience itself, in its concepts of politics and aesthetics, provoked a deep sociocultural view of the literary text. In other words, translation became an explicit tool with which they could question the received culture, politically and artistically. In this sense, these translations created a 'critical' culture as well as a creative one.
10. As an ongoing project, we can trace the impact of translation on most Arab contemporary writers. Most importantly, these pioneering translations opened the eyes of the new generations to the importance of translation for their own poetics.

Notes

Preface

1 An extract from this thesis was published in 2013 in Kufa Review, 2 (1).

Introduction

1 (s) is added to the translation because it comes in a plural form of 'آداب' in the original (see: *Kitāb al-Ḥayawān*, 1965: 75).
2 (not) is added to the translation because it comes in a negative form in the original: 'وبعضها ما انتقص شيئاً' (ibid.).
3 I only mention my additions to quotations. However, I do not mention insignificant changes (e.g. pronouns to noun). As for ellipses, I only mention those that are in the original.
4 Translations from Arabic into English are mine unless otherwise stated.

Chapter 1

1 This poem provided the basis on which Eliot was described as a homosexual poet by some of his critics such as John Peter in 'A New Interpretation of *The Waste Land*' (1952/1969) and James E. Miller Jr. in *T. S. Eliot's Personal Waste Land: Exorcism of the Demons* (1977) and 'T. S. Eliot's "Uranian Muse": The Verdenal Letters'. In the latter, which included Pound's poem, Miller interprets Eliot's relationship with his French friend Jean Verdenal as a homosexual one and he argues that this is clearly reflected in section IV of *The Waste Land*. However, Arab poet-translators did not accept this interpretation, either because they did not want to limit the readings of such a complex poem or because homosexuality is a taboo subject in Arabic culture.
2 Eliot's poem was also translated by other translators (we can call them critic-translators to distinguish them from poet-translators). Those critic-translators are Fā'iq Mattā (1966/1991); Yūsuf S. al-Yūsuf (1975/1986); 'Abd al-Wāḥid Lu'lu'a (1980/1995); Māhir Shafīq Farīd (1996); Muhammed Abdulsalām Manṣūr (2001), which is the only translation I have not seen yet; 'Adnān Abdulla and

Ṭalāl Abd al-Rāḥmān Ismā'īl (2006), which is a collaborative verse translation done by a poet and a scholar; Nabīl Rāghib (2011); Abdul Sattar Jawad (2014). Partially, *The Waste Land* was approached by many Arab translators and poets such as Jabrā who translated the opening and the ending stanzas of "The Burial of the Dead" (Jabrā, 1982: 195–6). Some of these works are used here to clarify certain translational issues.

3 This translation was sent by 'Awaḍ in 1964 to *Shi'r*, but the journal was suspended at that time and this delayed its publication until 1968. It was also published in *Fī al-Adab al-Ingilīzī al-Ḥadīth* (On modern English literature) in 1987, with the preface signed by 'Awaḍ as follows: Cairo: 13/5/1950. It seems that 'Awaḍ published some sections of the poem in the 1950s version of his book, and then when he translated the full poem in 1964, he sent it to *Shi'r*. The same translation also appears in the second edition of his book in 1987.

4 The impact of Andrewes on Eliot's works, and on his poem 'Journey of the Magi' in particular, will be explored in Chapter 3.

5 We will explore this issue in Chapter 3, which is devoted to al-Sayyāb's translational works.

6 This attempt is more complicated than his direct translation of St. John Perse's *Anabase* into English which influenced his poem 'Journey of the Magi', as we shall discuss in Chapter 3.

7 This is a mistake which was repeated in both versions of his translation. The correct form is شُطْآن.

8 For the Qur'ānic translations, I am using 'Abdallah Yūsuf 'Alī's *The Holy Qur'ān* unless otherwise stated.

9 As will be studied in Chapter 3, al-Sayyāb translated a poem by Pound using the Arabic metre *al-Kāmil*.

10 'Abd al-Ṣabūr also translated Eliot's 'The Love Song of J. Alfred Prufrock' and *The Hollow Men*.

11 Al-Sayyāb's relationship to the Iraqi Communist Party and his skilfulness of localizing the Western poetic techniques and themes will be studied in further detail in Chapter 3.

Chapter 2

1 This poem was translated by the Iraqi poet-translator Sargūn Būluṣ and published in *Shi'*r in October 1968. Ginsburg's famous poem 'Howl', which is considered by many to be a good example of the use of Whitman's style, was also translated by Būluṣ and published in *al-Karmal* in January 1992.

Chapter 3

1 Perse's poem was also translated into Arabic by Adūnīs in the middle of 1970s. That said, Adūnīs first tackled Perse in the middle of 1950s when he translated the ninth canto of Perse's poem *Amers* (Seamarks) under the title *Ḍayyiqah hiy al-Marākib*. In a lecture delivered in French at the Saint-John Perse Foundation in October 1993, then published in *Souffle de Perse* magazine in the same year, Adūnīs describes the importance of his translation, although controversial, in modern Arabic poetry:

> My translation [of *Anabase*] was discussed and criticized by many poets and translators. Some of them condemned it completely and described it as an execution of Perse's text . . . other went so far to say that they prefer the translation to the original. Here, I would like to add that this translation had become a central element in the conflict which took place then among various poetic trends, and among the poets and critics themselves.
>
> (Cited in Jihād, 2011: 529–30)

2 According to the Oxford English Dictionary, the term 'Pampean' is geological: Designating or relating to a series of sedimentary deposits of the Pleistocene epoch present across much of the pampas of South America, and the fauna (especially mammals) extant during their period of deposition.

Bibliography

Arabic*

Abbās, I., 1992. *Badr Shākir al-Sayyāb: Dirāsa fī Ḥayātih wa-Shiʿrih*. Bayrūt: Al-Muʾassasa al-ʿArabiyya lil-Dirāsāt wa-al-Nashr.

Abd al-Raḥmān, Ṭ., 2013. *Fiqh al-Falsafa: 1 al-Falsafa wa-Tarjama*. Bayrūt and al-Dār al-Bayḍāʾ: Al-Markaz al-Thaqāfī al-ʿArabī.

ʿAbd al- Ṣabūr, Ṣ., 1969. *Ḥayātī fī al-Shiʿr*. Bayrūt: Dār al-ʿAwda.

Adūnīs, ʿA. S., 1995. 'Bayān al-Ḥadātha'. In M. L. Yūsufī (ed.), *Al-Bayānāt*. Tūnis: Sarās. pp. 21–76.

Adūnīs, ʿA. S., 2010. 'Maḥmūd Darwīsh Shāʿir al-Muṣālaḥa ʿArifa Kayfa Yaruthinī wa-Jamāhīriyyatih Kānat Ḍidduh' part 4. *Jarīdat al-Ḥayāt* [online] 22 March 2010. Available from: http://www.alhayat.com/Details/120774 [Accessed 18 April 2017].

ʿAllūsh. N., 2005. 'Introduction'. In B. S. al-Sayyāb, *Dīwān Badr Shākir al-Sayyāb*. Bayrūt: Dār al-ʿAwda. pp. 3–87.

Aʿshā, M. i. Q., (n.d.). 'Al-Qaṣīda al-Thāmina lil-Aʿshā'. In Y. b. ʿA. Tabrīzī, *Sharḥ al-Qaṣāʾid al-ʿAshr lil-Tabrīzī*. Bayrūt: Dār al-Jīl. pp. 288–307.

ʿAwaḍ. L., 1974. *Thaqāfatunā fī Muftarq al-Ṭuruq*. Bayrūt: Dār al-Ādāb.

ʿAwaḍ. L., 1987. *Fī al-Adab al-Injilīzī al-Ḥadīth*. Al-Qāhira: Al-Hayʾa al-Miṣriyya al-ʿĀmma lil-Kitāb.

ʿAwaḍ, L., 1989. *Blūtūlānd: wa-Qaṣāʾid min Shiʿr al-Khāṣṣa*. Al-Qāhira: al-Hayʾah al-Miṣriyya al-ʿĀmma lil-Kitāb.

Azamah, N., 2004. *Badr Shākir al-Sayyāb wa- Idith Sītwal: Dirāsa Muqārana*. Dimashq: Dār ʿAlāʾ al-Din.

ʿAzzāwī, F., 2007. *Al–ʾAʿmāl al-Shiʿriyya*, V 2. Bayrūt: Manshūrāt al-Jamal.

Bashshūr, M., 1957. 'Arb 'ā' al-Ramād'. *Shiʿr* 1 (2): 51–66.

Basṛī, ʿA. D., 1966. *Badr Shākir al-Sayyāb Rāʾid al-Shʾir al-Ḥurr*. Baghdād: Dār al-Jumhūriyya.

Baṭal, ʿA., 1984. *Shabaḥ Qāyīn Baīn Idith Sītwal wa-Badr Shākir al-Sayyāb*. Bayrūt: Dār al-Andalus.

* I have used the original names of the Western poets in their Arabic translations. Likewise, I have kept the Arabic names in transliterations of the Arab poets in their English translations. I have used the definite article *al* in names of the Arab authors in the text but I omitted it from the bibliography.

Bayātī, 'A. W., 1995. *Al-A'māl al-Shi'riyya*. Bayrūt: Al-Mu'assasa al-'Arabiyya lil-Dirāsāt wa-al-Nashr.

Bayātī, 'A. W., 1998. *Kitāb al-Mukhtārāt*. M. Maẓūlm (ed.). Bayrūt: Dār al-Kunūz al-'Adabiyya.

Bullāṭa, 'Ī., 1981. *Badr Shākir al-Sayyāb: Ḥayātuhu wa-shi'ruhu*. Bayrūt: Dār al-Nahār.

Darwīsh, M., 2004. 'Sa'dī Yūsuf fī al-Sab'īn'. *Al-Karmal* (81): 1.

'Dhū al-Ḥuḍūr: Ti. As. Alyūt 1888-1965', 1967. *Shi'r* 9 (33–4): 189.

Eliot, T. S., (n.d.) [1955?]. 'Journey of the Magi' [Riḥlat al-Majūs] Translated from English by B. S. al-Sayyāb. In B. S. al-Sayyāb, *Qaṣā'id Mukhtāra min al-Shi'r al-'Ālamī al-Ḥadīth* (s. l.): (s. n.). pp. 9–12.

Eliot, T. S., 1958. 'The Waste Land' [Al- Arḍ al-Kharāb]. Translated from English by 'A. S. Adūnīs and Y. al- Khāl. In Y. al-Khāl (ed.), *Ti. As. Alyūt: Tarjamāt min al-Shi'r al-Ḥadīth*. Bayrūt: Dār Majallat Shi'r. pp. 129–48.

Eliot, T. S., 1968. 'The Waste Land' [Al- Arḍ al-Kharāb]. Translated from English by L. 'Awaḍ, *Shi'r* (40): 103–24.

Eliot, T. S., 2006. 'The Waste Land' [Al- Arḍ al-Kharāb]. Translated from English by A. K. Abdullah and Ṭ. 'A. Ismā'īl. In A. K. Abdullah and Ṭ. 'A. Ismā'īl, *Al- Arḍ al-Kharāb: Tarjama Shi'riyya ma'a Dirāsa Taḥlīliyya*. Al– Qāhira: Al-Sharika al-'Ālamiyya. pp. 24–129.

Eliot, T. S., 2017. 'The Waste Land' [Al- Arḍ al-Kharāb]. Translated from English by T. Ṣāyigh. In T. Ṣāyigh, *Ti. As. Alyūt al- Arḍ al-Kharāb ma'a al-Tafsīrāt al-Naqdiyya al-Ukhrā*. Tahqīq wa-Dirāsat M. Maẓlūm. Bayrūt: Manshūrāt al-Jamal. pp. 85–128.

Ibn al-'Arabī, M. A., 2005. *Tarjumān al-Ashwāq*. 'A. Al-Maṣṭāwī (ed.). Bayrūt: Dār al-Ma'rifa.

Ibn Manẓūr, M. i. M., 1955. *Lisān al-'Arab*. Bayrūt: Dār Ṣādir.

Jabrā, J. I., 1982. *Al-Ḥurriyya wa-al-Ṭūfān: Dirāsāt Naqdīyya*. Bayrūt: Al-Mu'assasa al-'Arabiyya lil-Dirāsāt wa-al-Nashr.

Jāḥiẓ, 'A. i. B., 1965. 'Kitāb al-Ḥayawān'. A. S. Ḥārūn (ed.). Miṣr: Sharikat wa-Maṭba'at Muṣṭafā al-Bābī al-Ḥalabī wa-'Awlādh.

Jihād, K., 2011. *Ḥuṣṣat al-Gharīb*. M. A. Ḥannā (tr.). Bayrūt: Manshūrāt al-Jamal.

Khāl, Y., 1958a. 'Introduction'. In Y. al-Khāl (ed.), *Tī. As. Alyūt: Tarjamāt min al-Shi'r al-Ḥadīth*. Bayrūt: Dār Majallat Shi'r. pp. 3–4.

Khāl, Y., 1958b. 'Walt Wītmān: Khams Qaṣā'id'. *Shi'r* 2 (7–8): 44–56.

Khāl, Y., 1958c. 'Preface'. In Y. al-Khāl, *Dīwān al-Shi'r al-Amīrkī*. Bayrūt: Dār Majallat Shi'r. pp. 7–10.

Khāl, Y., 1979. *Al-A'māl al-Shi'rīyah al-Kāmilah*. Bayrūt: Dār al-'Awda lil-Ṭibā'a wa-al-Nashr.

Khāl, Y., 1981. 'Preface'. In 'Ī. Bullāṭa, *Badr Shākir al-Sayyāb: Ḥayātuh wa-Shi'ruh*. Bayrūt: Dār al-Nahār. pp. 11–15.

Lu'lu'a, ʿA., 1995. *Ti. As. Alyūt, al- Arḍ al-Yabāb: Al-Shāʿir wa al-Qaṣīda*. Bayrūt: Al-Mu'assasa al-'Arabiyya lil-Dirāsāt wa-al-Nashr.

Madfa'ī, Q., 2015. 'Muqābala ma' Qaḥṭān al-Madfa'ī' by Shākir al-'Anbārī. Baghdād: *Jarīdat al-Madā, Mulḥaq ʿUrāqī'ūn* 12 (3262) 15 January: 8–9.

Mazlūm, M., 2017. 'Bain Makhṭūṭatay Alyūt wa-Tawfīq Ṣāyigh'. In T. Ṣāyigh, *Ti. As. Alyūt al- Arḍ al-Kharāb maʿ al-Tafsīrāt al-Naqdiyya al-Ukhrā*. Tahqīq wa-dirāst M. Mazlūm. Bayrūt: Manshūrāt al-Jamal. pp. 5–73.

Musṭafā, K. 'A., 2010. 'Al-Sayyāb wa-al-Shi'r al-Ṣīnī'. *Star Times* [online], 1 November 2010. Available from http://www.startimes.com/?t=25942767 [Accessed 6 December 2016].

Na'īma, M., 1964. *Al-Ghirbāl*. Bayrūt: Dār Ṣādir.

Perse, S. J., 1978. *Al-Aʿmāl al-Shiʿriyya al-Kāmila*. 'A. S., Adūnīs (tr.). Dimashq: Manshūrāt Wizārat al-Thaqāfa.

Pound, E. n. d. [1955?]. 'A Letter from the Wife of the River Merchant' [Risāla min Zawjat Tājir al-Nahr] Translated from English by B. S. al-Sayyāb. In B. S. al-Sayyāb, *Qaṣā'id Mukhtāra min al-Shiʿr al-'Ālamī al-Ḥadīth*. (s. l.): (s. n.). pp. 13–16.

Razzūq, A., 1959. 'Fi Al-Naqd'. *Shiʿr* 3 (9): 86–98.

Ṣāyigh, T., 1955. 'Al- Shi'r al-Ingilīzī Mu'āṣir'. *Al-Ādāb* 3 (1): 92–6.

Ṣāyigh, T., 1990. *Al-Aʿmāl al-Kāmila: Al-Majmūʿa al-Shiʿriyya*. London: Riad el-Rayyes.

Sayyāb, B. S., (n.d.) [1955?]. *Qaṣā'id Mukhtāra min al-Shiʿr al-'Ālamī al-Ḥadīth*. (s. l.): (s. n.).

Sayyāb, B. S., 1986. *Kitāb al-Sayyāb al-Nathrī*. Ḥ. Ghurfī (ed.). Fās: Manshūrāt Majallat al-Jawāhir.

Sayyāb, B. S., 1994. *Rasā'il al- Sayyāb*. M. al-Sāmarrā'ī (ed.). Bayrūt: Al-Mu'assasa al-'Arabiyya lil-Dirāsāt wa-al-Nashr.

Sayyāb, B. S., 2005. *Dīwān Badr Shākir al-Sayyāb*. Bayrūt: Dār al-'Awda.

Sayyāb, B. S., 2007. *Kuntu Shuyūʿīyan*. W. K. A. Ḥasan (ed.). Baghdād: Manshūrāt al-Jamal.

Sayyāb, B. S., 2012. *Badr Shākir al-Sayyāb: Aṣwāt al-Shāʿir al-Mutarjim*. Ḥ. Tawfīq (ed.). Duḥa: Wizārat al-Thaqāfa wa-al-Funūn wa-Turāth.

Sayyāb, B. S., 2013. *Min Nuṣūṣ al-Sayyāb al-Adabiyya al-Mutarjama*. K. 'A Muṣṭafā (ed.). Baghdād: Dār al-Shu'ūn al-thaqāfiyya al-'Āmma.

Shi'r, 1957. Musāhimūn fī Hādha al-'Adad. 1 (3): 117.

Shuraiḥ, Maḥmūd., 1989. *Tawfīq Ṣāyigh: Sīrat Shāʿir wa-Manfā*. London: Riad el-Rayyes.

Sitwell, E., 2013. 'The Shadow of Cain' [Shabaḥ Qābīl]. Translated from English by B. S. al-Sayyāb. In K. 'A. Muṣṭafā (ed.), *Min Nuṣūṣ al-Sayyāb al-Adabiyya al-Mutarjama*, B. S. Al- Sayyāb. Baghdād: Dār al-Shu'ūn al-thaqāfiyya al-'Āmma. pp. 95–104.

Suhrawardī, Y. i. H., 2005. *Dīwān al-Suhrawardi al-Maqtūl*. K. M. al-Shaybī (ed.). Baghdād: Maṭba'at al-Rafāh.

Tawfīq, Ḥ., 2012. 'Introduction'. In Ḥ. Tawfīq (ed.), *Badr Shākir al-Sayyāb: Aṣwāt al-Shā'ir al-Mutarjim*, B. S. al-Sayyāb. Duḥa: Wizārat al-Thaqāfa wa-al-Funūn wa-Turāth. pp. 7–44.

Yūsuf, S., 2010. 'Preface'. In S. Yūsuf (tr.), *Awrāq al-'Ushb*, W. Whitman. Bayrūt: Manshūrāt al-Jamal. pp. 5–23.

Yūsuf, S., 2014a. *Al–' A'māl al-Shi'riyya*, V 4. Bayrūt: Manshūrāt al-Jamal.

Yūsuf, S., 2014b. 'Udā'ib al-Qāri'', Interview with Bayat. Baghdād: *Majallat Bayat* (4): 65–9.

Yūsuf, S., 2014c. 'Kayfa Tasalla Lī Bū al-Shā'ir Ilaynā?', *Sa'dī Yūsuf's website* [online], 12. October 2014. Available from: http://www.saadiyousif.com/new/index.php ?option=com_content&view=article&id=1797:--q----q--&catid=19:---&Itemid=28 [Accessed 2 March 2016].

Yūsuf, S. Y., 1986. *Tī. As. Ilyūt*. 'Ammān: Dār Manārāt lil-Nashr.

Whitman, W., 1958. 'Song of Myself' [Ughniyyat Nafsī]. Translated from English by Y. al-Khāl. In Y. al-khāl, 1958b. 'Walt Wītmān: Khams Qaṣā'id'. *Shi'r* 2 (7–8): 44–56.

Whitman, W., 1982. 'Song of Myself' [Ughniyyat Nafsī]. Translated from English by J. I. Jabrā. In J. I. Jabrā, 1982. *Al-Ḥurriyya wa-al-Ṭufān: Dirāsāt Naqdiyya*. Bayrūt: Al-Mu'assasat al-'Arabiyya lil-Dirāsāt wa-al-Nashr. pp. 179–88.

Whitman, W., 2006. *Ughniyyat Nafsī*. 'Ā Ismā'il (tr.). Dimashq: al-Takwīn.

Whitman, W. 2010. *Awrāq al-'Ushb*. S . Yūsuf (tr.). Bayrūt: Manshūrāt al-Jamal.

English

'Abd al-Ḥai, M., 1982. *Tradition and English and American Influence in Arabic Romantic Poetry: A Study in Comparative Literature*. London: Ithaca Press.

Abdulla, A. K., 2011. 'On Translating Poetry into Arabic, with Special Reference to T. S. Eliot'. In *Other Words*: *The British Centre for Literary Translation* (23): 1–27. [online] Available from: https://www.researchgate.net/publication/281931592 [Accessed 2 August 2017].

Abel, R., 1973. 'The Influence of St.-John Perse on T. S. Eliot'. *Contemporary Literature* 14 (2): 213–39.

Adonis, 'A. S., 1990. *An Introduction to Arab Poetics*. C. Cobham (tr.). London: Saqi Books.

Adūnīs, 'A. S., 2004. *A Time between Ashes and Roses: Poems: Bilingual Edition*. S. M. Toorawa (tr.). Syracuse and New York: Syracuse University Press.

Allen, G. W., 1997. *A Reader's Guide to Walt Whitman*. Syracuse and New York: Syracuse University Press.

Alegria, F., 1995. 'The Worm Fence: Section 5 of 'Song of Myself', Whitman in Translation: A Seminar'. *Walt Whitman Quarterly Review* 13 (1): 158.

Asfour, J. M., 1992. *When the Words Burn: An Anthology of Modern Arabic Poetry: 1945–1987*. Cairo: The American University in Cairo Press.

Asseloneau, R., 1995. 'Whitman in Portugal'. In G. W. Allen and E. Folsom (eds), *Walt Whitman and the World*. Iowa City: University of Iowa Press. pp. 147–8. Available from: ProQuest Ebook Central. https://ebookcentral.proquest.com/lib/soasebocks/reader.action?docID=836768&ppg=160 [Accessed 4 April 2016].

'Azzāwī, F., 2003. *Miracle Maker*. K. Mattawa (tr.). Rochester and New York: BOA Editions Ltd.

Badawi, M. M., 1975. *A Critical Introduction to Modern Arabic Poetry*. Cambridge: Cambridge University Press.

Badenhausen, R., 2005. *T. S. Eliot and the Art of Collaboration*. Cambridge: Cambridge University Press.

Baker, M., 1992. *In Other Words: A Coursebook on Translation*. London and New York: Routledge.

Baldick, J., 1989. *Mystical Islam*. London: I. B. Tauris & Co Ltd.

Bassnett, S., 1998. 'Transplanting the Seed: Poetry and Translation'. In S. Bassnett and A. Lefevere, *Constructing Cultures: Essays on Literary Translation*. Clevedon: Multilingual Matters. pp. 57–75.

Bassnett, S., 2002. *Translation Studies*. London and New York: Routledge.

Berman, A., 2004. 'Translation and the Trials of the Foreign'. In L. Venuti, 2004 (ed.), *The Translation studies Reader*. London and New York: Routledge. pp. 276–89.

Birsanu, R., 2011. 'T. S. Eliot and the Modernist Approach to Translation'. *Scientia Traductionis* (9): 179–90.

Blake, W., 1988. *William Blake*. Oxford and New York: Oxford University Press.

Bloom, H., 2001. *How to Read and Why*. London: Fourth Estate.

Bloom, H., 2003. 'Introduction'. In H. Bloom (ed.), *Walt Whitman*. Broomall, PA: Chelsea House Publishers. pp. 1–4.

Bloom, H., 2005. *The Art of Reading Poetry*. New York: HarperCollins Publishers.

Boase-Beier, J., 2006. *Stylistic Approaches to Translation*. Manchester, UK; Kinderhook, [New York], USA: St. Jerome Pub.

Borges, J. L., 1975. 'Walt Whitman: Man and Myth'. *Critical Inquiry* 1 (4): 707–18.

Borges, J. L., 2000. *This Craft of Verse*. C. A. Mihailescu (tr.). Cambridge, MA and London: Harvard University Press.

Boullata, I. (1973). 'The Beleaguered Unicorn: A Study of Tawfīq Ṣāyigh'. *Journal of Arabic Literature* (4): 69–93.

Breslin, J. E. B., 1985. *William Carlos Williams: An American Artist.* Chicago and London: The University of Chicago Press.

Brown, S., 1995. 'The Case of Fernando Pessoa'. In G. W. Allen and E. Folsom (eds), *Walt Whitman and the World.* Iowa City: University of Iowa Press. pp. 148–53. Available from: ProQuest Ebook Central. https://ebookcentral.proquest.com/lib/soasebooks/reader.action?docID=836768&ppg=160 [Accessed 4 April 2016].

Buil, A. M., 2016. 'Poet-translators as Double Link in the Global Literary System'. *Translation and Interpreting Studies* 11 (3): 398–415.

Casale, F. D., 2009. *How to Write about Walt Whitman.* New York: Infobase Publishing.

Clej, A., 1997. 'The Debt of the Translator: An Essay on Translation and Modernism'. *Symplokē* 5 (1/2): 7–26.

Colla, E., 2015. 'Badr Shākir al-Sāyyb, Cold War Poet'. *Middle Eastern Literatures* 18 (3): 247–63.

Constantine, D., 2011. 'Serves Abroad: Hölderlin, Poet-Translator A Lecture'. *Translation and Literature* (20): 79–97.

Cowley, M., 1976. 'Introduction'. In M. Cowley (ed.), *Walt Whitman's Leaves of Grass, the First (1855) Edition.* London and New York: Penguin Books. pp. vii–xxxvii.

Delisle, J., and J., Woodsworth, 2012. *Translators through History* (Rev. edn). Amsterdam and Philadelphia: John Benjamins Pub. Co.

De Man, P., 1989. *Blindness and Insight: Essays in the Rhetoric of Contemporary Criticism* (2nd edn, rev.). London: Routledge.

De Man, P., 2000. '"Conclusions" on Walter Benjamin's "The Task of the Translator"', Messenger Lecture, Cornell University, 4 March 1983. *Yale French Studies* (97): 10–35.

DeYoung, T., 1993. 'A New Reading of Badr Shākir al-Sayyāb's "Hymn of the Rain"'. *Journal of Arabic Literature* 24 (1): 39–61.

DeYoung, T., 1998. *Placing the Poet: Badr Shakir al-Sayyab and Postcolonial Iraq.* Albany: State University of New York Press.

Dickins, J., S., Hervey and I., Higgins, 2002. *Thinking Arabic Translation: A Course in Translation Method: Arabic to English.* London and New York: Routledge.

Eco, U., 2004. *Mouse or Rat?: Translation as Negotiation.* London: Phoenix.

Einboden, J., 2013. *Nineteenth-Century U.S. Literature in Middle Eastern Languages.* Edinburgh: Edinburgh University Press.

Einboden, J., 2014. "Minding the Koran', in Civil War America: Islamic Revelation, US Reflections'. *Journal of Qur'anic Studies* 16 (3): 84–103.

Eliot, T. S., 1917. 'The Noh and the Image'. *Egoist* IV (7): 102–3.

Eliot, T. S., 1928. *For Lancelot Andrewes.* London: Faber & Gwyer.

Eliot, T. S., 1934. *After Strange Gods.* London: Faber and Faber.

Eliot, T. S., 1936. *Essays Ancient and Modern*. London: Faber and Faber.

Eliot, T. S., 1946. 'Preface'. In T. S. Eliot (tr.), *Anabasis*, S. J. Perse. New York and London: Harcourt Brace Jovanovich Inc. pp. 9–12.

Eliot, T. S., 1957. *On Poetry and Poets*. London: Faber and Faber.

Eliot, T. S., 1959. 'Introduction'. In E. Pound, *Ezra Pound Selected Poems*. London: Faber and Faber. pp. 7–21.

Eliot, T. S., 1960. *The Sacred Wood*. London and New York: Methuen.

Eliot, T. S., 1972. *The Waste Land and Other Poems*. London: Faber and Faber.

Eliot, T. S., 1975. *Selected Prose of T.S. Eliot*. London: Faber and Faber.

Eliot, T. S., 1978. *To Criticize the Critic*. London: Faber and Faber.

Eliot, T. S., 2011. *The Letters of T.S. Eliot*. V. Eliot and J. Haffenden (eds). New Haven, CT: Yale University Press.

Eliot, T. S., 2015. *The Poems of T. S. Eliot: Collected and Uncollected Poems*. C. Ricks, and J. McCue (eds). London: Faber and Faber.

Eliot, T. S., 2017. *The Complete Prose of T. S. Eliot: The Critical Edition: Tradition and Orthodoxy, 1934–1939*, V 5. I. Javadi, R. Schuchard and J. Stayer (eds). Baltimore: Johns Hopkins University Press.

Eliot, T. S., 2017. *The Complete Prose of T. S. Eliot: The Critical Edition: The War Years, 1940–1946*, V 6. D. E. Chinitz and R. Schuchard (eds). Baltimore: Johns Hopkins University Press.

Eliot, V., 1971. 'Introduction'. In T.S. Eliot, *The Waste Land a Facsimile and Transcript of the Original Drafts Including the Annotations of Ezra Pound*. V. Eliot (ed.). London: Faber and Faber. pp. Ix–xxx.

Emerson, R. W., 1971. 'Emerson's Letter to Whitman 1855'. In M. Hindus (ed.), *Walt Whitman: The Critical Heritage*. London: Routledge and Kegan Paul. pp. 21–2.

Emerson, R. W., 2010. *Essays: First and Second Series*. New York: Library of America Paperback Classics.

Erkkila, B., 1989. *Whitman the Political Poet*. New York and Oxford: Oxford University Press.

Faddul, A. Y., 1992. *The Poetics of T.S. Eliot and Adunis: A Comparative Study*. Beirut: Al-Hamra.

Fengmin, L., 2006. 'Walt Whitman and Arabic Immigrant Poet Gibran Khalil Gibran'. *Canadian Social Science* 2 (1): 63–8.

Fischbach, H., 1992. 'Translation, the Great Pollinator of Science'. *Babel* 38 (4): 193–202.

Folsom, E., 2012. 'Foreword'. WhitmanWeb. [online] available from: https://iwp.uiowa.edu/whitmanweb/en/writings/song-of-myself/section-1 [Accessed 2 April 2016].

Foucault, M., 1972. *The Archaeology of Knowledge*. A. M. S. Smith (tr.). London: Tavistock Publications.

Gentzler, E., 2001. *Contemporary Translation Theories*. Clevedon, UK; Buffalo: Multilingual Matters Ltd.

Ginsberg, A., 2009. *Collected Poems 1947-1997*. London: Penguin Classics.

Godelek, K., 1999. 'The Neoplatonist Roots of Sufi Philosophy'. *Muslim Philosophy*. Originally it was given at the Twentieth World Congress of Philosophy. Boston, Massachusetts from 10–15 August 1998. [online] Available from: http://www.musl imphilosophy.com/ip/CompGode.htm [Accessed 27 May 2016].

Gohar, S. M., 2008. 'Engaging T. S. Eliot's City Narratives in the Poetry Badr Shaker al-Sayyab'. *Studies in Islam and the Middle East* 5 (1): 1–20.

Greene, R., 1998. 'Introduction'. In R. Greene (ed.), *Selected Letters of Edith Sitwell*. London: Virago Books. pp. vii–xii.

Greenspan, E., 2005. 'Key Passages'. In E. Greenspan (ed.), *Walt Whitman's 'Song of Myself': A Sourcebook and Critical Edition*. London and New York: Routledge. pp. 126–40.

Greenspan, E., 2005. 'Contextual Overview'. In E. Greenspan (ed.), *Walt Whitman's 'Song of Myself': A Sourcebook and Critical Edition*. London and New York: Routledge. pp. 9–17.

Hass, R., 2010. 'Introduction'. In W. Whitman, *Song of Myself and Other Poems*, selected and introduced by R. Hass, with a lexicon of the poem by R. Hass and P. Ebenkamp. Berkeley: Counterpoint Press. pp. 3–6.

Hatim, B., and I., Mason, 1990. *Discourse and the Translator*. London: Longman.

Heaney, S., 1989. *The Government of the Tongue*. London and Boston: Faber and Faber.

Hindus, M., 1971. *Walt Whitman: The Critical Heritage*. London: Routledge and Kegan Paul.

Holmes, J. S., 1994. *Translated!: Papers on Literary Translation and Translation Studies* (2nd edn). Amsterdam: Rodopi.

Holy Bible, New International Version Arabic/English, 1999. Colorado: International Bible Society.

Homer, 1987. *The Iliad*. M. Hammond (tr.). London and New York. Penguin Books.

House, J., 2009. *Translation*. Oxford: Oxford University Press.

Huang, G., 1995. 'Participial Whitman: The Catalog Problem', Whitman in Translation: A Seminar. *Walt Whitman Quarterly Review* 13 (1): 1–58.

Huang, Y., 2002. *Transpacific Displacement: Ethnography, Translation, and Intertextual Travel in Twentieth-Century American Literature*. Berkeley, CA: University of California Press.

Hughes, T., 1992. *A Dancer to God: Tributes to T.S. Eliot*. London: Faber and Faber.

Huri, Y., 2006. *The Poetry of Saʿdī Yūsuf: Between Homeland and Exile*. Eastbourne: Sussex Academic Press.

Iskander, G. 2014. 'On Whitman'. Translated from Arabic by J. Hadfield. In R. V. Winkle and L. Pyott (eds), *This Room Is Waiting: Bilingual Edition*. Glasgow: Freight Books. pp. 102–5.

Iskander, G., 2016. *Gilgamesh's Snake and Other Poems: Bilingual Edition*. J. Glenday and G. Iskander (trs.). Syracuse and New York: Syracuse University Press.

Jabra, I. J., 1971. 'Modern Arabic Literature and the West'. *Journal of Arabic Literature* (2): 76–91.

Jackson, S., 1984, 'Al-Jahiz on Translation'. *Alif: Journal of Comparative Poetics* (4): 99–107.

Jāḥiẓ, 'A. i. B. 1969. *The Life and Works of Jāḥiẓ: Translations of Selected Texts*. C. Pellat (ed.) and D. M. Hawke (tr.). London: Routledge and Kegan Paul.

James, W., 1902. *Varieties of Religious Experience: A Study in Human Nature*. London and New York: Longmans, Green, and Co.

Jayyusi, S. K., 1977. *Trends and Movements in Modern Arabic Poetry*. Leiden: Brill.

Jayyusi, S. K., 1987. *Modern Arabic Poetry: An Anthology*. New York and Oxford: Columbia University Press.

Katz, D., 2004. 'Jack Spicer's After Lorca: Translation as Decomposition'. *Textual Practice* 18 (1): 83–103.

Katz, D., 2007. *American Modernism's Expatriate Scene: The Labour of Translation*. Edinburgh: Edinburgh University Press.

Kenesei, A., 2010. *Poetry Translation through Reception and Cognition: The Proof of Translation is in the Reading*. Newcastle upon Tyne: Cambridge Scholars Publishing.

Kenner, H., 2007. 'The Waste Land'. In H. Bloom (ed.). *T.S. Eliot's The Waste Land*. New York: Infobase Publishing. pp. 7–34

Khouri, M. A., 1970. 'Lewis ʿAwaḍ: A Forgotten Pioneer of the Free Verse Movement'. *Journal of Arabic Literature* (1): 137–44.

Khouri, M. A., 1987. *Studies in Contemporary Arabic Poetry and Criticism*. Piedmont, CA: Jahan Book Co.

Kinnell, G., 2006. 'Introduction'. In G. Kinnell (ed.), *The Essential Whitman*. New York: HarperCollin. p. 6.

Kuspinar, P., 2000. 'Perception: A Way to Perfection in Sadra'. *Transcendent Philosophy* 1 (2): 41–63.

Lawrence, H. D., 1971. *Studies in Classic American Literature*. Harmondsworth: Penguin.

Lefevere, A., 1975. *Translating Poetry: Seven Strategies and a Blueprint*. Amsterdam: Van Gorcum.

Lefevere, A., 1992. *Translating Literature: Practice and Theory in a Comparative Literature Context*. New York: The Modern Language Association of America.

Lewis, C. D., 1969. *A Hope for Poetry*. Folcroft, PA: Folcroft.

Lewis, C. D., 2017. *Golden Bridle: Selected Prose*. A. Gelpi and B. O'Donoghue (eds). Oxford: Oxford University Press.

Lorca, F. G., 1990. *Poet in New York*. G. Simon and S. F. White (trs.). London and New York: Penguin Books.

McAuley, D. E., 2012. *Ibn 'Arabī's Mystical Poetics*. Oxford: Oxford University Press.

Malinowski, B., 1935. *Coral Gardens and Their Magic: A Study of the Methods of Tilling the Soil and of Agricultural Rites in the Trobriand Islands*. London: George Allen & Unwin.

Masefield, J., 1978. *Selected Poems*. London: Book Club Associates.

Mattawa, K., 2014. 'Skyping with Saadi, Channeling Li Po'. *Banipal* 51 (1): 50–3.

Mey, J. L., 1993. *Pragmatics: An Introduction*. Oxford: Blackwell.

Mills, S., 2003. *Michel Foucault*. London: Routledge.

Moody, A. D., 1994. *Thomas Stearns Eliot: Poet*. Cambridge and New York: Cambridge University Press.

Moreh, S., 1988. *Studies in Modern Arabic Prose and Poetry*. Leiden: Brill.

Morrisson, M. S., 2002. 'Edith Sitwell's Atomic Bomb Poems: Alchemy and Scientific Reintegration'. *Modernism/Modernity* 9 (4): 605–33.

Musawi, M. J., 2006. *Arabic Poetry: Trajectories of Modernity and Tradition*. London: Routledge.

Nida, E. A., 1964. *Toward a Science of Translating: With Special Reference to Principles and Procedures Involved in Bible Translating*. Leiden: Brill.

Norton, C. E., 1971. 'Charles Eliot Norton's Review 1855'. In M. Hindus (ed.), *Walt Whitman: The Critical Heritage*. London: Routledge and Kegan Paul. pp. 24–7.

Nouryeh, C., 1993. *Translation and Critical Study of Ten Pre-Islamic Odes: Traces in the Sand*. Lewiston: Edwin Mellen Press.

Oser, L., 1998. *T. S. Eliot and the American Poetry*. Missouri and London: University of Missouri Press.

Oxford University Press, 2017. *Oxford English Dictionary online*. Oxford: Oxford University Press.

Paz, O., 1990. *On Poets and Others*. M. Schmidt (tr.). New York: Arcade Publishing.

Pearce, R. H., 1962. *Whitman: A Collection of Critical Essays*. Englewood Cliffs, NJ: Prentice-Hall, Inc.

Pearson, J., 1989. *Façades: Edith, Osbert, and Sacheverell Sitwell*. London: Papermac.

Perse, S. J., 1946. *Anabasis*. T. S. Eliot (tr.). New York and London: Harcourt Brace Jovanovich Inc.

Pinion, F. B., 1989. *A T. S. Eliot Companion*. London: Papermac.

Pound, E., 1950. *The Selected Letters of Ezra Pound, 1907–1941*. D. D. Paige (ed.). New York: New Directions Publishing.

Pound, E., 1959. *Selected Poems*. London: Faber and Faber.

Pound, E., 1962. 'The Open Road' In R. H. Pearce (ed.), *Whitman: A Collection of Critical Essays*. Englewood Cliffs, NJ: Prentice-Hall, Inc. pp. 8–10.

Pound, E., 2004. 'Guido's Relations' In L. Venuti (ed.), *The Translation Studies Reader*. London and New York: Routledge. pp. 86–93.

Railton, S., 1995. '"As If I Were with You"—The Performance of Whitman's Poetry'. In E. Greenspan (ed.), *The Cambridge Companion to Walt Whitman*. New York: Cambridge University Press. pp. 7–26.

Richards, I. A., 1960. *Principles of Literary Criticism*. London: Routledge & Ken Paul Ltd.

Rose, M. G., 1997. *Translation and Literary Criticism: Translation as Analysis*. Manchester: St. Jerome.

Rumeau, D., 2014. 'Federico García Lorca and Pablo Neruda's Odes to Walt Whitman: A Set of Choral Poetry'. *Comparative Literature Studies* 51 (3): 418–38.

Sandburg, C., 1921. 'Introduction'. In W. Whitman, *Leaves of Grass*. New York: Modern Library. PP. iii–xi.

Sayyāb, B. S., 2013. 'Unshūdat al-Maṭar' [The Hymn of Rain]. Translated from Arabic by G. Iskander. In G. Iskander, *Translating Sayyab into English: A Comparative Study of Unshudat al-Matar*. London: Dar Alhikma & Iraqi Cultural Centre. pp. 65–71.

Schleiermacher, F., 1992. 'On the Different Methods of Translating'. In R. Schulte and J. Biguenet (eds),. *Theories of Translations: An Anthology of Essays from Dryden to Derrida*. Chicago and London: The University of Chicago Press. pp. 36–54.

Sitwell, E., 1961. *Collected Poems*. London: Macmillan & Co Ltd.

Sitwell, E., 1998. *Selected Letters of Edith Sitwell*. R. Greene (ed.). London: Virago Books.

Skwara, M., 2008. 'The Poet of Great Reality: Czeslaw Milosz's Reading of Walt Whitman'. *Walt Whitman Quarterly Review* 26 (1): 1–22.

Smith, G., 1956. *T.S. Eliot's Poetry and Plays: A Study in Sources and Meaning*. Chicago and London: University of Chicago Press.

Southam, B. C., 1996. *A Guide to the Selected Poems of T. S. Eliot*. New York: A Harvest Original.

Spender, S., 1975. *Eliot*. Glasgow: Fontana/Collins.

Steiner, G., 1975. *After Babel: Aspects of Language and Translation*. London: Oxford University Press.

Stockwell, P., 2009. *Texture: A Cognitive Aesthetics of Reading*. Edinburgh: Edinburgh University Press.

Sullivan, J., 1961. 'The Poet as Translator: Ezra Pound and Sextus Propertius'. *The Kenyon Review* 23 (3): 462–81.

Tamplin, R., 1988. *A Preface to T S Eliot*. London and New York: Longman.

Toury, G., 1995. *Descriptive Translation Studies -- And Beyond*. Amsterdam and Philadelphia: Benjamins.

Venuti, L., 1995. *The Translator's Invisibility*. London and New York: Routledge.

Venuti, L., 1998. 'Strategies of Translation'. In M. Baker and K. Malmkjær (eds), *Routledge Encyclopaedia of Translation Studies*. London and New York: Routledge. pp. 240–4.

Venuti, L., 2004. 'Introduction'. In L. Venuti (ed.), *The Translation studies Reader* (2nd edn). London and New York: Routledge. pp. 1–9.

Virgil. 2003. *The Aeneid*. D. West (tr.). London: Penguin.

Weissbort, D., 1989. 'Preface'. In D. Weissbort (ed.), *Translating Poetry: The Double Labyrinth*. Houndmills, Basingstoke, Hampshire and London: Macmillan Press LTD. pp. ix–xiv.

West, D. 2003. 'Introduction'. In Virgil, *The Aeneid*. Translated with an introduction by D. West. London: Penguin. pp. vii–xlii.

Whitman, W., 1971. 'Whitman's Anonymous Self-Reviews, 185–6'. In M. Hindus (ed.), *Walt Whitman: the Critical Heritage*. London: Routledge and Kegan Paul. pp. 34–48.

Whitman, W., 1976. *Leaves of Grass, the First (1855) Edition*. M. Cowley (ed.). London and New York: Penguin Books.

Whitman, W., 1982. *Whitman, Poetry and Prose*. J. Kaplan (ed.). New York: Library of America.

Whitman, W., 1984. *Notebook and Unpublished Prose Manuscripts*. E. F. Grier (ed.), 6 vols. New York: New York University press.

Whitman, W., 2001. *Leaves of Grass*. New York: Modern Library.

Williams, C. W., 1967. *The Autobiography of William Carlos Williams*. New York: New Directions Publishing.

Williams, C. W., 2001. 'Introduction'. In W. Whitman, *Leaves of Grass*. New York: Modern Library.

Williams, W. 1987. 'America, Whitman, and the Art of Poetry'. *William Carlos Williams Review* 13 (1): 1–4.

Xie, M., 1999. *Ezra Pound and the Appropriation of Chinese Poetry: Cathay, Translation, and Imagism*. New York: Garland Publishing IVC.

Yao, S. G., 2002. *Translation and the Language of Modernism: Gender, Politics, Language*. London: Palgrave Macmillan.

Yücesoy, H. 2009. 'Translation as Self-Consciousness: Ancient Sciences, Antediluvian Wisdom, and the 'Abbāsid Translation Movement'. *Journal of World History* 20 (4): 523–57.

Yūsuf Ali, ʻA., 1969. *The Holy Qur'ān: Text and Translation*. Kuala Lumpur: Islamic Book Trust.

Yūsuf, S., 2002. *Without an Alphabet, Without a Face*. K. Mattawa (tr.). Saint Paul, Minnesota: Graywolf Press.

Zweig, P., 1984. *Walt Whitman: The Making of the Poet*. New York: Basic Books.

Index

50 Poems from American Contemporary Poetry (Pound) 28

'Abbās, Iḥsān 105, 109, 113, 114, 132
'Abdul-Hai, Muhammad 25
Abdullah, Adnān K. 45, 46
Abel, Richard 116
'Abr al-Arḍ al-Bawār (Through the waste land, Ṣāyigh) 28
'abstract' concepts 68
al-'Abṭa, Maḥmūd 107
Abū Ghailān (*Ghailān* is his son, al-Sayyāb) 102
Abū Nuwās 10
Abū Tammām 10
Adrīs, Suhayl 132
Adūnīs, 'A. S. 6, 7, 10–12, 23, 25–7, 31, 32, 35, 46, 52–4, 56, 94–6, 121, 123, 145, 155 n.1
Aeneid (Virgil) 1, 73
Affifi, A. E. 76
affinity 6, 7, 13, 54, 57, 147, 150
After Babel Aspects of Language and Translation (Steiner) 123
After Strange Gods (Eliot) 24
Aghānī Mihyār al-Dimashqī (*The Songs of Mihyar, the Damascene,* Adūnīs) 27
al-Ādāb 118
Al-'Arḍ al-Kharāb ('Awaḍ and Ṣāyigh) 23, 29, 47, 57, 148
Al-Arḍ al-Yabāb (Lu'lu'a and Ṣāyigh) 28, 29
Al-Asliḥa wa al-Aṭfāl (The weapons and children, al-Sayyāb) 135, 136
Al-Bi'r Al-Mahjūra (*The Deserted Well,* al-Khāl) 53
al-Ghirbāl (Na'īma) 5
Al-Ḥubb fi Sān Lāzār (Love in St. Lazare, 'Awaḍ) 48
al-Ḥuriyya 111
Al-Ḥuriyya wa al-Ṭūfān (Freedom and the flood, Jabrā) 69
Al-Ḥuzn ('The Sadness,' al-Ṣabūr) 50
al-Jamal Publishing House 23
al-Kāmil metre 124, 140, 149
al-Karmal 97
Al-Kātib al-Miṣrī 23
Al-Kūlīra (Cholera, al-Malā'ika) 146
Allah, Ibrāhīm Shukr 25
Allen, Gay Wilson 59, 62, 64
'Allūsh, Nājī 104, 108
al-Mahjar (the diaspora). *See al-Rābiṭah al-qalamiyyah* (the pen league)
Al-Mulk Lak (al-Ṣabūr) 49
Al-Mūmis al-'Amyā (The blind whore, al-Sayyāb) 135
Al-Mutawaḥḥishūn (The savages, Simonov) 111
al-Nahr wa-al-Mawt (The river and death, al-Sayyāb) 139
Al-Qaṣīda K (Ṣāyigh) 54
al-Rābiṭah al-qalamiyyah (the pen league) 65–7
'Al-Sayyāb wa-al-Shi'r al-Ṣīnī' (Al-Sayyāb and the Chinese poetry, Muṣṭafā) 138
al-Sha'b (The people) 110
Al-Shā'ir wa-al-Mukhtari' wa-al-Kulūnīl (The poet, inventor and colonel, al-Sayyāb) 102
Al-Shi'r al-Ḥurr (free verse) 13, 48, 49, 54, 57, 60, 65, 66, 70–2, 124, 142, 145, 146
'al-shi'r al-mutlaq' 68
al-shi'r al-mursal (blank verse) 68, 69
al-Taḍāmun (Solidarity) 128
al-Thabāt 107
al-Thaqāfa al-Waṭaniyya (The national culture) 114
al-Yanābī' al-Thaqāfiyya (The cultural sources, 'Abbās) 109

'America, America' (Yūsuf) 94, 96
'America, Whitman, and the Art of Poetry' (Williams) 61
American civilization 94
American Civil War (1861–5) 68, 80
American Phrenological Journal 64
American Poetry and Prose (Forester) 102
Amers (Seamarks, Perse) 155 n.1
'amūd al-shi'r 10
Amūt Shahīd al-Jirāḥ (I die a martyr of my afflictions, 'Awaḍ) 48
Anabase (Perse) 116
Andrewes, Lancelot 115, 116
'Animula' (Eliot) 115
'The April Rain' (Sitwell) 126, 136
Arab modernists 11, 12, 16, 17, 23, 25, 27, 35, 49, 54–7, 67, 70, 145–51
Aragon, Louis 108
'Araq wa-Qiṣaṣ Ukhrā (Wine and other stories, Jabrā) 28
Archaeology of Knowledge, The (Foucault) 13
Arḍ al-Ḍayā' (The land of loss, Rāghib) 29
'Arial' (Eliot) 115
Artaud, Antonin 8
Asāṭīr (Myths, al-Sayyāb) 124
Ash Wednesday (Eliot) 24, 25, 27
'"As if I Were with You" – The Performance of Whitman's Poetry' (Railton) 75
Asselineau, Roger 92
'Awaḍ, Lūwīs 13, 23–6, 31–41, 43–5, 47–9, 51, 56, 104, 147, 154 n.3
Awrāq al-'Ushb 70–2, 79
al-'Aẓamah, Nadhīr 114
Azhār Dhābila (Withered flowers, al-Sayyāb) 106
al-'Azzāwī, Fāḍil 97, 98

Badawi, M. M. 12
Badenhausen, Richard 20
Badr Shākir al-Sayyāb: al-Rajul wa-al-Shā'ir (Badr Shākir al-Sayyāb: The man and the poet) 105
Badr Shākir al-Sayyāb: Aṣwāt al-Shā'ir al-Mutarjim (Badr Shākir al-Sayyāb: The voices of the poet-translator, Tawfīq) 117
Badr Shākir al-Sayyāb: Dirāsa fī Ḥayātih wa-Shi'rih (Badr Shākir al-Sayyāb: A study in his life and poetry) 105
Badr Shākir al-Sayyāb: Ḥayātuh wa-Shi'ruh (Badr Shākir al-Sayyāb: His life and poetry, Bullāṭa) 108
Baker, Mona 31
Bashshūr, Munīr 25
al-Baṣrī, 'Abd al-Jabbār Dāūd 102, 110, 112, 113
Bassnett, Susan 10, 14
al-Baṭal, 'Alī 114, 135
Baudelaire, Charles 6–8, 40, 41, 106, 149
Baudelaire (Pichois) 7, 8
Bayān al-Ḥadātha (Manifesto of Modernity, Adūnīs) 11
al-Bayātī 35, 46, 94–6, 108, 109
Bayn al-Rūḥ wa-al-Jasad (Between the soul and the body, al-Sayyāb) 106
Bayt al-Ḥikma (the House of Wisdom) 2
Benjamin, Walter 7
Birsanu, Roxana 8, 11
Birth of Freedom, The (Eifert) 102
Black Stallion, The (Farley) 102
Blake, William 103, 104
Bloom, Harold 61, 75, 76, 90
Boase-Beier, Jean 93
'bold conception' 61
Borges, Jorge Luis 6, 61, 62
Boullata, I. 54
Bowra, Cecil Maurice 128
Breslin, James E. B. 61
Breton, Andre 27
'Bright Star' (Keats) 104
Brooke, Rupert 106, 109
Brooklyn Daily Times 74
Bruetts, Herman 62
Buil, Ana Mata 6, 7
Bullāṭa, 'Īsa 108, 113
Būluṣ, Sargūn 154 n.1
'Burnt Norton' (Eliot) 24

Caliph al-Ma'mūn 2
'The Canticle of the Rose' (Sitwell) 126
Casale, Frank D. 62, 72
Catford, J. C. 17
Cathay (Pound) 123
Chamoun, Camille 54
Chapman, George 4
Clej, Alina 8

cognitive context 13, 15, 24, 47–56, 91–8, 101, 132–42, 145
Collected Poems (Sitwell) 127
colloquial technique 39, 47–50
communicated aesthetics 54
communism 102, 110
comparative analysis 13, 14
Conrad, Joseph 36
Constantine, David 4
'continuity' 15, 16, 48, 57, 92, 148
correlative and inner experiences 54
Cowley, Malcolm 59, 63, 77
Criterion, The 19, 20
culture
  Arabic 2, 4, 6, 10, 11, 14, 49, 52, 68, 99, 130, 132, 146–50
  target 5, 12, 14–17, 82, 148–50
  Western 6, 11, 53, 69
Cummings, E. E. 12

Daniel, Arnaut 30
Dans le Restaurant (Eliot) 41, 42
Darbelnet, J. 17
Dār Majallat Shi'r 25
Darwīsh, Maḥmūd 12, 46, 97
Davies, William Henry 109
Ḍayyiqah hiy al-Marākib (Perse) 155 n.1
de Man, Paul 8
Derrida, Jacques 39, 45
DeYoung, T. 105, 108
Dial, The 19, 22
Dickens, Charles 21
Dickins, James 82
Ḍikrā Liqā' (Memory of a date, al-Sayyāb) 104
'Dirge for the New Sunrise' (Sitwell) 126
discourse 8, 15, 142
  analysis 16, 99, 145
  definition 13, 14
  'foreign' 142–3
discursive process 13, 15, 16, 142, 145
Dīwān al-Sayyāb ('Allūsh) 108
Dīwān al-Shi'r al-Amīrkī (Divan of American poetry, al-Khāl) 69, 70
Donne, John 36
Dryden, John 4
Dry Salvages, The (Eliot) 24

Eco, Umberto 12, 13
Edith Sitwell: A Biography (Elborn) 105
'Edith Sitwell's Atomic Bomb Poems: Alchemy and Scientific Reintegration' (Morrisson) 127
Eifert, Virginia 102
Einboden, Jeffrey 72, 82, 88
Elborn, Geoffrey 105
Eliot (Spender) 20
Eliot, T. S. 7–9, 11–14, 17, 19–42, 45, 47–57, 60, 61, 66–8, 95, 99, 101, 102, 104, 109, 114–16, 121, 123, 132, 140, 142, 145, 147–50, 153 n.1
Eliot, Valerie 20, 21
Emerson, Ralph Waldo 60, 61, 77, 87
'enrichment,' concept of 6
Epic of Gilgamesh 1
Erkkila, Betsy 68
'experientialism' 15, 16, 92
experimental language 49
experimental techniques 51
Ezra Pound Selected Poems (Pound) 60, 123

Fajr al-Salām (Dawn of peace, al-Sayyāb) 135
Farīd, Māhir Shafīq 114
Farley, Walter 102
Fenollosa, Ernest 123
Fī al-Adab al-Ingilīzī al-Ḥadīth ('Awaḍ) 24, 154 n.3
First World War (1914–18) 14, 21, 52, 56, 147
Fischbach, Henry 2
FitzGerald, Edward 5, 6
Fleurs du Mal (The flowers of evil, Baudelaire) 41, 106
'Follow Me' (Shelley) 104
Folsom, Ed 77
Forester, Norman 102
For Lancelot Andrewes (Eliot) 24
Foucault, Michel 13–14
Four Quartets, The (Eliot) 12, 24, 28, 54, 57
'fragmentariness' 21–2
free verbalization 54
From Ritual to Romance (Weston) 21
Frost, Robert 12
'The Funeral of New York' (Hazo) 94

'generalization' 15, 48, 57, 92, 93, 142, 148

Gentzler, Edwin 9
Gibran, Gibran Khalil (Jubrān Khalīl Jubrān) 65–7, 70, 93
Ginsberg, Allen 13, 91, 92
Godelek, Kamuran 76
God that Failed, The 102
Goethe, Johann Wolfgang von 86
'A Grave for New York' (Toorawa) 94–6
Greene, Richard 137
'gymnosophist' 87, 88

al-Ḥaidarī, Bulānd 25, 105, 106
Hale, Edward Everett 59
Hal Kān Ḥubban? (Was it love?, al-Sayyāb) 146
Hall, Donald 42
Hass, Robert 64–5
Ḥaṭṭimū 'Amūd al-Shi'r (Break the pattern of poetry, 'Awaḍ) 48
Ḥayātī fi al-Shi'r (My life in poetry, al-Ṣabūr) 49
Hazo, Samuel 94
Heaney, Seamus 22
Hervey, Sandor 82
Hesse, Hermann 21
Higgins, Ian 82
Ḥikmat, Nāẓim 102, 108, 110
Hölderlin, Friedrich 4, 5
Hollow Men, The (Eliot) 24, 25, 27
Holmes, J. S. 35
Homer 1, 4, 73
Honig, Edwin 28
Hope for Poetry, A (Lewis) 25
House, Juliane 47
How to Read and Why (Bloom) 75
Huang, G. 90
Hughes, Ted 22, 34
Ḥusayn, Ṭāhā 23
Hutāf al-Awdiya (Hymns of the valleys, al-Rīḥānī) 65
ḥuwwilat 2

Ibn 'Arabī 76, 80
Ibrāhīm, Ḥāfiẓ 67
Ilḥāḥ (Insistence, Yūsuf) 141
Iliad (Homer) 1
'The Influence of St.-John Perse on T. S. Eliot' (Abel) 116
Introduction to Arab Poetics, An (Adūnīs) 10
Iraqi Communist Party (ICP) 25, 109, 110
Ismā'īl, 'Ābid 65, 84, 87
Ismā'īl, Muḥammad 'Alī 103
Ismā'īl, Ṭalāl 'A. 45, 46
Itba'īnī ('Follow Me,' al-Sayyāb) 104

Jabrā, Jabrā Ibrāhīm 13, 22, 25, 28, 47, 55, 65, 68, 69, 71, 73–5, 79–86, 88–91, 99, 103, 121, 145, 148
'Jack Spicer's After Lorca: Translation as Decomposition' (Katz) 89
al-Jāḥiẓ, Abū 'Uthmān 2, 3, 5
Jakobson, Roman 17
al-Jawāhirī, Muhammad Mahdī 67, 107
Jayyusi, S. K. 53
Jihād, Kāẓim 39
'Journey of the Magi' (Eliot) 101, 102, 114–22, 132, 133, 142, 149

Katz, Daniel 9, 89, 90
Keats, John 104, 107, 109
Kenesei, Andrea 14
al-Khāl, Adūnīs Yūsuf 12, 23, 25–7, 31–41, 43–5, 47, 53, 54, 56, 57, 65, 69, 71, 73, 79–85, 88, 90, 91, 99, 113, 121, 145, 147, 148
Khouri, Mounah A. 65, 66
Kinnell, Galway 62
'kosmos' type 91, 94
Kunt Shiyū'iyyan (I used to be a communist, al-Sayyāb) 25, 111
Kuspinar, Bilal 78

'Lament of Frontier Guard' (Li Po) 139
Larbaud, Valery 21
Later Poems (from 1940 onward) (Sitwell) 126
Lawrence, D. H. 61
Leaves of Grass (Whitman) 59–64, 69–72, 75, 77, 80, 85, 90–2
Lefevere, Andre 2, 17, 46, 99
Les Sept Vieillards (Baudelaire) 40
Les yeux d'Elsa (The eyes of Elsa, Aragon) 108
Lewis, C. D. 22, 25
Lincoln, Abraham 68
Lindsay, Jack 127
Lin Fengmin 66
Li Po 123, 124, 139–43

literary writing styles 37
literature
American 64
Arabic 69, 70, 101, 108, 146
history of 1
Western 108, 132
Lorca, Federico Garcia 91, 92, 97, 109
love 66, 77, 80, 84
'The Love Song of J. Alfred Prufrock' (Eliot) 24, 25, 27
'Lullaby' (Sitwell) 126
Lu'lu'a, ʿA. 29, 31, 34, 38, 45

MacLeish, Archibald 12
al-Madfaʿī, Qaḥtān 105
al-Malā'ika, Nāzik 12, 146
Malinowski, Bronislaw 15, 16
Manzil al-Aqnān (The house of slaves) 140
Marshall Plan 111
Marzouq, Salim 142
Masefield, John 106, 107
'A Mass for New York' (al-Bayātī) 94, 95
Mattawa, Khaled 94, 141, 142
Maud and Other Poems (Tennyson) 64
Maẓlūm, Mūḥammad 23, 40
metaphor 34
metrical system 46, 122, 124, 142, 143, 146
Mey, Jacob L. 15
Mills, Sara 14
Milosz, Czeslaw 95
Milton, John 65
mimetic form 35
mimetic strategy 146
'"Minding the Koran" in Civil War America: Islamic Revelation, US Reflections' (Einboden) 88
Min Nuṣūṣ al-Sayyāb al-Adabiyyah al-Mutarjamah (From al-Sayyāb's translational literary texts) 128
'Modern Arabic Literature and the West' (Jabrā) 22
modernist movement 9, 146
modernist poets 7, 9, 10, 60, 66, 70, 92, 98, 101
modernity 4, 8, 10–13, 15, 17, 19, 22–5, 27, 34, 51, 53, 57, 60, 91, 99, 101, 114, 119, 132, 143, 145, 147, 148, 150
modernization 52
Moody, A. David 117
Moreh, S. 93
Morrisson, Mark S. 127
'A Mother to Her Dead Child' (Sitwell) 102, 126
Muʿallaqat Tawfīq Ṣāyigh (Ṣāyigh) 54
Murder in the Cathedral (Eliot) 25, 27
al-Musawi, M. J. 12
Muṣṭafā, Khālid ʿAlī 128, 138, 139
mysticism 71, 77, 79

Naʿīma, Mīkhā'īl 5
al-Naqāsh, Waḥīd 109
narrative technique 34, 115, 117
Neoplatonism 76, 78
Neruda, Pablo 91, 92, 110
Neuffer, Christian Ludwig 4
'A new Reading of Badr Shākir al-Sayyāb's 'Hymn of the Rain'' (DeYoung) 138
New York Daily Times 59–60
Nida, Eugene 17
'The Night Wind' (Sitwell) 126
Nineteenth-Century U.S. Literature in Middle Eastern Languages (Einboden) 72
Norton, Charles Eliot 59
Notebooks and Unpublished Prose Manuscripts (Whitman) 75
nuqilat 2

'Ode to Walt Whitman' (Lorca and Neruda) 92
Omar Khayyam 5
'oneness' 76
'On Translating Poetry into Arabic, with Special Reference to T.S. Eliot's *The Waste Land*' (Abdulla) 46
'The Open Road' (Pound) 60
Our Mutual Friend (Dickens) 21
'the Over-soul' (Emerson) 76, 87
Ovid 4

'paratactic syntax' 117
Paris Review, The 42
Paulham, Jean 116
Paz, Octavio 87
Pearson, John 127

'Perception: A Way to Perfection in Sadra' (Kuspinar) 78
Perse, S. J. 6, 7, 27, 115, 116, 155 n.1
Pessoa, Fernando 91, 92, 95
Petronius, Gaius 29
'Philip Massinger' (Eliot) 140
Pichois, Claude 7, 8
Pinion, F. B. 22
Plūtūlānd (Plutoland, 'Awaḍ) 48
Poe, Edgar Allan 6, 7, 109
Poeta en Nueua York (Poet in New York, Lorca) 92
poetic/poetics 113
  Arabic 10, 12, 38, 93, 98
  authorship 1
  cognitive 15, 99
  concept 54, 56, 149
  English 15
  European traditions 72
  form 3, 63, 67, 69, 98, 110, 119, 149
  language 49, 51, 91, 99, 150
  schools 13, 93, 99
  style 70–1, 87
  technique 22, 25, 38, 101
  theory 65
  Western 11
poetry
  Arabic 3, 4, 10–14, 16, 17, 22, 23, 26–8, 46, 49, 50, 55, 56, 65, 66, 74, 91, 97, 99, 101, 104, 109, 114, 124, 132, 137, 142, 143, 145–50, 155 n.1
  Chinese 138–9
  concept of 26, 64
  democratic 62, 64
  English 12, 16, 24, 27, 65, 91, 101–14, 123, 124, 132, 142, 143, 150
  modern 16, 19, 22, 26, 27, 46, 49, 56, 91, 97, 101, 104, 109, 123, 132, 143, 145, 148, 155 n.1
  'romantic' 67
  style 62
  Western 101, 113
poet-translators 4–7, 13, 14, 17, 23, 29, 31, 47, 55, 56, 93, 101, 117, 128, 143, 145–7, 150, 153 n.1
'Poet-translators as Double Link in the Global Literary System' (Buil) 6
Pope, Alexander 4
Pound, Ezra 3, 8–10, 13, 17, 20, 25–8, 30, 32, 35, 41, 53, 54, 57, 60, 83, 86, 101, 102, 114, 123, 124, 138, 140–3, 145–7, 149–51
prose 3, 10
prose poems/poetry 48, 65–7, 71, 93, 97, 122, 145, 146
Putnam's Monthly 59

Qabr min Ajl New York (Grave for New York, Adūnīs) 53
Qāfilat al-Ḍayā' (The convoy of loss, al-Sayyāb) 117, 132, 133, 136
Qaṣā'id Mukhtāra min al-Shi'r al-'Ālamī al-Ḥadīth (Selected poems from modern world poetry, al-Sayyāb) 102, 113, 114
qaṣīdat al-nathr (prose poem) 71
Qīthārat al-Rīḥ (The lyre of wind) 106
Quinn, John 19

Rāghib, Nabīl 29
Raḥal al-Nahār (The day has gone, al-Sayyāb) 126, 140
al-Raḥmān, Ṭāha Abd 74
Railton, Stephen 75
Razzūq, As'ad 47
Reader's Guide to Walt Whitman, A (Allen) 59
'Reflections on Vers Libre' (Eliot) 48
'renaissance' 27
'Revolutionaries and Poetry' (Lewis) 25
Richards, I. A. 22
al-Rīḥānī, Amīn 65–8, 71, 93, 99, 149, 150
Riḥlat al-Majūs (al-Sayyāb) 116, 122, 131
Rimbaud, Arthur 8
Risāla min Zawjat Tājir al-Nahr (A letter from the wife of the river merchant, al-Sayyāb) 124, 131, 140
'The River-Merchant's Wife: A Letter' (Pound) 101, 102, 114, 123–6, 140–2, 145, 149
Roman poets 1
Romantic Movement 67
romantic poets 25, 67, 105
Rose, Marilyn Gaddis 6
Rossetti, Dante Gabriel 6, 29, 31
Rubaiyat, The (Omar Khayyam) 5, 6
al-Rūṣāfī, Ma'rūf 67

al-Ṣabūr, 'Abd 46, 49–51, 54, 109
Sadra, Mulla 78
'Sage Homme' (Pound) 20
Sallām, Rif 'at 65
'Salutation to Walt Whitman' (Pessoa) 92
Sandburg, Carl 64
Sartre, Jean-Paul 69
Satyricon (Petronius) 29
Ṣāyigh, Tawfīq 12, 23, 27–8, 31–41, 43–5, 47, 54–6, 145, 147, 148
al-Sayyāb, Badr Shākir 7, 13, 17, 25, 35, 46, 51, 52, 56, 115–22, 124–6, 128–43, 145, 149–51
  engagement with English poetry 101–14
Sa 'dī Yūsuf fī al-Sab'īn (Sa 'dī Yūsuf at seventy, Yūsuf) 97
Schiller, Friedrich 86
Schleiermacher, Friedrich 5
Second World War 14, 23, 52, 54, 56, 67, 105, 110, 112, 136, 145, 147
Selected Letters of Edith Sitwell (Greene) 137
Shabaḥ Qābīl (Ghost of Qābīl, al-Sayyāb) 128, 131
Shabaḥ Qāyīn Baīn Idith Sītwal wa-Badr Shākir al-Sayyāb (The shadow of Cain between Edith Sitwell and Badr Shākir al-Sayyāb, al-Baṭal) 135
Shadow of Cain, The (Sitwell) 12, 101, 102, 114, 126–31, 142, 145, 149
Shakespeare, William 65
Shanq Zahrān (Hanging *Zahrān*, al-Ṣabūr) 49
Shauqī, Aḥmad 67
al-Shawwāf, Khālid 103
Shelley, Percy Bysshe 103–5, 109
Shi'r 4, 12, 23, 25, 26, 53, 69, 106, 154 nn.3, 1
shi 'r mursal (blank verse) 71
Shuraiḥ, Maḥmūd 28
Simonov, Konstantin 111, 112
situational context 13–15, 23–8, 56, 65–72, 101–14, 142, 145
Sitwell, Edith 12, 13, 17, 101, 102, 105, 106, 109, 110, 114, 126, 128, 130–2, 134, 135–8, 142, 145, 149, 150
Smith, Grover 29, 38, 39, 115
'Some Notes on my Own Poetry' (Sitwell) 127
'A Song for Simeon' (Eliot) 115
'The Song of Ch'ang-kan' (Waley) 124
Song of Myself (Whitman) 12, 17, 59, 62–5, 68–9, 71–7, 80, 82, 85, 88, 90, 93–5, 98–9, 145, 148
Sophocles 4, 5
Souffle de Perse 155 n.1
source text (ST) 7, 13, 14, 17, 30, 32–6, 38–40, 45, 46, 56, 91, 118–22, 125, 126, 129–31
Southam, B.C. 35, 37, 38
Spender, Stephen 20, 21, 41, 109
Statue of Liberty 94, 95
Steiner, George 6, 123, 124, 134, 140
Stephenson, Ethel M. 36
Stevens, Wallace 12
Stewart, D. 25
'Still Falls the Rain' (Sitwell) 110, 126, 136–8
Stockwell, Peter 15, 48, 92
'Street Song' (Sitwell) 126
Studies in Classic American Literature (Lawrence) 61
Studies in Contemporary Arabic Poetry and Criticism (Khouri) 65
Studies in Modern Arabic Prose and Poetry (Moreh) 93
'stylistics' 15, 16, 92
Sufism 76, 78, 79, 84, 85, 88
"A Supermarket in California" (Ginsberg) 92
Swinburne, Algernon Charles 6

taf 'īla (metrical foot) 48
Tammām, Abū 109, 110
Tammūzī movement 121
Tamplin, Ronald 21
Tao Yuan Ming 138
target text (TT) 7, 13, 30, 34–6, 38, 39, 45, 46, 56, 57, 79, 82, 118–22, 125, 129–31
Tarjumān al-Ashwāq (*Interpreter of Desires,* Ibn 'Arabī') 80
Tawfīq, Ḥasan 117, 118
Tennyson, Alfred 36, 64
Thalāthat Qurūn min al-Adab (al-Sayyāb) 103

Thalāthūn Qaṣīda (Thirty poems, Ṣāyigh) 28, 54
Thaqāfatunā fi Muftaraq al-Ṭuruq (Our culture at the crossroads, 'Awaḍ) 37
Thawrat al-Lugha (Revolution of the language, 'Awaḍ) 37
Thinking Arabic Translation (Dickins, Hervey and Higgins) 82
Thomas Stearns Eliot: Poet (Moody) 117
'Three Poems of the Atomic Age' (Sitwell) 102, 110, 126, 127
Tī. As. Ilyūt: Tarjamāt min al-Shi'r al-Ḥadīth (T. S. Eliot: Translations from modern poetry, al-Khāl) 25, 26
Time between Ashes and Roses, A (Adūnīs) 94
'To C. L. M' (Masefield) 106
'To-En-Mei's "the Unmoving Cloud"' (Tao Yuan Ming) 138
Toorawa, Shawkat M. 94
'To Summer' (Blake) 103
'To the Reader' (Baudelaire) 41
Tradition and English and American Influence in Arabic Romantic Poetry ('Abdul-Hai) 24–5
Translating Literature (Lefevere) 99
translation 1–2, 5, 16, 37, 47, 48, 56, 90, 99, 101, 108, 114, 131, 142, 143, 145, 146, 149, 150
  literary 4
  metrical 46
  of poetry 3, 4, 7, 9, 11, 14, 17, 31, 32, 34–6, 39, 44, 47, 102, 124
  technique 39
Tristan und Isolde (*Tristan and Isolde*, Wagner) 37, 38
T. S. Eliot and the Art of Collaboration (Badenhausen) 20
T. S. Eliot Tarjamāt min al-Shi'r al-Hadīth (al-Khāl) 44
T. S. Eliot The Waste Land: A Facsimile and Transcript of the Original Drafts including the Annotations of Ezra Pound (Eliot) 20
al-Ṭu'ma, Ṣāliḥ Jawād 106
turjumat 2

Ughniyyat Nafsī (Jabrā) 69
'Umārah, Lamī'a Abbās 106
United States Review 63
Unity of Existence. *See Wahdat al-Wujūd* (the Oneness of Being)
Unshūdat al-Maṭar (Hymn of the rain, al-Sayyāb and Badr) 27, 35, 46, 51, 52, 56, 106, 109, 113, 137–9, 148
'Uyūn Ilzā (*Les Yeux d'Elsa*, al-Sayyāb) 102

Varieties of Religious Experience (James) 77
Venuti, Lawrence 1, 38
verbal context 13–15, 28–47, 56, 72–91, 114–32, 142, 145
'verse to prose' strategy 45
'verse to verse' strategy 45
Vers Libre. See Al-Shi'r al-Ḥurr (free verse)
Vinay, J. P. 17
Virgil 1, 4, 73

Wagner, Richard 37
Wahdat al-Wujūd (the Oneness of Being) 76
'Wait for Me' (Simonov) 112
Waley, Arthur 124
'Walt Whitman and Modern Poetry' (Eliot) 60
'Walt Whitman and the Arabic Immigrant Poet Gibran Khalil Gibran' (Lin Fengmin) 66
Walt Whitman: The Critical Heritage (Hindus) 63, 64
Walt Whitman: The Making of the Poet (Zweig) 62
Waste Land, The (Eliot) 12, 14, 17, 19–28, 32, 56, 57, 95, 106, 132, 145, 147–9
  'The Burial of the Dead' 32–41, 154 n.2
  'Death by Water' 28, 41–7
  'The Fire Sermon' 37–8, 50
  'A Game of Chess' 38
  title, epigraph and dedication 28–32
  'What the Thunder Said' 28, 51–2, 61
Weissbort, D. 3
West, David 1, 4

Western civilization 21, 52, 53, 112, 147
Weston, Jessie L. 21
'What I Feel about Walt Whitman' (Pound) 60
Whitman, Walt 12, 13, 17, 35, 48, 51, 53, 59–99, 145, 148–50
'Whitman' (Lawrence) 61
'Whitman in Translation' (Huang) 90
Whitman the Political Poet (Erkkila) 68
Williams, William Carlos 12, 22, 51, 61
Wordsworth, William 106

Yao, Steven G. 4, 9
Yā Sālim al-Marzūq (O *Sālim al-Marzūq*, Yūsuf) 141
Yerma (Lorca) 109
Yücesoy, Hayrettin 2
Yūsuf, Sa'dī 13, 25, 35, 65, 71, 72, 75, 78–91, 94, 96, 97, 99, 109, 141, 145, 148, 150
al-Yūsuf, Yūsuf S. 29, 31, 45

Zhao Luorui 90
Zweig, Paul 62

www.ingramcontent.com/pod-product-compliance
Lightning Source LLC
Chambersburg PA
CBHW070641300426
44111CB00013B/2195
* 9 7 8 0 7 5 5 6 3 9 9 3 9 *